Margaret Scanlan is Visiting Professor of English at Indiana University.

Traces of Another Time

Traces of Another Time

HISTORY AND POLITICS IN
POSTWAR BRITISH FICTION

Margaret Scanlan

PRINCETON UNIVERSITY PRESS

PRINCETON, NEW JERSEY

Library of Congress Cataloging-in-Publication Data

Scanlan, Margaret, 1944–
Traces of another time : history and politics in postwar British fiction /
Margaret Scanlan.
p.   cm.
Includes bibliographical references.
1. English fiction—20th century—History and criticism.
2. Historical fiction, English—History and criticism. 3. Political
fiction, English—History and criticism. 4. Northern Ireland in
literature. 5. Ireland in literature. I. Title.
PR888.H5S3   1990   823'.91409358—dc20   89-35996

ISBN 0-691-06824-0 (alk. paper)

To John, Christopher, Patrick, and Andrew

Contents

Acknowledgments

I WOULD LIKE to express my appreciation to Indiana University at South Bend for supporting my research with three summer faculty fellowships and a sabbatical. During that sabbatical in 1982–1983 I was a visiting faculty fellow at Princeton University, where the original drafts of four chapters of this book were written; I am grateful to the Department of Comparative Literature for providing this status, which made possible my research in the Firestone Library. I have also twice benefited from National Endowment for the Humanities seminars at Princeton. In 1975–1976 I held a Fellowship in Residence for College Teachers and participated in a seminar taught by Victor Brombert. That long-ago seminar on ideology in nineteenth-century French fiction is everywhere and nowhere in this book on history in the postwar British novel, and I remain indebted to Professor Brombert for providing a model of how one might approach the question posed by Stendhal's famous gunshot at the concert, as well as for his many kindnesses over the intervening years. In the summer of 1988 I participated in a seminar on "Literature as a Socially Constructed Reality" directed by Alvin Kernan. I am more indebted to Professor Kernan than I can easily express, specifically for his lucid reading of the manuscript of this book and his encouragement at a critical time and more generally for his warmth, humor, and intelligence. I am also grateful to Professor David Leon Higdon of Texas Tech University for a careful reading that gave me the benefit of his broad expertise in contemporary British fiction.

Several colleagues at Indiana University, both in South Bend and Indianapolis, have read parts or all of this manuscript. I would especially like to thank Lawrence Clipper, Gloria Kaufman, Richard Turner, and William Touponce for their critical insight and support. James Blodgett not only read all of it but sustained its author with his good sense and humor, managing to make me laugh on even the dreariest Tuesdays in November.

My husband John read every draft of every chapter and provided indispensable commentary on all of them. Perhaps he cannot hope to compete with the monograph wife of the 1950s, at least as memory enshrines her: "My wife Mildred typed five versions of this manuscript, prepared the index, proofread the galleys. . . ." Nonetheless, in the pantheon of liberated husbands he ranks high indeed, having functioned as an unpaid computer consultant, a tireless expert on the complex theology of word processing—Conversion to 5.0, the Index function, Widows and Orphans Protect. To their credit, our three sons, Christopher, Patrick, and Andrew, have yet to demonstrate a heartfelt interest in postwar British fiction, but they have been remarkably patient with the writer of this book and have cheered her on in all her endeavors. My talented brother-in-law, Peter Scanlan, has generously contributed the cover illustration.

Earlier versions of the following chapters appeared in the following journals: Chapter 1: "Fiction and the Fictions of History in Iris Murdoch's *The Red and the Green*," *Clio* 9, no. 3 (Spring 1980): 365–78; Chapter 2: "Rumors of War: Historical Indirection in Elizabeth Bowen's *Last September* and J. G. Farrell's *Troubles*," *Eire/Ireland* 20, no. 2 (Summer 1985): 70–89; Chapter 3: "The Unbearable Present: Northern Ireland in Four Contemporary Novels," *Etudes Irlandaises* 10 (December 1986): 145–61; Chapter 4: "Philby and His Fictions," *Dalhousie Review* 62, no. 4 (Winter 1982–83): 533-53; Chapter 5: "Histories in Fiction: The Problem of the Past in Iris Murdoch's *Nuns and Soldiers*," *Renascence* 38, no. 3 (Spring 1986): 170–82; Chapter 6: "The Disappearance of History: Paul Scott's *The Raj Quartet*," *Clio* 15, no. 2 (Winter 1986): 153–70. Finally, I would like to express my gratitude to Robert Brown, literary editor at Princeton University Press, for his help in bringing this manuscript to press and to Jenna Dolan, its skillful and amiable copy editor.

Abbreviations

EDITIONS cited in the text are indicated below. Except where otherwise noted, translations in the text are my own.

AD   Murdoch, Iris. "Against Dryness: A Polemical Sketch." *Encounter* 16 January 1961, 16–20. Reprinted in *The Novel Today*, edited by Malcolm Bradbury. Manchester: Manchester University Press, 1977.

AOK   Foucault, Michel. *The Archaeology of Knowledge*. Translated by A. M. Sheridan Smith. New York: Pantheon, 1972.

BC   Kilroy, Thomas. *The Big Chapel*. London: Faber, 1971.

C   MacLaverty, Bernard. *Cal*. New York: Braziller, 1983.

CE   Greene, Graham. "The Spy." In *Collected Essays*. London: Bodley Head, 1969.

CP   Yeats, William Butler. *The Collected Poems of William Butler Yeats*. 2d ed. New York: Macmillan, 1951. References in the text are by page number.

DS   Scott, Paul. *A Division of the Spoils*. Vol. 4 of *The Raj Quartet*. 4 vols. 1975. New York: Avon, 1979.

EH   Certeau, Michel de. *L'écriture et l'histoire*. Paris: Gallimard, 1975.

EHN   Fleishman, Avrom. *The English Historical Novel*. Baltimore: Johns Hopkins University Press, 1971.

EWN   Burgess, Anthony. *The End of the World News*. New York: McGraw-Hill, 1983.

FGC   Lessing, Doris. *The Four-Gated City*. Vol. 5 of *Children of Violence*. 5 vols. 1969. New York: Bantam, 1970.

FS   Murdoch, Iris. *The Fire and the Sun: Why Plato Banished the Poets.* London: Oxford University Press, 1977.

FWK   Fleishman, Avrom. *Fictions and the Ways of Knowing: Essays on British Novels.* Austin: University of Texas Press, 1978.

HF   Greene, Graham. *The Human Factor.* New York: Simon and Schuster, 1978.

HN   Lukács, George. *The Historical Novel.* Translated by Hannah and Stanley Mitchell. New York: Humanities Press, 1965.

HS   Farrell, J. G. *The Hill Station: An Unfinished Novel, and an Indian Diary.* Edited by John Spurling. London: Weidenfeld and Nicolson, 1981.

II   Swinden, Patrick. *Paul Scott: Images of India.* New York: St. Martin's Press, 1980.

JC   Scott, Paul. *The Jewel in the Crown.* Vol. 1 of *The Raj Quartet.* 4 vols. 1966. New York: Avon, 1979.

L   Lessing, Doris. *Landlocked.* Vol. 3 of *Children of Violence.* 5 vols. 1958. New York: Plume-NAL, 1970.

LS   Bowen, Elizabeth. *The Last September.* 1929. New York: Avon, 1979.

MQ   Lessing, Doris. *Martha Quest.* Vol. 1 of *Children of Violence.* 5 vols. 1952. New York: Plume-NAL, 1970.

MSW   Philby, Kim. *My Silent War.* London: McGibbon and Kee, 1968.

NS   Murdoch, Iris. *Nuns and Soldiers.* New York: Viking, 1980.

OG   Derrida, Jacques. *Of Grammatology.* Translated by Gaytari Chakravarty Spivak. Baltimore: Johns Hopkins University Press, 1976.

P   Kiely, Benedict. *Proxopera.* London: Victor Golancz, 1977.

PC   Page, Bruce, David Leitch, and Phillip Knightley. *The Philby Conspiracy.* New York: Signet-NAL, 1968. Published in England as *Philby: The Spy*

Who Betrayed a Generation. London: Sphere, 1967.

PHP   Cruise O'Brien, Conor. *Parnell and His Party.* Oxford: Clarendon, 1957.

PM   Lessing, Doris. *A Proper Marriage.* Vol. 2 of *Children of Violence.* 5 vols. 1954. New York: Plume-NAL, 1970.

PS   Hone, Joseph. *The Private Sector.* New York: Dutton, 1972

RG   Murdoch, Iris. *The Red and the Green.* New York: Bard-Avon, 1965.

RS   Lessing, Doris. *A Ripple from the Storm.* Vol. 4 of *Children of Violence.* 5 vols. 1965. St. Albans: Panther-Grenada, 1966.

S   Scott, Paul. *The Day of the Scorpion.* Vol. 2 of *The Raj Quartet.* 4 vols. 1968. New York: Avon, 1979.

SC   Leitch, Maurice. *Silver's City.* London: Secker and Warburg, 1981.

SG   Murdoch, Iris. *The Sovereignty of Good.* London: Routledge and Kegan Paul, 1970.

SH   Deighton, Len. *Spy Hook.* New York: Knopf, 1988.

SK   Farrell, J. G. *The Seige of Krishnapur.* London: Weidenfeld and Nicolson, 1973.

SM   Lévi-Strauss, Claude. *The Savage Mind.* No translation given. London: Weidenfeld and Nicolson, 1966.

SPV   Lessing, Doris. *A Small Personal Voice: Essays, Reviews, Interviews.* Edited by Paul Schlueter. New York: Knopf, 1974.

T   Farrell, J. G. *Troubles.* New York: Knopf, 1971.

TCD   Forster, E. M. *Two Cheers for Democracy.* London: Penguin, 1965.

TS   Scott, Paul. *The Towers of Silence.* Vol. 3 of *The Raj Quartet.* 4 vols. New York: Avon, 1979.

TTSS   le Carré, John. *Tinker, Tailor, Soldier, Spy.* New York: Bantam, 1975.

UC   Burgess, Anthony. "The Democracy of Prejudice." In *Urgent Copy.* London: Jonathan Cape, 1968.

WBJA   Amis, Kingsley. "A New James Bond." In *Whatever Became of Jane Austen?* London: Jonathan Cape, 1970.

WWW   Queneau, Raymond. *We Always Treat Women Too Well*. Translated by Barbara Wright. New York: New Directions, 1981.

Traces of Another Time

Introduction

SAY "HISTORICAL NOVEL" to most people, and they will immediately think of a loosely defined, outmoded genre practiced by Sir Walter Scott, Leo Tolstoy, and Barbara Cartland: a product of romanticism, nationalism, and the nineteenth century's enthusiasm for history. Yet as Hans Vilmar Geppert argues persuasively, there was always an "other historical novel": skeptical, ironic, and "discontinuous," seeking to exploit rather than cover up the boundaries between history and fiction.[1] Such a novel, to take the first major example in English, is William Makepeace Thackeray's *Vanity Fair*. Written in the generation immediately following Scott's, when romantic history was in its heyday, Thackeray's novel offers its profound skepticism about the British Empire and Victorian morality in the form of a history of the glorious battle that paved the way for the ascendancy of both over the immoral French. The weak selfishness of George Osborne gives lie to the heroism of the fallen, as the cowardice of his brother-in-law, "Waterloo Sedley," does to that of the empire builders; the stubborn, plodding virtue of the eponymous Dobbin makes the moral of chaste, virtuous devotion unattractive; and, ascendent over them all, shrewd and amoral, Becky Sharp embodies the spirit of reckless adventurism and insatiable avarice that energizes the culture. Avrom Fleishman, who has written brilliantly about this novel, says that it is "outside the canons of historical fiction"(*FWK*, 53); rather, perhaps, he should have said that it is the prototype of the contemporary skeptical historical novel. For such novels, like Thackeray's, are by their nature decentered, domestic, given to marginalizing the great events that occupy the center stage of more traditional books. When he says that *Vanity Fair* is more interested in the "enactment of the processes by which historical events are

[1] *Der "andere" historische Roman: Theorie und Strukturen einer diskontinuierlichen Gattung* (Tübingen: Max Niemeyer, 1976), 1.

assimilated into consciousness and behavior" (*FWK*, 53) than in the events themselves, he accurately evokes the tendency of contemporary British historical novels. One might even say that in a few instances, the consciousness of history is able to operate in contemporary British novels despite the significant—and eloquent—absence of events.

That a considerable body of postwar British fiction interests itself in the past is clearly demonstrated by three recent books, David Leon Higdon's *Shadows of the Past in Contemporary British Fiction* (University of Georgia Press, 1985), Patrick Swinden's *The English Novel of History and Society, 1940–1980* (St. Martin's Press, 1986), and Neil McEwan's *Perspective in British Historical Fiction Today* (Longwood Academic, 1987). Higdon argues that in the postwar period the modernist preoccupation with personal relationships and timeless moments of intense emotional experience (exemplified in D. H. Lawrence, Virginia Woolf, and E. M. Forster) was replaced by an interest in the past: "No longer a nightmare to be fled, no longer an irrelevancy to be ignored, at some point following World War II, the concept of and attitude toward the past changed . . ." (3). Other recent books, such as Alex Zwerdling's *Virginia Woolf and the Real World* and James Longenbach's *Modernist Poetics of History*, contradict Higdon's assumption that the major British writers of the early twentieth century lacked an interest in history. As an experimental historical novel, Woolf's *Orlando* may be an exception to the usual modernist practice, but one should not lightly dismiss the role of the First World War in *Mrs. Dalloway*, or forget that, even as Stephen Dedalus flies over the net of Irish nationalism, James Joyce depends on our ability to identify Parnell and the Gaelic League. Just as Joyce's Dublin shadows all subsequent Irish fiction, the powerful critiques of imperialism in Joseph Conrad's *Heart of Darkness* and Forster's *A Passage to India* resonate in subsequent fictions about England's colonies. Modernism, as we shall see, bequeaths to contemporary British historical fiction a host of techniques for representing the world as seen through a situated consciousness, for disrupting ordinary perceptions of time, and for keeping narratives open.

Yet even so, contemporary British novelists often display a more overt interest in the public past than their modernist predecessors did. One could argue that the massive changes in British society and the diminishment of Britain's political power that followed the war created the sort of sharp break with the recent past that promotes a greater consciousness of history or historical processes. That argument might seem more convincing were it not for François Furet's claim that the same forces made for the antihistorical tendencies of French writers and thinkers after 1945: "Cette France, expulsée de l'histoire, accepte d'autant mieux expulser l'histoire."[2] More important perhaps, contemporary treatments of the past have a distinctive flavor. As Longenbach demonstrates, when modernist writers were not distinctly antihistorical in the manner of Nietzsche, they stressed the power of the imagination to make the past come alive in the present. This resurrection of the past, which he analyzes at length in T. S. Eliot and Ezra Pound, is familiar to readers of Proust, whose narrator offers a moving and convincing reconstruction of the love affair of Swann and Odette that took place several years before his birth. The desire for such a reconstruction animates William Faulkner's *Absalom, Absalom!*, while in the novels of Virginia Woolf characters experience moments of heightened emotion in which their personal pasts appear vividly present. In the postwar novel such moments seem illusory or undesirable.

Indeed, in his "Fictions of History" Bernard Bergonzi defines a sober respect for the public past that resists imaginative transformation as setting English novels apart from American novels, which tend to treat "history as a text of low and uninteresting organization, infinitely malleable" (45). Where a Thomas Pynchon or a Joyce Carol Oates might turn to fabulation, almost as if assuming that the past can become what-

---

[2] "This France, expelled from history, is all the more eager to expel history" (*L'Atelier de l'histoire*, 42).

ever we wish it to be, the British novelist is more likely to see that assumption itself as a problem to be critiqued.[3] Yet the British novelist is equally distrustful of the kind of clear progress from past to present, the too easily mapped historical roads of popular history or, for that matter, of classical Marxism. "History" is not seen as a force compelling change along inevitable lines, but as the dispersed contents of the past, an outcome of ignorance, fanaticism, and accident that, in Michel Foucault's words, "cannot be reduced to the general model of a consciousness that acquires, progresses, and remembers" (*AOK*, 8).

Within that large body of British fiction that concerns itself with the past about which Swinden, Higdon, McEwan, and Bergonzi write, we find a rebirth and development of the skeptical and critical historical novel that Thackeray wrote. Such fiction looks back to a public past, most often to the world wars or to conflicts in countries like India and Ireland once under English rule. The particular moments chosen are mostly inglorious or violent; the novels are more likely to evoke defeats than victories, stupidity and arrogance than heroism. All concern themselves with the question of how pri-

[3] The major exception to Bergonzi's rule is probably D. M. Thomas's *The White Hotel*. The question of plagiarism aside, Thomas's awarding of Dina Pronicheva's eyewitness testimony about Babi Yar to Lisa Erdman, a fictional character whose masochistic sexual fantasies ("she wanted to be hurt more," [*WH*, 48]) have previously been detailed at great length, seems to many readers an unconscionable violation of the text of history. This violation will seem especially troubling to readers who associate such fantasies with the bayonet rape of Lisa at Babi Yar, and with stereotypes of passive Jews needlessly complying with their murderers' commands. Linda Hutcheon, in "Subject in/of/ to History and His Story" (*Diacritics* 16, no. 1 [Spring 1986]: 78–91), however, argues that such objections are "to some extent . . . displacements, for this is a profoundly anti-humanistic novel that problematizes the same issues as post-structuralist theory. . . ." (83). She sees *The White Hotel* as a successful "historiographical metafiction" (79) about "how we produce meaning in fiction and in history" (83) when older assumptions about the continuity of both consciousness and history have become implausible. Hutcheon's general argument about "historiographical metafiction" is highly perceptive; one suspects, however, that to be termed "militantly antihumanistic" (90) would hardly seem high praise to the British novelists whom Bergonzi describes.

vate lives and consciousnesses intersect with public events; how it is that we experience our history. In one way or another, all are preoccupied with the insight that J. G. Farrell's Collector expresses at the end of *The Siege of Krishnapur*: that "a people, a nation does not create itself according to its own best ideas, but is shaped by other forces, of which it has little knowledge" (*SK*, 343). In the process, the novels become a field of exploration, a space in which the shared epistemological concerns of literary modernism and contemporary historiography meet. With both its terms problematized—for, as Nathalie Sarraute long ago convinced us, it is no easier to write fiction in a world overwhelmed by events whose horror defies the imagination than it is to write history in a period in which a prestigious historiographer, Michel de Certeau, claims that "the past is a fiction of the present" (*EH*, 17)—the historical novel, an open, skeptical form, seeks to tell us the fictions by which we know our history.

As Avrom Fleishman explains, traditionally conceived historical fictions are anchored in a romantic, synthetic view of history in which "the past is seen as a peculiarly national affair, as having a direct connection with the present fortunes of the nation, and as an organically intertwined and self-validating system of institutions and values" (*EHN*, 19). Such a notion of history can lead to sentimental idealization, as in the popular Gothic, or to the patriotic and propagandistic excesses that characterize, for example, Thomas Dixon's *The Clansman*, where a highly biased evocation of the Reconstruction years barely disguises a summons to the reader to join forces with the Ku Klux Klan in preventing black suffrage and school integration. Yet the traditional conception is also compatible with irony. Fleishman perceives a debunking element even in *Ivanhoe*, a "thorough-going critique of medieval civilization, akin to the Enlightenment view and anticipating that in *A Connecticut Yankee in King Arthur's Court*" (*EHN*, 57). More central to the tradition than idealization is a sense of the past as whole, finished, and knowable; in Foucault's vocabulary, "continuous":

> Continuous history is the indispensable correlative of the founding function of the subject: the guarantee that everything that has eluded him may be restored to him; the certainty that time will disperse nothing without restoring it in a reconstituted unity; the promise that one day the subject—in the form of historical consciousness—will once again be able to appropriate, to bring back under its sway, all those things that are kept at a distance by difference, and find in them what might be called his abode. (*AOK*, 12)

Thus Fleishman says of historical novels generally that their "aesthetic function . . . is to lift the contemplation of the past above both the present and the past, to see it in its universal character, freed of the urgency of historical engagement" (*EHN*, 15). This transformation—which Fleishman admires—of historical event into privileged moment or epiphany cannot, as he says, survive the assaults of "the changed conception of reality in the age of Freud and Einstein" (*EHN*, 233). "With the passing of the sense not only of progress but even of comprehensible relationships among historical events," he adds, "the historical novelist is all but put out of business. . . . His fictional plots show themselves to be rather artificial when no historical plot or order can be assumed behind them" (*EHN*, 207). Thus, Fleishman concludes that "the historical novel in our time will probably join the experimental movement of the modern novel or retire from the province of serious literature" (*EHN*, 255).

But examining serious contemporary historical fiction means going beyond the outdated historiography that underlies much criticism of the genre. We do well at the outset to recall that the doyen of the historical novel, George Lukács, objected strenuously to what he called "this soulless, ossified, this thoroughly bureaucratic classification" (*HN*, 240) of the historical novel as a subgenre, believing that all novels ought to see life historically; to him, there is no essential difference between *Anna Karenina* and *War and Peace* (*HN*, 242). The ossified definitions that still surface—for example, even Fleishman talks about restricting the term to novels written about events that occurred "forty to sixty years before" the time of their composition and insists on the presence in the fiction of at least one "historical personage" (*EHN*, 3)—seem to reflect an old notion of history as a subject matter or as a story about famous people. Such views have collapsed under the pressures of recent theory. To the contemporary historian, the notion of recovering the past is an immensely complicated project, fraught with the anxiety that we may not be able to recognize and account for our biases, with the problematics of establishing documentation, with the knowledge that most of the evidence has already been lost. Social historians of the *Annales* school, along with many feminists, question traditional ideas of subject matter, suggesting the need to look at previously ignored dimensions of past experience, that life in the home or factory ought to be as meaningful to history as military campaigns, acts of Parliament, or the evolution of great ideas about the Noble Savage or the death of God. Natalie Zemon Davis's *The Return of Martin Guerre*, for example, totally ignores the splendors of François I's court and the annexation of Brittany in favor of a close analysis of a single case of imposture that offers insight into the social assumptions of peasants in sixteenth-century France. Similarly, Robert Darnton's *The Great Cat Massacre* moves away from "the high road of intellectual history" (3) to explore the shadowy underside of France in the Enlightenment; once we have read about police inspectors who compile dossiers on the sex lives of writers and apprentices who ritually slaughter cats, the Age of Reason will never seem so reasonable again. More fundamentally, the notion that history has any distinctive subject matter has been attacked by Claude Lévi-Strauss, who, in his *The Savage Mind*, described history as a "method without an object" (*SM*, 262) that analyzes phenomena in terms of a "code of before and after" (*SM*, 260). Moreover, "writing history," Foucault, in Mark Poster's words, "threatens every canon of his craft." A category as basic as "man" becomes, in *The Order of Things*, "a recent invention."[4] The conventional

[4] *Foucault, Marxism, and History: Mode of Production versus Mode of Information* (Cambridge: Polity Press, 1984), xxiii, 73.

logic of influence fails in Foucault's vision of human beings and their texts caught in an epistemological "web of which they are not the masters, of which they cannot see the whole, and of whose breadth they have a very inadequate idea" (*AOK*, 126).

This fragmentation and dispersal of the subject of history has its parallel in many contemporary English novels. Although some are set in the midst of identifiable historical events such as the Sepoy Mutiny of 1857 or the Easter Rebellion of 1916, writers generally present history in the decentered manner we can associate with the history of mentalities. Well-known personages, and the attendant idea that great men (or, rarely, women) *make* history are conspicuously absent. Although even Thackeray wrote about the Battle of Waterloo, the contemporary novelist tends to put his or her characters in contact with less well-known, marginal events; or to display the lives of people who live through a great historical event in virtual ignorance of its significance to their lives; or to leave out the event altogether, substituting for it a symbolic, even caricatural or parodic event. Thus, in *An Ice Cream War* William Boyd writes not about the Somme but about an obscure conflict between Germans and Englishmen in colonial Africa; in *The New Confessions*, when Boyd's hero does reach the horrors of trench warfare at Ypres, he is promptly rescued by his uncle and put to work making uplifting propaganda films with Harold Faithfull, a prosperous director who sedulously avoids any contact with real troops or live ammunition. J. G. Farrell describes a group of Anglo-Irish men and women who sit out the years of Michael Collins and the Black and Tans in a backwater hotel on the Irish seacoast; Isabel Colegate's *Shooting Party* is first "about" a group of Englishmen hunting pheasants, yet it clearly derives its ironies and interest from the heavily foreshadowed Great War that will follow in less than a year. Such a decentered view of history permits the writer to pay attention to what seem to be the more important questions of how ordinary people assimilate their private lives to public history. What makes these novels historical is the text's own interest in the "code of before and after" and in the intersection of a private consciousness with the unique, unrepeatable events of its own time.

Among the many ways in which a novel can encode the before and after, two most characteristic of contemporary British fiction are deliberate anachronism and what might be called the historical variant of dramatic irony. The novelist frequently exploits the reader's awareness of the future that awaits characters who are secure in their certainty that "Nuremburg is a city of tolerance" or that England will never surrender her claim to Singapore, India, Egypt, or Ireland. Part of the humor of *The Siege of Krishnapur* comes from the narrator's deadpan chronicling of the more bizarre theories of Victorian medicine. The multiple time shifts, characteristic of modernist fiction, in a historical novel similarly tend to keep both past and present visible, thus preventing the comfortable escape into the past that is characteristic of romantic fiction. Deliberate anachronism—a matter perhaps of calling Trotsky a Trotskyite in 1917—reinforces this effect. Shuttled between their own time and that of the characters, readers become implicated in the past. This collapsing of clear distinctions between past and present is neither in the service of Nabakovian nostalgia (*Speak, Memory*) or Proustian euphoria. Since few of the serious novels treat heroic incidents, this sense of involvement is especially disturbing. The reader cannot be inspired to imitation, but neither has he or she been given a lofty perspective from which to judge or even learn from the lessons of history. The past still seems alive in his or her own mistaken complacencies, vestigial racism, facile acceptance of scientific views that, doubtless, from the perspective of the future will seem as absurd as the notion that cholera is spread by poisonous clouds.

To keep the reader from retreating into a comfortably finished time, the writers often splice the fictional with the actual in obtrusive or at least highly visible ways, as when Anthony Burgess describes Alfred Adler as having a voice resembling that of one of his own fictional characters or Iris Murdoch houses one of her characters on a street whose Joycean associations are inevitable. Tonal shifts, from the nearly romantic to unadulterated farce, recur in both Burgess and Farrell. The discomforts these techniques engender underline the problems of understanding the past and indeed of experiencing ourselves as people whose private lives intersect public events and bear a connection, itself not easily described, with a public past.

The contemporary English novel often emphasizes the difficulties of knowing the truth about the past. Whether we are reading Paul Scott's descriptions of his narrator's efforts to discover the truth about a rape in the face of the death or disappearance of most of the people who knew the facts or Anthony Burgess's account of an editor who recovers a manuscript, wrapped in a plastic bag, from its author's bathroom, we are aware that knowledge of the past is always mediated. Multiple narration often accentuates the vulnerability of the past to interpretation; like Stanley Fish's Milton scholars, the readers of history never seem to agree on a common text. The Irish peasant and her English landlord scarcely seem to live in the same time and place. When eye witnesses can be located, they prove unreliable; it is not only that people forget, but that *even at the time* their own fantasy mechanisms, their absorption in the minutiae of private life, prevent them from understanding the larger political and social contexts of an event in their lives. Failing to discover, to give the reader the real presence of the historical text, the novel concentrates instead on the process by which people become aware—or more often, defer becoming aware—of the public life of their time.

That human beings so readily misunderstand their history is partly attributable, so these novels argue, to their reliance on narratives whose sources, always difficult to specify, include literature. Both conscious formulations of the kind found in political speeches and unconscious assumptions about one's place in the world and its history are essentially mythic: highly selective narratives into which the random events of contemporary life must be fitted, often with violence. These myths, persuasive, consoling, lethal, are what the novelist must expose and to which he or she must oppose another, inevitably narrative, vision. Thus, novelist after novelist in effect deconstructs an attractive mythology: the myth that English civilization is superior to pagan culture; that colonialism exists to enlighten the masses; the myth that Ireland is a beautiful mother who demands the sacrifice of her children; as well as the myth that Irish peasants, humorous and dirty, love their elegant landlords. Allusions to the literary sources or affirmations of such myths, in the instances noted—for example, to Rudyard Kipling, William Butler Yeats, and the Somerville and Ross stories—abound in recent British novels. Yet although Paul Scott, in his *The Raj Quartet*, clearly is interested in replacing one myth with another, "truer" one, most novelists seem essentially distrustful of finished narratives. To avoid the complicity of literature in myth making, they go to great lengths to present history as it is experienced by its participants who, lacking all knowledge of its outcome, are frequently wrong about what is going on ("the British will never give up India") and can experience its impact on their lives only fitfully and at random.

The recognition that narratives falsify does not, however, imply that we can do without them. Indeed the view of Hayden White, who argues in his *Metahistory* and elsewhere that all histories are narrative (those that do not appear to be so being ironic) and implicate themselves in the processes of selection, emphasis, and tone that characterize other narratives, receives strong theoretical confirmation from Jacques Derrida. As is well known, Derrida has argued persuasively against the simple bipolar oppositions that have, in his view, characterized Western thought since Plato: reason versus emotion, male versus female, presence versus absence, and so on. In his *Of Grammatology*, Derrida defines the most fundamental of these, the one that enables the others, as the opposition between the signifier and the signified, the sign and its referent. "That the signifier is originarily and essentially (and not only for a finite and created spirit) trace, that it is *always already in the position of the signifier*, is the apparently innocent proposition within which the metaphysics of the logos, of presence and consciousness, must reflect upon writing as its death and its resource" (OG, 73). For Derrida then, the opposition between the world of events and the text is meaningless: "il n'y a pas de hors-texte"; "there have never been anything but supplements, substitutive significations which could only come forth in a chain of differential references, the 'real' supervening, and being added only while taking on meaning from a trace and from an invocation of the supplement, etc." (OG, 159). This view could be taken to mean that history is inconsequential, easily juggled away (as in Yale criticism at its most extreme), just as the view that literature has ceased to offer us timeless real presence can lead to a reduction of fiction to mere verbal play, an endless manipulation of rhetoric. Yet, as Frank Lentricchia argues persuasively, deconstruction need not lead away from historicism; Derrida himself has remarked, "I don't destroy the subject; I situate it."[5] For Lentricchia, Foucault's "naked statement of his goals as a historian is . . . evidence . . . of a passionate belief that genuine history-writing is not only possible, but is *made possible* by Derrida's revision of traditional thought in general and of structuralism in particular."[6] Derrida's theory need not mean that history does not exist, that the Holocaust did not happen or that we can live as if the hydrogen bomb were a figment of the imagination, but that we always experience our history through texts.

From the perspective of historical fiction, we might say that history and fiction cannot be figured as absolute oppositions between "what really happened" and what some writer invented; to quote Fleishman, "This puts literature and life, signs and objects, so equably on the same plane that they enter the night in which all cats are grey" (FWK, 12). What happened can never be seen without the aid of language, which is always, in Derrida's sense "written," secondary; moreover, the actors in history can never encounter it pure, as if for the first time. When Margaret Thatcher perceives that England's

[5] Quoted in Frank Lentricchia, *After the New Criticism* (Chicago: University of Chicago Press, 1980), 174.

[6] Ibid., 191.

colony in the Falklands is threatened, she acts in terms of a script, a text that is one version of England's self-image, notions of empire, civilizing privileges, naval domination, and so on that have their sources in popular historical narrative and even in literature. Derrida's theory can encourage us to see a historical fiction that is conscious of the fictivity of our historical experience as a powerful instrument of representation and cultural criticism. Moreover, fictions are in Derrida's sense a necessary supplement to the gaps in our knowledge of history. Every written history must to some extent reconstruct the always absent past, and the most sophisticated historian's hypothesis about if or in what sense Minoan culture was matriarchal differs in degree, but not in kind, from a fictional hypothesis, accompanied by imagined characters and invented dialogue, that we might find in a Mary Renault novel.

Indeed, just as the equation of history with major historical events would seem naive to a contemporary historian whose field is constantly being renegotiated by sociohistorians, so the contemporary novelist seeks to discard limiting notions of history. The idea that we ought to pay attention to the "unspeakable," to the repressed, to the signifying absences in our discourse, that matter so much to contemporary theoreticians—whether of a deconstructionist, Marxist, or psychoanalytic bent—clearly corresponds to the practices of several recent British novelists. We see this tendency already in Elizabeth Bowen, when she uses her reader's knowledge of the outcome of the Irish struggle for independence to create a sense of irony about what her complacent Anglo-Irish family does not want to, cannot see; it reaches its fullest development in Iris Murdoch's *Nuns and Soldiers*, where the omission of all contemporary references to public life—in contrast to a textual obsession with the history of Poland before 1945 and repeated references to the characters' obsession with their personal pasts—signals an ominous absence, an inability of the characters to connect themselves to the English past and public present they all share that, whether they will it or not, shape their lives.

History as presented in the contemporary British novel is neither glamorous nor consoling. It is too diffuse to offer lessons, too unfinished to constitute a space into which we can escape; and we ourselves, implicated in the failures of the past, cannot even enjoy its ironies comfortably. Whatever the authors' professed politics, their novels resonate with a profound pessimism about the consequences of public action. What actuates these fictions is not, then, a confidence that the past will teach us how to behave, but a quieter conviction that it is better to know than to remain ignorant, even though what we learn is the enormous difficulty of understanding our lives historically.

. . .

The chapters that follow consider the movement of historical consciousness in more than a dozen British novels, all but one written since the war. The first section, "Troubles in Ireland," looks at fictional representations of England's difficult history in her oldest colony. The Easter Rising, memorialized in Yeats's "Easter 1916," is the topic of Iris Murdoch's *The Red and the Green*, a novelistic deconstruction of Yeats that seeks to make a shapeless and unfinished history visible to an audience that knows it as a well-made story. The guerilla war that followed the execution of the Easter rebels is the subject both of Elizabeth Bowen's *The Last September* and J. G. Farrell's *Troubles*. Both novels present that war obliquely, from the perspective of the Protestant upper classes, but although Bowen's novel is a comedy of manners, Farrell's is blacker, closer to farce. Yet the real subject of both books is the Anglo-Irish consciousness struggling, like Freud's dreamer, to remain oblivious to external stimuli. As the Protestant-Catholic conflict continues in Northern Ireland, several contemporary writers have contributed novels that testify to the problems of treating what is clearly felt to be an unbearable present in the mode of social realism. Thomas Kilroy's *The Big Chapel*, a historical novel set one hundred years before the renewal of the Irish troubles in 1969, uses history, in Lion Feuchtwanger's phrase, as a disguise for an analysis of the present. Kilroy's picture of a small Irish village torn apart by a Catholic bishop's attempt to close a secular school suggests that the divisions of Irish history, although fiercely defended, are not fixed in the very nature of things.

In the years since World War II, England has not only lost an empire, but has been subject to a series of espionage scandals that have weakened public confidence in the nation's leadership. The story of Kim Philby has become as mythic to postwar British writers as the story of Bonnie Prince Charlie was to earlier generations. "Philby and His Fictions" analyzes several works, including Philby's own autobiography, that attempt to account for his motives, drawing a relationship between his story and the story of England's decline. That the loss of public confidence relates to a loss of a shared history or even a shared connection to public life is a central theme in Iris Murdoch's *Nuns and Soldiers*. This story of outsiders—a Jewish philosopher, a Polish refugee, an American nun are among its chief characters—looks at the ways in which "the alienating necessities" of history, in Fredric Jameson's phrase, "will not forget us," however much we might prefer to ignore them.[7]

The final section, "Apocalypse," begins with Paul Scott's *The Raj Quartet* (1966–1975), which, like Murdoch's *The Red and the Green*, interests itself in the role of myths in shaping public behavior. Closer to modernism than Murdoch, Scott ends by creating a countermyth of escape from history into timelessness. The last historical scene in Scott's novel is a description of the religious massacres that followed India's independence, rendered apocalyptically as the end of British, Hindu, and Muslim illusions about public life. Doris Lessing's *Children of Violence* series (1952–1968) ends with something closer to a real apocalypse, the destruction of Britain by a nuclear accident. By symbolically ending history, the novel enacts the anger of women who have been excluded from partic-

---

[7] *The Political Unconscious: Narrative as a Socially Symbolic Act* (Ithaca, N.Y.: Cornell University Press, 1981), 102.

ipation in public history and ignored by history texts; further, it suggests that the passivity and madness traditionally assigned to women (one must either stay home drinking tea or be thought a crazy suffragette) have become characteristic of all twentieth-century human beings facing their history. Finally, we will look at a straightforward apocalypse, Anthony Burgess's *The End of the World News* (1983). This novel splices together two historical narratives—the life of Sigmund Freud and an episode in the life of Leon Trotsky—and a science fiction narrative about the destruction of the planet Earth. The spatialized history that results offers a powerful critique of what Burgess sees as the ahistorical tendencies of contemporary culture, be it the preference for synchrony over diachrony in some literary criticism or the trivializing of the past in television programming.

Taken as a whole, these novels witness the power of postwar British fiction to identify the problems of understanding and responding to history in the twentieth century and the ability of a disparate group of writers, through modernist concerns with consciousness and the distinctive accents of individual voices, to examine those problems. Certainly the writers examined here are not the only British writers whose works demonstrate a marked consciousness of public history. With the exception of Burgess—and even he makes much of Ernest Jones and Freud's exile in London—these writers are all preoccupied with their own country's history; Britain as a colonizer of Africa, India, and Ireland provides the subject for six of the nine novels treated at length. In this respect they differ from novels such as D. M. Thomas's *White Hotel*, Sybille Bedford's *A Legacy*, Gabriel Fielding's *The Birthday King*, or the first two volumes of Richard Hughes's *The Human Predicament*, which reveal the attempts by English writers to imagine a foreign past. Yet the novels considered have more than local significance, testifying as they do their authors' understanding of an intellectual universe in which we all live—one in which the subject of history is fragmented and uncertain and from which the ungrounded imagination no longer seems to offer an escape. This intellectual universe corresponds to some of the features of the political and historical world the writers describe: the sense of victimization by history seen in our inability to end ancient tribal conflicts such as the one in Northern Ireland, our greatly diminished sense of the importance of Western culture in the world, and especially our fear that we and our sonnets and our history will be blown to fragments on some not-too-distant day. In their unillusioned portrayal of the consequences of such anxieties, these novelists testify to the still vital role of fiction in shaping our understanding of history.

PART ONE

Troubles in Ireland

CHAPTER ONE

Iris Murdoch's *The Red and the Green*

To SELECT, to simplify, to arrange elements in the patterns most congenial to itself: these are temptations the novel always faces when it attempts to draw an unfinished public history within the boundaries of finished form. The deep suspicion of narrative that attaches itself to this perception, and the resultant struggle to write historical fiction that avoids fictionalizing history, can be felt in many contemporary English novels. No one argues more persistently against the consolations of form than Iris Murdoch, whose plots are always characterized by what A. S. Byatt has called a "respect for the contingent," by accidents, coincidences, and surprises intended to suggest the limits of authorial knowledge and the density of real experience. In the only one of her novels that fits conventional definitions of historical fiction, *The Red and the Green*, Murdoch confronts these problems explicitly. Her novel takes place during Easter Week 1916; in other words, it describes a rebellion immortalized by W. B. Yeats in a time and place immortalized by James Joyce. To find "other words," to deconstruct the attractive mythology of Easter Week in the service of a larger criticism of literature's complicity in the violence of public history, is the novel's goal.

In his perceptive essay on "Le roman historique et l'histoire," André Daspré argues that the interest of the historical novel lies in the oxymoronic nature of its fictional world, "composé à la fois d'éléments fictifs et d'éléments réels," where real history must be assimilated to a fictional story. According to Daspré, the historical novelist seeks out "la confrontation directe entre le monde réel et le monde fictif, a l'intérieur même du roman."[1] Thus, the critical reader must

---

[1] The historical novel is "composed at the same time of fictive and real

consider not only the relation between the fictional world and reality, but the relation between reality and fiction *within* the novel's imaginary world. If we apply his suggestion to *The Red and the Green*, then the critical problem is not so much to see how faithful or vivid the portrait of the Easter Rebellion is, but to see how it is integrated with the lives of Murdoch's characters, and to what effect. But that problem hinges on another, for Murdoch's fictional world is full of literary fragments that add a third term: at the center of her novel, the real and the imagined confront the imagined worlds of other works of literature. Millie fights at Boland's Mill, but afterward goes to live on Eccles Street. And while Murdoch's fictional world is not always a successful assimilation of its literary and historical sources—Donna Gerstenberger is justified in deploring the "educational symposia"[2] on Irish politics in the early chapters—a confrontation of literature and history is the novel's central theme. For, in *The Red and the Green*, Murdoch uses historical fiction as a device for examining the relationship between fiction and history. She analyzes the relationship between artistic and revolutionary impulses, the role of literature in creating public events, and the fictional nature of much public history. In the end, she suggests that literature cannot be free from the historical world, any more than the revolutionary can be free from the fictions that shape his or her perception of history.

The choice of the Easter Rebellion was anything but accidental for a writer concerned with the involvement of literature in history. Outside Ireland, of course, the rebellion is chiefly remembered as the occasion for a few Yeats poems and for O'Casey's *The Plough and the Stars*. Indeed, in the early twentieth century the Irish independence movement was extraordinarily literary. Three of the fifteen "Easter martyrs"— Pearse, MacDonagh, and Plunkett—were poets, part of a literary renaissance that Conor Cruise O'Brien sees as a dis-

---

elements." One finds in them a "direct confrontation between the real world and the fictive world, at the very interior of the novel." From *Revue d'Histoire Littéraire de la France* 75 (1975): 235, 240.

[2] *Iris Murdoch*, 57.

placement of the Parnellite movement, which "deviated from politics into literature" (*PHP*, 356). Perhaps, as Sean O'Casey puts it, the "Plunkets" (*sic*) and "MacDonaghs" merely "paddled in the summer-time in the dull waters of poor verse," failing to appreciate and therefore rioting at the first performance of *The Playboy of the Western World* and in Yeats's work caring only for "the dream which fashioned the little play about Cathleen ni Houlihan."[3] Yet, Yeats himself was to wonder in "The Man and the Echo" if "that play of mine set out / Certain men the English shot," an act to which the poor verse contributed as well (*CP*, 337).[4] William Irwin Thompson argues that the Irish rebels were failed artists who attempted "to make of the state a work of art," who "lived as if they were in a work of art." What the artist imagined of Irish independence was translated into action, which is a reversal of the process by which the artist is usually seen "portraying" history. As Thompson says, "Easter 1916 is a public event which became a private imagination in the art of A.E., Yeats, and O'Casey. But to regard the historic event as the known with which we solve for the unknown of the work of art is to misunderstand history and art by distorting the relationship between them. The event of Easter 1916 is itself a work of imagination, and to understand the event we must take into account the manner in which private imagination . . . became part of the process of public event."[5]

Throughout *The Red and the Green*, "the event of Easter 1916" is treated as a paradigm of all past events—including literary works—that give rise to the imagination and, at the same time, it is presented as the outcome of such imagining, and the standard against which to measure those literary characters who are portrayed as bringing it into being. Historical

[3] *Drums under the Windows* (New York: Macmillan, 1956), 350–51. It is possible that O'Casey's *Autobiographies* is one of the sources for *The Red and the Green*; "The Red above the Green," the song over which Cathal and Pat Dumay argue, gives its title to a chapter in *I Knock at the Door*.

[4] From "The Man and the Echo."

[5] William Irwin Thompson, *The Imagination of an Insurrection: Dublin 1916* (New York: Oxford University Press, 1967), ix, 115, 235.

figures are overheard, or have reported conversations with the characters, but they are never on stage. Each character is assigned a political role and a set of political opinions, which are often reflected in his or her name: Barney the Celtic revivalist, Pat the Irish Volunteer, Andrew the unwilling officer of the anachronistic cavalry, Millie the Constance Markievicz soldier-woman, Kathleen the apolitical victim who echoes MacNeill's warning that "there is no such person as Caitlin Ni Uallachain" when she cries, "She! Who is Ireland indeed. . . . There is no such thing as dying for Ireland" (RG, 193). Motives for political action are inseparable from personal, psychological intentions. Pat's aversion to women, for example, is closely linked to his adoration of Pearse: "Pat approved of the absence from [Pearse's] life of women and all that they represented" (RG, 76). Similarly the impact of a political crisis, for many characters, is largely personal: Kathleen and Frances grieve for Pat, whom they love, and not for the Rising, to which they are indifferent. Finally, as Peter Kemp indicates, historical relationships between England and Ireland are written into the relationships among members of the "incestuous" Anglo-Irish family to which the major characters belong: "family tensions and quarrels illustrate the forces which, on a larger scale, keep the countries apart: jealousies, temperamental antagonisms, religious intolerance. The language of international affairs . . . is used . . . of lesser events—'Millie's difficulty would be Christopher's opportunity' " (RG, 64).[6]

This skewed version of a political aphorism is but one of the many literary allusions that are woven into the lives of the novel's characters, its setting, and its language. The novel's sense of a literary past is an extension of its historical consciousness and reminds the reader of how other writers have viewed public events. In reimagining Easter 1916, Murdoch may very well, as R. B. Kershner, Jr., points out, have borne in mind We Always Treat Women Too Well, a 1947 novel by

[6] Peter Kemp, "The Fight Against Fantasy: Iris Murdoch's The Red and the Green," Modern Fiction Studies 15 (1969): 404.

Raymond Queneau, to whom she dedicated *Under the Net*.
Queneau's novel, also set in Easter Week 1916, describes the
fictitious occupation of a branch post office by a band of rebels
whose password is "Finnegans wake." In a Dublin constructed entirely of literary allusions (mostly to Joyce), Gertie
Girdle, held hostage and subjected to what might be termed
consensual rape, awaits rescue by her sterling fiancé, Sidney
Cartwright, who, at the end of the novel, commands the firing
squad that executes her remaining captors. Queneau's is a
world full of evident misinformation ("the codpiece" is glossed
as "a part of the masculine costume, extremely common in
Ireland") and anachronism (when a character remarks, "Anyone can see we're in the land of James Joyce," the author adds
a footnote: "Caffrey, being illiterate, could not have known in
1916 that *Ulysses* had not yet appeared" [*WWW*, 83; 66]).
But, as Valerie Caton argues in her introduction to the English translation, although Queneau's playful novel may well
be deadly serious about combating the "glorification of the
power instinct" in popular fictions about rape and murder,[7] it
is not at all serious about Irish history. Murdoch seems to
have taken from Queneau the notion of liberating oneself from
the grip of a literary work by displacing, rearranging, and
reinventing it, but, for her, the purpose of doing so is to enable the reader to see the historical world that literature for-
malizes.

Murdoch's most extensive allusions are to Irish writers, especially Joyce and Yeats.[8] Alluding to these two figures, from

[7] From *We Always Treat Women Too Well*, trans. Barbara Wright (New
York: New Directions, 1981), 5.

[8] See Howard German, "Allusions in the Early Novels of Iris Murdoch,"
Modern Fiction Studies 15 (1969): 361–77, and "The Range of Allusions in the
Novels of Iris Murdoch," *Journal of Modern Literature* 2 (1971): 57–81. The
latter article treats *The Red and the Green*; German points out that Barney
Drumm is linked to the life and works of Oliver St. John Gogarty, and to a
character in George Moore's *The Lake* named Oliver Gogarty (75). Millie,
whom Barney adores, repeats the key words "bottom" and "yes" from Molly's
soliloquy and, like Yeats's Cathleen ni Houlihan, proposes to sell herself.
German points to a number of other Yeatsean allusions—to "Easter 1916,"
"Sailing to Byzantium," *A Herne's Egg*—and finds the novel's animal im-

whom most of Murdoch's readers have taken their ideas about
Ireland in the early twentieth century, helps to create a recognizable setting. But Murdoch's allusions do more. By creating a world in which it is possible to encounter a character
of obviously Joycean extraction described in language that
echoes Yeats, the allusions violate the formal unity of Joyce's
or Yeats's world. Such violations compel us to note that
Joyce's Dublin or Yeats's Holy Ireland is but one version of
Ireland, a unified vision of a more complicated reality. Yet, as
the novel succeeds in making us aware of how Yeats, Joyce,
or the artist generally impose a perspective on history, it also
insists that the revolutionary imposes, in very similar ways,
an equally limited perspective.[9]

The Joycean allusions in *The Red and the Green* are easily
recognized. That the novel provides an alternative perspective on his more familiar Dublin becomes clear when we note
the number of echoes of Joyce's settings, images, and characters. To be sure, Dublin is so much Joyce's city that any novel
set there would seem to echo him; clearly, Joyce is not the
sole proprietor of Howth, Clontarf, or even Findlater's
Church. But that the revolutionary Pat Dumay lives on Bles-
sington Street, one street north of Eccles Street, while Sandycove, with the Martello Tower always visible (*RG*, 5, 9, 187),
is his English cousin's home, is more than coincidental. The
sense of being once more in Joyce's world is also owed in part
to the novel's colors, which are those of *Dubliners* and *A Portrait of the Artist as a Young Man*. The "red" and "green" of

---

agery, which stresses the mind-body split, an echo of Swift (76–77). Gerstenberger develops the allusion to "Easter 1916," demonstrating that the novel's
structure "mirrors Yeats' poem in its general form" from the initial "casual
comedy" to the "transfiguration through sacrifice with its catalog of the heroes' names" (53).

[9] See Murray Krieger, "Fiction, History, and Empirical Reality," in *Theory
of Criticism* (Baltimore: Johns Hopkins University Press, 1976), 149–75, for a
discussion of this point. Noting that "imagination—as a form-giving power—
must give even history's raw data their intelligible contours," Krieger says
that "prior intercourse with fictions" conditions the imagination to "see form
in history's casual sequence. . . . Thus the imagination collapses history into
the categories of human form: in effect, it turns history itself into a fiction."

the title, frequently iterated, are more than national emblems. These colors recall Dante's press box, with its green brush for Parnell and maroon for Davitt and the chain of images they generate—the "green rose," the picture of the green world with maroon clouds, the holly and ivy of the Christmas dinner. Frances's sash, as she walks across the green lawn, is mauve (*RG*, 25), and Millie is twice described wearing mauve (*RG*, 157, 161), although she is usually associated with red—red shawl, reddish-brown hair, a house painted with powdery red wash (211, 56, 53). Christopher picks her a "lovely green rosebud" (119). As in *Dubliners*, brown is the color of dull materialism devoid of imagination: Kathleen wears it (*RG*, 43, 128); her drawing room is brown with brownish-white curtains (*RG*, 42); to Barney the Liffey looks a "dark, dirty brown" and the clouds above it are "whitish brown" (*RG*, 128).[10] Quite naturally, after MacNeill cancels the Rising, the moon seems to Pat to shine "through a brown haze" (*RG*, 202). Similarly, as in Joyce, yellow is associated with what is both sensual and repellent: while Barney is reflecting on the lies he told Frances about frequenting Dublin's brothels, the sky over Kingston seems "yellowish" (*RG*, 97); the rocks "remained senselessly jagged and yellow" (*RG*, 102). In a scene at Millie's when Pat's visit is interrupted by Barney, her light is yellow (*RG*, 84); after Millie's proposition, Andrew looks up at a "thin papery yellow" sky (*RG*, 163).[11] Similarly, words that acquire a special significance in

[10] On Joyce's use of brown in *Dubliners* see Brewster Ghiselin, "The Unity of Joyce's *Dubliners*," in *Dubliners: Text, Criticism, and Notes*, ed. Robert Scholes and A. Walton Litz (1969; Harmondsworth: Penguin, 1976), 318. "Brown, like green, is associated with the limitations of life in Dublin, but much more emphatically. It recurs many times in the stories. It is mentioned as the tint of Dublin streets and is found in the freckled face and in the eyes of Miss Ivors, in 'The Dead' . . . who is militantly Irish."

[11] In *A Portrait of the Artist as a Young Man*, note a "thick yellow scum" on the water at the Dublin quays, "the yellow gasflames" of the prostitutes' quarter, "the yellow lamps . . . of the brothels," "a soft cocoon of yellowish haze" around the city as Stephen sees it immediately after his vision of the "hell of lecherous goatish fiends" waiting to punish his sexual excesses. James

Joyce are repeated: Pat, Andrew, and Cathal are "paralyzed" (*RG*, 152, 159, 233); Andrew in bed with Millie is "like a paralytic" (*RG*, 239).[12] Cathal, like Heron, resembles a bird (*RG*, 106, 134); his face "like a piece of ivory" (*RG*, 106) recalls Eileen's hands and the "Tower of Ivory" images of *A Portrait of the Artist*.

But these attempts to reimagine Joyce's world would be less significant were it not for the fact that two of the novel's characters, Barney Drumm and Pat Dumay, are based on Joyce's characters. Barney certainly resembles Leopold Bloom; Howard German notes that he wears a skullcap that makes him "look like a Jew" (*RG*, 130);[13] he has a platonic infatuation with a woman named Millie that recalls Bloom's marriage to Molly (Molly's daughter, of course, is named Milly), and is stepfather, if not exactly Odysseus, to Pat's Telemakhos. Any attempt to seize the significance of his relationship to Bloom must take into account, however, that he buys his skullcap at Finnegan's store and resembles Stephen in a number of ways, most notably in his desire to write and his renunciation of a priestly vocation. Qualities that in *Ulysses* are seen as opposites are merged in *The Red and the Green* and yet form the basis of a credible character. Perhaps a view of Barney as a pastiche of Stephen and Bloom is, in fact, more important than his separate relation to each. Like the Dumay's house, one street north of Eccles Street, Barney's character is not a reproduction but a reimagining of its original that generates new possibilities: what if Bloom had been Catholic, what if Stephen were middle-aged?

These questions are precisely those that Joyce, with his conception of the novel as a unified object detached from the historical world, does not want the reader to ask. By prompt-

---

Joyce, *A Portrait of the Artist as a Young Man* (Harmondsworth: Penguin, 1976), 66, 100, 102, 138.

[12] For a discussion of paralysis as a theme in *Dubliners*, see Ghiselin, 318–19. Joyce, in a famous letter to Grant Richards (6 May 1906), called Dublin "the centre of paralysis." (Scholes and Litz, *Dubliners*, 269).

[13] "The Range of Allusions in the Novels of Iris Murdoch," *Journal of Modern Literature* 2 (1971): 77.

ing them, Murdoch suggests a fallacy in the aesthetic of the early modernist novel, more specifically, in that aesthetic as articulated in extreme form by Stephen at the end of *A Portrait of the Artist*. We see the point most clearly when we compare the famous scene in *A Portrait of the Artist* where Stephen, having just renounced his ambition to join the Jesuits, takes the walk along the sea that culminates in the epiphany of the bird-woman, with a similar scene in *The Red and the Green*. In Murdoch's novel, Barney, the spoiled priest, retraces Stephen's path and, like him, looks back at Dublin but, unlike Stephen, sees there "the two tall rival spires at Kingstown, Catholic and Protestant, shifting constantly in their relation to each other except when from the Martello tower at Sandycove they could be seen superimposed" (*RG*, 98). For a lyrical affirmation of the artist's vocation and his flight over the nets of church and country, Murdoch substitutes an acknowledgment of the complexities of real experience. The view from the Martello tower, although attractively unified, is an optical illusion. That criticism of Stephen's aesthetic—that too many people and issues are subsumed to the single vision of formal perfection—is implicit in the novel's fragmented point of view as well. By focusing on Frances, Millie, Christopher, and Andrew, as well as on Pat and Barney, Murdoch reinforces the suggestion that the real world is made up of conflicting egos and interests that cannot, except by illusion, be subordinated to the claims of one vision.

Although the scene we have just examined suggests a fallacy in a vision of art that detaches it from the historical world, Murdoch's characterization of Pat Dumay offers the idea that it is equally fallacious to think of the revolutionary as someone who, choosing to act in the historical world, has nothing in common with the artist. Pat is consistently linked to Stephen Dedalus. Like Stephen, he seeks furtive pleasures in the "dark doorways off the Dublin quays" (*RG*, 78). His revolutionary vocation consistently recalls Stephen's artistic one; gun smuggling succeeds because of "cunning" (*RG*, 80); Pat's decision to join the Volunteers is "lonely and secret" (*RG*,

81).[14] His patriotism is "some distilled essence of romanticism, something bitter, dark, and pure" (73)—a description that would serve equally well for Stephen's aesthetics at the end of *A Portrait of the Artist*. The Ireland Pat loves is "the refined purified counterpart of his Irishness": "If he could have believed himself a poet, a creator of any kind, capable of lifting out of the muck and mess of life some self-contained perfect object, this would have seemed to him a goal worthy of his powers" (*RG*, 78). Thus, Pat, who idolizes Patrick Pearse, seems to embody Thompson's view of that Irish martyr as a poet who attempted to "make of the state a work of art."[15] The connection with Stephen, like the emphasis on Pat's latent homosexuality, undercuts his revolutionary ardor, implying that it substitutes for deeper impulses.

Less visible than the Joyce allusions are allusions to Yeats throughout *The Red and the Green*. Most refer the reader to poems in which Yeats questions the meaning of politics; often they comment on a character's behavior or more generally call action into question. Thus, the allusion to "Sailing to Byzantium" that German notes: Christopher Bellman watches his daughter walking in the "monumentally quiet" garden, her still figure seeming to be "gathered into the dim morning silence where not even a bird was stirring" (*JML*, 76). This reference to a poem that envisions a timeless world of artifice as an alternative to the changing and ultimately decaying world of the "young / In one another's arms" (*CP*, 191) suggests that the cause of Frances's strange behavior is fear that the young man she loves will die. Similarly, Andrew's fumbling attempts to recover Millie's lapis lazuli earring predict and comment upon his death at Passchendaele. They underscore his incompatibility with the ideal world of art as seen in the carving of Yeats's "Lapis Lazuli," with its "longlegged bird, / A symbol of longevity" (*CP*, 293). Christopher, contemplating Millie's precarious wealth, thinks "But all this must shortly vanish like

---

[14] ". . . using for my defence the only arms I allow myself to use—silence, exile, and cunning" (Joyce, *A Portrait of the Artist as a Young Man* [1916; Harmondsworth: Penguin, 1976], 247).

[15] From *Imagination of an Insurrection*, ix.

a dream" (*RG*, 66), which suggests the lines from Yeats's "The Blood and the Moon": "And God-appointed Berkeley that proved all things a dream / That this preposterous pig of a world, its farrow that so solid seem, / Must vanish on the instant if the mind but change its theme" (*CP*, 233).

So, too, Barney is described as feeling "sunk and drowned like a fly in treacle" (*RG*, 167) in his love for Millie; Yeats's "Ego Dominus Tuus" asks, "What portion in the world can the artist have?" and images action as "the struggle of the fly in marmalade" (*CP*, 159). Thus, Barney's futile passions comment on the futility of Irish politics; Millie herself in the epilogue, pathetically boasting of her bravery during Easter Week, recalls Yeats's description of Constance Markievicz in "In Memory of Eva Gore-Booth and Con Markiewicz": "When withered old and skeleton gaunt / An image of such politics" (*CP*, 229). Yeats's mystical vision of a timeless world is also suggested in Andrew's characterization of his family as "the snake that eats its own tail" (*RG*, 13); the syntax recalls Stephen's characterization of Ireland, but the words are from Yeats's "There": "There all serpent-tails are bit" (*CP*, 284). Barney's desire to "purge his imagination of these pictures of violence" (*RG*, 184) and his conviction that "Easter must purge" the imagery of Good Friday (*RG*, 223) echo the language and theme of Yeats's "Byzantium." A more explicit condemnation of Irish politics is found in Frances's question to Barney, "What will Home Rule do for that woman begging in the street?" with its realistic answer, "Nothing. . . . They'll have the pleasure of being exploited by P. Flanagan instead of J. Smith" (*RG*, 101). This dialogue seems a prosy echo of Yeats's "Parnell": "Ireland shall get her freedom and you still break stone" (*CP*, 309).

Yet the novel does not adopt Yeats's pose of the mystic turning away from the historical world any more than it adopts Stephen Dedalus's version of that impulse. Indeed, its epilogue is in part a gloss on Yeats's famous "Easter 1916" and, although Frances's emotions accord with those of the poem, Murdoch's observations on the whole suggest that Yeats glamourized this historical event. Yeats's resonant conclusion, with its conviction that the dead rebels are "changed utterly" ("Easter 1916," *CP*, 180) is mocked in an earlier passage in which Andrew Chase-White mistakenly believes that he "has changed utterly" (*RG*, 155) because Frances refused to marry him. One's sense of Ireland, in the epilogue of *The Red and the Green*, is not of an oppressed country transformed "utterly" into terrible beauty, but of a poor country being recolonized. The dead rebels' rooms are rented by their mother to a retired major in the British army; their cousin's house, Finglas, is painted pink and renamed Hillcrest by its new English owners. Frances's catalog of the rebels—"They shot most of them. Pearse, Connolly, MacDonagh, MacDermott, MacBride, Joseph Plunkett—And they hanged Roger Casement" (*RG*, 271–72)—resembles only superficially Yeats's lines from "Easter 1916": "And what if excess of love / Bewildered them till they died? / I write it out in a verse—MacDonagh and MacBride / And Connolly and Pearse" (*CP*, 179). By attributing death to guns and hangmen, and by refusing to echo Yeats's meter, the novel suggests a less attractive reality behind Yeats's famous interpretation of Easter Week.

The novel's allusions to Yeats and Joyce, then, define some limitations of the visions of revolutionaries and artists. But they do more. They suggest resemblances, points of collusion, between the two groups: a tendency to simplify reality, a willingness to glamourize violent death. The words of Barney's journal at first seem to run through his head "all pure and glittering like a clear brook," but then he thinks "perhaps the words were stones in the brook . . . which through a trembling translucent medium he saw steadfastly arrayed before him" (*RG*, 86). In Yeats's "Easter 1916," political fanaticism is the stone that troubles "the living stream" in a world where all life changes "minute by minute" (*CP*, 179). In a more general way, most of the literary allusions in *The Red and the Green* have a similar function: to suggest that "history" and "literature" are not two self-contained categories, but continually react to and contaminate each other.

Indeed, the title of the novel comes from a passage that centers on the relationship of art to historical reality and the possibility that fictions create history. At the beginning of chapter 8, Cathal sings: "Charge it again, boys, charge it again / *Pardonnez-moi je vous en prie*, As long as you have any ink in your pen, / With never a penny of money!" (*RG*, 104). In the context of the novel, the pun in the first line is disturbing. The younger brother of the hero who goes off to die in Yeats's play *Cathleen ni Houlihan* is named Patrick. The play strongly suggests that he will be part of the next generation to die for Ireland; in *The Red and the Green*, Patrick Dumay's younger brother will die in the civil war of the next generation. As long as writers have ink in their pens, suggests the song, Irish boys will be killed. Pat tells Cathal to stop singing that song, so he begins another: "Sure 'twas for this Lord Edward died and Wolfe Tone sunk serene / Because they could not bear to leave the red above the green" (*RG*, 104). Pat objects to this song as well, arguing that death is not "sinking serene," that "bad poetry is lies" (*RG*, 104). But Cathal has already absorbed too much of the lie: in imitation of the song's narrator, he has already been to Bodenstown to lie on the grave of Wolfe Tone. "I'm going to die young," he affirms (*RG*, 108).

"Bad poetry" is not the only kind of literature that influences political history, nor is such influence the property of any one nationality. Some of the greatest works are susceptible of being read as simplified political statements, and these include English as well as Irish works. Millie quotes a line from *Henry IV*, Part 1, act 2—"Thou wilt not utter what thou dost not know, and thus far will I trust thee"—and discusses with Andrew the meaning of rue and rosemary ("That's for remembrance" [*RG*, 57]); Pat is nicknamed "Hotspur" (*RG*, 84, 57, 75). These allusions, along with references to Malory and Arthurian legend (*RG*, 7, 154), are glossed by the text itself. Thinking back on the evolution of "his *persona* as a soldier . . . Andrew would have blushed to admit how much his zeal depended on early impressions of the more patriotic passages of Shakespeare and a boyish devotion to Sir Lancelot" (*RG*, 9). Clearly the debate about whether English is "the language of Shakespeare" or "the language of Cromwell" (*RG*, 45) is meant to be pointless, for our experience of even the greatest writers is not pure. The confusion of literature with history is matched by the human tendency to perceive history as if it were a work of art. Christopher Bellman, the scholar killed during Easter Week, "mocked . . . the *'tragic woman,'*" but "there was more than a touch of heated gallantry in his reaction to the whole miserable *story* . . . with the sensibility of an artist he apprehended an *epic* splendour . . . in the *tragedy* of Ireland" (*RG*, 195, emphasis added).

In the novel we see the source of this confusion of history and art as the difficulty human beings generally have in distinguishing the real from the imagined. Christopher, for example, does not see his self-deception when he tells Millie that Frances will not mind their marriage. The engagement had "gained its own historical momentum," and Frances's haunted figure seems only a ghost: "this sunny garden and its certainties were the real world" (*RG*, 119). Andrew is astonished when his proposal to Frances, "rehearsed . . . so often in imagination," is rejected: "the real Frances had just broken through a screen upon which a picture of her had been painted" (*RG*, 138, 140). Significantly, a similar image describes Pearse's proclamation at the General Post Office: "There was something . . . improbable about this scene, as if the line between dream and reality had been crossed in a blundering manner and almost unaware" (*RG*, 261).

The novel's only writer, Barney, finds reality especially problematic: "Tracts of time were blotted out and he was not always sure where the link came between what he had imagined and what was real . . ." (*RG*, 96). An historian of sorts, Barney studies the Celtic church in its controversy with Rome over the dating of Easter and contemplates writing a book called *The Significance of Brigid.* By 1916 he is reduced to writing a personal memoir that consistently distorts the truth about himself, his buffoonery transmogrified into "my own congenital gaiety," his impotence attributed to his wife's bad grooming (*RG*, 122). Recognizing that the memoir is "his greatest sin," a "wicked lie," Barney briefly contemplates changing the names and turning it into a novel (*RG*, 168, 181). But a journal of lies does not make a truthful novel. Clearly, we are meant to admire Barney's destruction of the memoir when he decides to join the rebellion. Barney's journal provides a model of the way in which facts are distorted almost as quickly as they occur. Such falsifications too easily become the basis for action: "a most alarming document" (*RG*, 107), a forgery claiming that the British are about to disarm the Volunteers and the Citizen's Army, helps precipitate the Easter Rising. Hearing that the Rebellion is about to take place, Christopher feels "the warm, quick movement of Irish history risen out of books, alive, alive-o" (*RG*, 209).

The epilogue, which Edward Weeks calls an "anti-climax"[16] and which Gerstenberger believes is "hand-cuffed" to the novel,[17] actually sustains and develops the theme of the relationship of art to history. Set in the time of the Spanish Civil War, so closely linked with the names of Lorca, Picasso, Hemingway, Orwell, Malraux, and Gironella, the epilogue is a new perspective on the Easter Rebellion, which has already become history. The novel's criticism of the fictions of history is articulated by Frances's husband, who offers the ironic view that the Easter Rebellion was unnecessary, that Cathleen ni Houlihan was a bore, and that contemporary Ireland is a dead country supported by German capital. There is, he says, "no such thing as European history. . . . Each country tells a selective story creditable to itself" (*RG*, 269). Although Frances does not entirely agree, she recognizes the role of art in shaping our perception of history; she remembers Fontenoy because of a poem about the Wild Geese, and of the Spanish Civil War "people will only remember Guernica, and that will be because of Picasso" (*RG*, 269). The epilogue also strongly suggests that Frances's "tall son," who looks like Cathal and echoes his words about the value of fighting oppression, will soon go to Spain and suffer a fate like his. The gaze of "guilty . . . complicity" (*RG*, 269) that Frances shares with her son is

---

[16] Review of *The Red and the Green*, *Atlantic Monthly*, December 1965, 138.

[17] From *Iris Murdoch* (Lewisburg: Bucknell University Press, 1975), 68.

morally significant for, by refusing to debunk the Easter heroes, Frances encourages him to imitate them.

Yet there is, as Halio and Gerstenberger agree, a shift of tone in the novel's final pages. Having deconstructed Yeats's "Easter 1916" by acknowledging the revolutionaries' motives and their suffering, Murdoch, like Frances, seems to affirm their "terrible beauty" and the "glorious things . . . justice, freedom, Ireland" for which they died (*RG*, 272). "Young and perfect forever," the executed rebels, in the novel's last description of them, have once more become the heroes of a story. But such a transformation is not necessarily a contradiction. The novel suggests that the artist and the revolutionary are never entirely free from each other, that they share a common impulse to shape reality. In doing so, they necessarily impose on the novel the limitations of their own perspectives: lying novels and bad poems are dangerous; human beings can derive harmful fantasies even from Shakespeare. Yet the novel stops short of saying that these evident human limitations invalidate either art or political struggle. It would be reductive to say that the novel's logic in effect makes Frances's husband the raisonneur, so that we ought to agree to be bored with Ireland. The ironic view too readily becomes the *realpolitik* of his last speech: "In this century the small nations have got to pack up. . . . You've got to belong to a big show nowadays, and you may as well do it with sense and good grace" (*RG*, 269). Such a dismissal of small nations—and by implication of individual human beings—is not the conclusion of a novel that minutely observes the struggles and eccentricities of a large cast of characters and rejects the optical illusion of the Martello tower in favor of the "constantly shifting" realities of Dublin. To say that "people will only remember Guernica, and that will be because of Picasso" suggests that there is a loss when people remember a work of art instead of, rather than in addition to, its larger historical context, but the loss would be greater if people forgot both. Indeed, "Guernica," which does not glamorize violence, might serve as a model of the kind of art Murdoch values.

Central to *The Red and the Green*, then, is that "concern

for the way we know history" that Fleishman sees as characteristic of all serious historical novels (*EHN*, 12). By creating a fictional world that mediates Irish history and literature, Murdoch suggests that they are inextricably related. Most history is fictional; much of our literature promotes illusions about history; literature can never be independent of the historical world. The artist, like the historian, must be willing to listen to the liturgical injunction that moves Barney to destroy his false memoir: "attendite et videte," attend and see (*RG*, 166). Having deconstructed a more glamorous version of Easter Week 1916, Murdoch ends by convincing us that hers—sober, secular, and, by comparison, prosy—is that sort of attentive witness she so evidently admires.

CHAPTER TWO

Elizabeth Bowen's *The Last September* and J. G. Farrell's *Troubles*

IN THE INTRODUCTION to his *The English Novel of History and Society, 1940–1980*, Patrick Swinden decries the "imaginative anaemia and provincialism" (1) that characterized British fiction in the 1950s and 1960s, when "civilized," "genteel" writers like Barbara Pym, Elizabeth Taylor, and L. P. Hartley placed "English fiction in a sort of quarantine," isolating it from the experiments and ambitions of American and continental writing (3). Swinden is especially critical of Elizabeth Bowen, whose "deplorably limited view of life" he finds crystallized in her observation that "when we remember habit it seems to have been happiness" (2). Questioning whether Solzhenitsyn might feel this happiness recalling habits contracted in "the labour camps and cancer wards of Gulag," Swinden remarks that "one sees what she means in the context of a view of life that fails to relate private feelings that are conversable about the public catastrophes that seem not to be" (2). Yet the subject of Bowen's first novel is precisely this inability of the privileged to understand their own historicity. *The Last September*, set in Ireland during the Irish troubles of 1919–1921, plots out the mental processes by which members of the Ascendancy defer the knowledge that the guerrillas lurking in the shadows of their Big Houses will shortly succeed in burning them to the ground. What at first appears to be a novel of manners ends as a novel deeply anchored in history, an elegy to a dying civilization that is tempered with irony about its characters' blindness to their fate.

Some forty years after the publication of *The Last September*, another Anglo-Irish novelist, J. G. Farrell, published *Troubles*, a novel set in the same period and similarly concerned with the blindness of the Ascendancy to its already certain defeat. Farrell himself had apparently not read *The Last September* until 1971,[1] the year that its author published an enthusiastic review of *Troubles*, implicitly contrasting Farrell's novel with her own by remarking that Farrell's choice of subject could not be accounted for by "nostalgic compulsion."[2] Although Bowen's novel celebrates upper-class Protestant values, affirming the "people of Burke and of Grattan" as stoutly as Yeats might have done, Farrell, whose work decenters the myth of the Ascendancy, is ironic where Bowen is elegiac. The contrast between the two novels moves us to the heart of those concerns and techniques that make the treatment of history in the postwar English novel distinctive.

To dramatize the failure of awareness is no easy matter for historical fiction: the reader is asked to understand, perhaps even identify with, people who refuse to learn what the reader already takes for granted. As Farrell does after her, Bowen chooses to reflect historical events and processes through the minds of characters who not only do not participate in them, but are constantly involved in strategies to put off knowing about them. To borrow Harry Henderson's terminology, Anglo-Irish traditions create a "counter-history," a system of explanation that, when abetted by psychic needs, becomes all but impenetrable.[3] Through indirection and rumor, accident and, at last, catastrophe, the novelists present a history that their characters avoid. On a realistic level, *The Last September* presents one segment of historical awareness directly, the perspective of the Anglo-Irish landowning family headed by Lord and Lady Naylor. The novel's slight story line revolves around the courtship of their niece, Lois Farquar, by Gerald Lesworth, a British officer, and the distractions offered by the flirtation of a pair of houseguests. To the extent that

---

[1] In a diary entry for February 20, Farrell, who was traveling in India, wrote, "The hotel has a supply of books lent by the British Council. I have seized a splendid one by Elizabeth Bowen, *The Last September*, set in Ireland at the time of *Troubles*" (*HS*).

[2] Ronald Binns, *J. G. Farrell* (London: Methuen, 1986), 25.

[3] *Versions of the Past* (New York: Oxford University Press, 1974), 207.

the Naylors and their guests are aware of their political views,
they are ambivalent, as Bowen notes in her 1952 preface: "the
position of . . . an Anglo-Irish landowning Protestant family
. . . was not only ambiguous but was more nearly heartbreaking than they could bear to show" (LS, xi). Class and tradition
suggest loyalty to England; benevolence to their own tenants
blinds the Naylors to any real grievances of the Irish people.
To the American reader at least, comparisons with white fictions about the antebellum South become inevitable. Danielstown cares for its tenants in a manner indistinguishable from
Gone with the Wind's Katie O'Hara's benevolence to the field
hands, so that the unsanitary housing, malnutrition, and sickness that make public health statistics so grim for Ireland in
the period occur elsewhere and are someone else's responsibility.[4] The novel's point of view is so rigorously controlled
that the reader sees Irish Catholics always as the Naylor's did:
the deferential Michael Connor, for example, needs only
blackface to settle down happily at Tara: " 'And yourself's
looking lovely, Miss Lois; a fine strong lady, glory be to
God' " (LS, 76). Only later do we glimpse another perspective
in the revelation that Connor had been hiding his son Peter,
a fugitive from the British. The only rebel Irishman who does
have lines, if not a name, is the hungry gunman whom Lois
and her friend Marda stumble across at an abandoned mill.
His warning that the Naylors should " 'keep within the house
while y'have it' " (LS, 54) is promptly forgotten. The gunman's isolation itself removes any connection to a defensible

[4] The Report of the American Committee for Relief in Ireland (New York:
n.d.), a contemporaneous document, states that in 1921 a "commission in
Cork City" had determined that the minimum "living wage" for a family was
fourteen dollars a week. "The present prevailing wage for ordinary unskilled
labor in Ireland ranges from $9–$24 a week . . . farm laborers rarely [receive]
more than $8." Some one hundred thousand people were living on a diet of
bread and tea supplemented with soup two or three times a week (80). "Economic stagnation," aggravated by the "burning of homes" and the "destruction of industry," was blamed for these conditions (84). The high mortality
rates, low wages, bad housing, and primitive sanitation of pre–World War I
Dublin are ably chronicled in the first chapter of David Krause's Sean
O'Casey: The Man and His Work, enlarged ed. (New York: Macmillan, 1975).

political movement. Still, the older Naylors prove anything but enthusiastic about the British army's policy in their country. At several points a Naylor expresses guarded disapproval of reprisals, a vague sense that if the British " 'danced more and interfered less . . . there would be less trouble in the country' " (*LS*, 203). The Naylors' opposition to Lois's engagement to Gerald is largely a snobbish disapproval of his unimaginable social origins, but is doubtless influenced by their dislike of British military activity. Sir Richard Naylor greets the news that Gerald has just captured Peter Connor coldly: " 'I'm sorry to hear that. . . . His mother is dying' " (*LS*, 113). Clearly, the Naylors, to some extent, fear their defenders: hearing a lorry full of drunken Black and Tans pass by, they feel "exposed and hunted" (*LS*, 192). The military see the Naylors as equally alien: " 'When one thinks those are the people we are defending!' " remarks an officer's wife in the consciousness of having been socially slighted (*LS*, 242–43). When Daventry appears at Danielstown to announce Gerald's death, "it seemed to him odd that there should be nothing to search for, nobody to interrogate," and the Naylors "felt instinctively that he had come . . . to search the house" (*LS*, 249, 251).

Yet, Bowen's representation of such conscious and unfocused attitudes forms only one, and perhaps not the most important, part of the novel's historical texture. Mary Lascelles has noted that one of the risks of the historical novel is that it may become a kind of costume drama, "figures of familiar fiction in unfamiliar clothes."[5] Lascelles argues that the solution is for characters in historical novels themselves to have a well-developed sense of the past. Bowen seems more interested in embedding this sense of the past in the narrative itself. In her preface, Bowen points out that she had wished the "mood and cast" of her characters, "and their actions . . . to reflect the glow of a finished time." It was highly important that the "reader . . . look—and more . . . be aware of looking—backward, down a perspective cut through the years." For this purpose, "the ordinary narrative past, so much in use as to be taken for granted" seemed inadequate. For this reason, Bowen writes, she added a verbal "pointer," the phrase "in those days" that begins the description of Lois's ribbons, which "lead into history" (*LS*, ix). This sense of a "finished time" is continuous, if elusive, in the novel, for Bowen is too subtle to disrupt the narrative with explicit commentary of the "little did they know then" variety. Instead, she continues to find ways of emphasizing the past tense, as when she cuts off Lady Naylor's conversation with Gerald and supplies a summary set in a double past: "As Lady Naylor said at the time, . . . And as she said afterwards . . ." (*LS*, 117). There are characters, most notably the Montmorencys, who are pure period pieces: she, the Invalid and he, the Professional House Guest. Hugo Montmorency's preoccupation with Laura, Lois's long-dead mother, further makes the past thematic. The characters seem to feel that they are living in an historical backwater, survivors of "all the dear boys who . . . had been killed in that dreadful war" (*LS*, 87).

The sense of finished time is created also by an elegiac tone associated with descriptions of nature and the house and by the novel's attitudes toward its heroine's youth. The description of the end of an autumn evening, "such a particular happy point of decline in the short curve of the day, the long curve of the season" (*LS*, 255), underscores a pattern of nature images that emphasizes the beauty and the impermanence of the last days before winter. Seen during the day, the landscape seems idealized, fragile: "the light pink road crushed under wheels like sugar"; "as they mounted they seemed to be striking deeper into the large mild crystal of an inverted sea; "over the parching heather shadow faded and folded tone on tone, and was drawn to the sky on delicate brittle peaks" (*LS*, 73). An elegant repository of Anglo-Irish tradition, Danielstown is already seen nostalgically at the beginning of the second chapter, when Francie Montmorency reflects on how the happiest days of her life had been spent in that house where "time, loose-textured, had had a shining undertone, happiness glittered between the moments" (*LS*, 13).

Homeless and aimless, Francie and her husband are limited even in imagination to unfulfilled plans of building their own bungalow, "an eternal present for them . . . never able to shine in retrospect" (*LS*, 229). This language confirms the truth of Elizabeth Hardwick's criticism of Bowen's "complicated theology of objects."[6] A veritable Mansfield Park West, Danielstown is despised only by vulgar types like the British officer's wife who complains, " 'It smells of damp. Myself, I do like a house to be bright and homey' " (*LS*, 246). While it may be too impatient to talk, as Hardwick does, of "the moral intransigence of the interior decorator," it is quite clear that: "Peace is a well-lit drawing room, purity is light, airy, spacious and in its presence the glasses shine and the flowers are forever fresh."[7] Even an inferior version of Danielstown, Mount Isabel, when assimilated to the fragile daytime Anglo-Irish landscape, is seen elegiacally: "Light slid over the heavy burnished trees; the cream facade of the house was like cardboard, high and confident in the sun—a house without weight, an appearance, less actual than the begonias' scarlet and wax-pink flesh. Begonias, burning in an impatience of colour, crowded over the edge of heart-shaped beds (*LS*, 143). History seen in such metaphors, where a bed of begonias enacts the behavior of the IRA, is very much attenuated, but by no means absent.[8]

[6] From "Elizabeth Bowen's Fiction," *Partisan Review* 16 (1949): 1116.
[7] Ibid.
[8] Deirdre Laigle notes a similar passage in which natural phenomena suggest political violence: "behind the trees, pressing in from the open and empty country like an invasion, the orange bright sky crept and smouldered" (*LS*, 23). She points out that:

> This is a war of superimposed worlds striving to occupy the same terrain, and organised military defence, like legal rights and wrongs, is made to appear ludicrously irrelevant and insufficient. The image used by Miss Bowen to characterise the countryside, and by extension its people, implies that their uprising against the Ascendancy has the inevitable, irresistible violence of natural law: moreover, the invasion of the demesne, identified with the sunlight, has already taken place. ("Images of the Big House

Most of *The Last September* is seen through the eyes of nineteen-year-old Lois, whose position in the novel's "theology of objects" Bowen emphasizes in the preface: she is the "niece only, and not the child" of Danielstown (*LS*, xii). Her disqualifications for serving as the central consciousness of a historical novel are many. Not only is she ignorant of politics but, as an orphan educated in England, she is cut off from a personal past as well. Lois never thinks of her father. Her mother impinges on her consciousness—and on that of other characters—as a splendid ghost of her own age in comparison with whom Lois pales. Her inability to feel that she loves Gerald matches an incapacity to "conceive of her country emotionally" (*LS*, 37). Her response to the burning of a Royal Irish Constabulary barracks is typical: " 'I might at least have felt something' " (*LS*, 56). In " 'this country that ought to be full of such violent realness,' " she feels that " 'there is nothing for me but clothes and what people say' " (*LS*, 56). History that crosses such a mind must be either extremely violent or very much deformed. For a long time Lois is aware of events only as they fit into the more compelling story of Anglo-Irish social life. A "Sinn Fein" raid means that all the telephone wires are down, "quite a relief" because it puts off having to do anything about a guest's lost luggage (*LS*, 96). This mentality forms part of Lois's environment, where people talk about guerrilla war as if they were discussing a reception: Ireland, remarks Mrs. Vermont, is a "country where the most extraordinary people died" (*LS*, 59). The possibility of putting up sandbags behind the shutters is a joke that they "all shared" (*LS*, 24). Lady Naylor thinks Lois needs to see her school friends from England, " 'but it's so unlucky, they're never allowed to come over. Something said in the English press has given rise to the idea that this country's unsafe' " (*LS*, 66).

The real dangers of her encounter with an armed rebel make less of an impression on Lois than the drama of Hugo

Montmorency's infatuation with Marda that reaches its dé-
nouement there. Laurence is briefly jolted out of his under-
graduate ennui by being robbed of his watch by three armed
men; "then he limped home to dinner and an audience con-
siderably cheered" (*LS*, 234). When the watch is returned
three days later, his Uncle Richard notes "with satisfaction"
that it is still ticking; "But that was a day of confusion: nobody
listened" (*LS*, 234).

Since Lois and, indeed, most of the others cannot be relied
upon to listen or notice, the novelist allows the events to enter the fiction indirectly, through metaphor and the slightest
suggestion of allegory. Early in the novel, nature, which is so
pleasant during the day, becomes threatening at night. Even
when Lois walks in the shrubbery at Danielstown, "on her
bare arms the tips of the leaves were timid and dank like
tongues of dead animals. Her fear of the shrubberies tugged
at its chain, fear behind reason, fear before her birth, fear like
the earliest germ of her life . . ." (*LS*, 36). Raids and reprisals
and even the two direct encounters between the IRA and the
people at Danielstown already noted take place at night.
Eventually, even in the day the Irish landscape comes to
seem inseparable from the guerrillas who hide in it. Laurence
feels exposed at Mount Isabel to the gaze of an imagined
watcher in the mountains and turns away: "But the unavoidable and containing stare impinged to the point of a transformation upon the social figures with orderly, knitted shadows,
the well-groomed grass and the beds in their formal pattern"
(*LS*, 147). The threatening possibilities of nature become even
clearer later when Lois returns to the guest room after Marda's departure: "Through the defenceless windows came in the
vacancy of the sky; the grey ceiling had gone up in remote-
ness. More wind came through, flowers moved in the vases,
the pages of a book left open beside the bed turned over hur-
riedly" (*LS*, 172).

Passages such as these indicate the increasing if unconscious acknowledgment of the family at Danielstown that its
way of life is doomed. The political activities of the time are
figured to some extent in the disruptions caused by the arrival

of Marda, an accident-prone guest who, in Lois's words, " 'annoys Aunt Myra by being unfortunate in ways that are far more trying for other people than for herself' " (LS, 92). In spite of being determined to marry an Englishman and settle into the most British sort of life imaginable, Marda has a long history of reckless independence including a chain of broken engagements. Her latest engagement ring is emerald for the country of her birth: " 'I had no idea I had such an expensive nationality' " (LS, 99).

The most nearly allegorical element in the novel, however, is the party at the Rolfes that follows Marda's return to England. The Rolfes are British army people, well below the Naylors socially, and their party, which features a loud gramophone, is just the sort of vulgar, modern exhibition Lady Naylor would like her husband's niece to avoid. In the midst of growing conflict, this party seems "not only criminal but lunatic" to the father of Moira Ralte, who herself mindlessly remarks that it would be " 'a rag . . . if they tried to fire in at the windows while we were dancing' " (LS, 177). This last-ditch effort to keep reality at bay already embodies the disintegration of Anglo-Irish social standards; worse depredations are suggested as the dreary frantic evening proceeds—the guests speaking and dancing "with a kind of exalted helplessness" and the hostess laughing constantly "you would have said with despair" (LS, 186). Electric lights wobble, walls crack, even the gramophone is finally wrecked. Through this damage stalks Mr. Daventry, not completely recovered from shell shock, who seems to Lois to "laugh like Satan" (LS, 195).

The drunken behavior of the guests mimes the activities of combatants in the guerrilla war they are trying not to think about: Moira Ralte wonders aloud if the popping balloons sound like a "bombardment" and "David Armstrong leaned from his partner wildly and struck Gerald over the head with a red balloon" (LS, 192). The knowledge that Gerald will be shot through the head by the end of the month lurks unrecognized in this line.

The threat that has built throughout the novel is finally carried out in its last chapter. Archly entitled "The Departure of

Gerald" to match the first two sections, "The Arrival of Mr. and Mrs. Montmorency" and "The Visit of Miss Norton," the last section ends with Gerald killed and Danielstown in ashes. There is an apparent abruptness to Bowen's presentation of both events. Gerald's death is introduced not by a description of his last patrol, nor by an account of military strategy, but by the observation that: "The world did not stand still, though the household at Danielstown and the Thompson's lunch party took no account of it" (*LS*, 246). On the other hand, the natural imagery Bowen had used earlier provides a link with the rest of the novel; the news of Gerald's death "crashed upon the unknowingness of the town like a wave" and "crept down streets . . . like a dull wind" (*LS*, 246): "In Gerald's room some new music for the jazz band, caught in a draught, flopped over and over" (*LS*, 247). Repeating the earlier image of "defenceless windows" these lines anticipate the last view of Danielstown, its door standing "open hospitably upon a furnace" (*LS*, 256).

Watching that furnace, the Naylors, "not saying anything, did not look at each other, for in the light from the sky they saw too clearly" (*LS*, 256). What they see, what they had willed not to see, has been the historical content of the novel. Ireland 1920–1921, as seen in *The Last September* is a myth of inattention, of violence without discernible causes, a myth without heroes and almost without a plot. Bowen's novel radically differs from the traditional war novel not only because it pays so much attention to social detail—Tolstoy had his tea parties too—but because the war it describes was fought without pitched battles. Guerrilla war against a system that reasonable people had been taught to equate with civilization— " 'What do you mean by the point of view of civilization?' 'Oh—ours' " (*LS*, 114)—was newer in 1920 than it seems now. The process by which Michael Collins and his soldiers wear down the British will to resist is arguably well imitated in the process by which reality is borne in upon the family at Danielstown.

If, in this respect and in her faithful portrayal of Anglo-Irish attitudes, Bowen has been truthful to the facts of her period, there is certainly much that she omits. She has not avoided, very possibly did not wish to avoid, the *Gone with the Wind* syndrome that haunts so many novels of the American South. Her Irish Catholic characters have as little depth as Butterfly McQueen's Prissy; the injustices on which Bowen herself saw Anglo-Irish life to have been founded[9] are not subjects over which her Protestant characters brood at secondhand, as Jack Burden or Quentin Compson brood over slavery. To read, for example, Frank O'Connor's *An Only Child* in tandem with *The Last September* is to experience a sense of shock at the discovery that throughout his childhood O'Connor's mother earned one-shilling-and-sixpence for a twelve-hour day as a cleaning woman.[10] Aware of such poverty, can a reader seriously be expected to grieve over the death of a house or feel sympathetic with the collapse of a set of values that it symbolizes? Of Bowen's Anglo-Ireland, Barbara Brothers says what has so often been said of Faulkner's South: "Bowen was suggesting not so much that we return to it, as that we take from it a model of what is needed to provide a pattern for man to withstand the void."[11] But it is precisely the articulation between the model and the injustice on which it depended for survival that the critic must debate. The question of whether literally or figuratively, Big Houses can exist without women willing to clean them for a few cents an hour is an issue Bowen never raises.

The issue of the degree to which English culture, when imposed on an alien people, can be equated with civilization, is raised in all three of the novels—*The Siege of Krishnapur*, *Troubles*, and *The Singapore Grip*—that constitute J. G. Farrell's remarkable trilogy on British colonialism. The very inclusion of Ireland in the trilogy constitutes a political state-

---

[9] Bowen's point of view emerges most clearly in her autobiographical *Bowen's Court*; for example, she says of her own family that "Having obtained their position through an injustice they kept it through privilege" (455).

[10] *An Only Child* (New York: Knopf, 1961), 122.

[11] "Pattern and Void: Bowen's Irish Landscapes and *The Heat of the Day*," *Mosaic* 12, no. 3 (1978): 138.

ment, but *Troubles* hardly embodies the Irish patriotic story one finds in a work like Ulick O'Connor's *A Terrible Beauty is Born: The Irish Troubles, 1912–1922.* Like *The Last September,* Farrell's novel radically limits the reader's access to major events and the actors in them, offering relatively little in the way of explanation of political processes. Its central consciousness, "the Major," Brendan Archer, is an Englishman suffering from shell shock whose symptoms are a partial loss of memory, a sense of being in a "state of narcosis," of looking at the world through a "bubble of bitterness . . . inches thick like plate glass" (*T*, 80). Moreover, the Major's benign attempts to understand the situation in Ireland are opposed by the strong misreading of the present offered by Edward Spencer, his nearly mad, fanatically pro-British landlord and prospective father-in-law. Thus, as in *The Last September,* history reaches the reader through refraction and indirection.

Like Bowen in *The Last September,* Farrell went to pains to set his novel in an unmistakable past, reinforcing the ordinary narrative past with semantic signals. Bernard Bergonzi has already described the effectiveness of the first paragraphs and, indeed, the first sentences of Farrell's colonial novels in "focus[ing] attention on the places that are the physical locations of the novels' action, and, equally, their metaphorical centres."[12] Also remarkable in *Troubles* is the complexity of the time scheme that Farrell introduces:

> In those days the Majestic was still standing in Kilnalough at the very end of a slim peninsula covered with dead pines leaning here and there at odd angles. At that time there were probably yachts there too during the summer since the hotel held a regatta every July. These yachts would have been beached on one or other end of the sandy crescent that curved out towards the hotel on each side of the peninsula. But now both pines and yachts have floated away and one day the high tide may very well meet over the narrowest part of the peninsula, made narrower by erosion. As for the

[12] "Fictions of History," *The Contemporary English Novel,* ed. Malcolm Bradbury and Davis Palmer (London: Edward Arnold, 1979), 59.

regalia, for some reason it was discontinued years ago, before the Spencers took over the management of the place. And a few years later the Majestic itself followed the boats and preceded the pines into oblivion by burning to the ground—but by that time, of course, the place was in such a state of disrepair that it hardly mattered. (*T*, 9–10)

The first sentence seems almost to have been written to illustrate Käte Hamburger's contention that one of the chief differences between history and historical fiction is that fiction never answers precisely the question "When?"[13] The phrase "in those days" evokes the Bible and the never-never time of legend; still, the reader at first assumes that the question of when will be answered by the story—that "those days" will be the time of the fiction. Yet, the yachts that beached there "at that time" had already disappeared by another unspecified time, when the Spencers bought the Majestic. "Now"—another unspecified time—even the "then" dead pines and yachts have disappeared; at another unspecified time in between, the Majestic hotel "followed" the one and "preceded" the other "into oblivion." Structurally, the paragraph seems to show great concern with placing the narrative in time, yet the lack of precise answers to the question "When?" puts the reader in the vague time of myth. In this first paragraph, the elegiac tone is straight; through the "erosion" the time of pines and yachts has been lost forever, worn away until even its obliteration "hardly mattered."

Strong distancing of Farrell's story from contemporary life and from facticity is the first of many gestures aimed at the *irréalisation* of the historical narrative. Farrell clearly wishes to keep the reader alert to his or her own distance from the time of the narrative and to the problems of a facile identification with people and events of the past. To paraphrase Walter Cronkite, "you" are not "there," wherever you are. What is there, and the problematics of the reader's relation to it, are thematic concerns that are reflected in the novel's fuzzi-

[13] *The Logic of Literature*, trans. Marilynn J. Rose, 2d ed. (Bloomington: Indiana University Press, 1973), 70.

ness about times and proper names, in its shifting perspectives, and in the play between the journalistic and the fantastic in which neither element remains uncontaminated.

These problems of telling the story are themselves made thematic in a number of ways. Before coming to Ireland, the Major had relied heavily on the letters of his fiancée, Angela, to create a picture of her country. Her copious letters were filled with the minutiae of daily life, the names of the family's many dogs, stores in Dublin where she shopped; they were "precise and factual . . . filled . . . with an invincible reality as hard as granite" (*T*, 24). Yet, even in the early days the Major had sensed Angela's tendency to omit unpleasant details: "There would be a list of Edward's dogs again, for example: Rover, Toby, Fritz, Haig, Woof, Puppy, Bran, Flash, Laddie, Foch and Collie. But where, he would wonder, is Spot? Where are you, Spot?" (*T*, 113).

And then the Major realized that Spot had died. Even the rawest fact, then, required of him an imaginative act of interpretation: "In this way, thread by thread, he embroidered for himself a colourful tapestry of Angela's life at the Majestic" (*T*, 13). The rudest shock to his faith in the granite reality of Angela's letters comes with her death, when the Major finally realizes that her illness had been not some temporary indisposition but leukemia, and that she had known all along that she was dying. In her last letter, which the Major can only bring himself to open months after her death, the multiplication of concrete details seems not reassuring but horrible, a bizarre accretion of meaningless facts to which he reacts as Roquentin might have: "the detail in it is intolerable" (*T*, 156).

Many of the details of life in Ireland are, from the Major's point of view, intolerable. Sartrean nausea rises repeatedly to his throat, the awful viscosity of fact defeating his vague attempts to come to terms theoretically with his experiences. On his first night, the Major finds a sweetish, rotting sheepshead in his chamberpot, harbinger of the sty with its "rotting" floor, mud, excrement, and "intolerable stench" (*T*, 145), of the tutor's boils, and of his own loathsomely detailed head cold. Vomitings too various to mention, whether of brown soup and steamed bacon and cabbage or of a "thick yellow liquid" (*T*, 346), might always be said to be done "enormously, volcanically" (*T*, 362). In this world of perennially steady rain, the blankets always feel damp; no wonder that Mortimer, the public school Auxie (Auxiliary) imagines a "vast dough of white grease" (*T*, 360) falling from the ceiling into the bed where he shrinks from the touch of Edward's daughter, Faith, "whose ample bosom fle[es] silkily in all directions, quivering like a beef jelly" (*T*, 360). Long deferred, water torture and bloodshed seem, when they finally do occur, only an extension of the general nastiness.

Lacking any discernible cause and producing a sensation of helpless subjugation to the "forces of history," the gluey, reeking horrors of Irish life are abetted by Gothic descriptions of the Majestic itself. On the literal level, the novel's Big House is a fairly large resort hotel that has seen better days, its decline hastened by the guerrilla fighting that has made Ireland an unlikely vacation spot. But, as evoked in the novel, the rotting hotel is an impossibly vast, cavernous hulk in which long-time guests can never be certain they will not lose themselves and stumble across some room that has not been seen for generations. Try as he might, the Major cannot discover, during her lifetime, Angela's room. The kitchen, to take another example, is fearsome; from its walls hang "an armoury of giant pots and pans"; lurking within, an "extremely fat" cook chops onions "with extraordinary speed and ferocity, using a kitchen knife as big as a bayonet" (*T*, 52–53). The hotel is crumbling before our eyes: in a semiotic catastrophe, the giant letter "M" tumbles from the Majestic's sign, shattering a table at which a "very old and very deaf lady" sits with her eyes closed (*T*, 286). Deconstructed, the sign resists interpretation: the Englishwoman fails to recognize "this strange, seagull-shaped piece of cast iron" that has robbed her of her tea. Further dangers abound: even at the beginning, the Major feels apprehensive in the Palm Court, where palms "had completely run riot, shooting out of their wooden tubs . . . hammering . . . against the greenish glass"; where foliage leap[s] out to seize any unwary object that remained in one place for too long" (*T*, 20–21). Less than half-way through the novel, this Irish jungle, this "advancing green tide," has completely covered up such vestiges of civilization as its own pots and the electric light (*T*, 151–53).

An outrageously obvious symbol, the "advancing green tide" manages to include the Sinn Féin and a strong suggestion of Farrell's concern with larger colonial themes as well. As in *The Last September*, but more grotesquely, a nightmarish history is borne in on people who seek to avoid it. Farrell nearly allegorizes the battle with the British in the story of the Majestic's cats. The numerous dogs seen milling around the sheepsheads in the early sections, with their fine British names and propensity for hunting, Farrell clearly associates with the Ascendancy. As the novel progresses, an especially fertile breed of cats, led by a ferocious orange female with "bitter green eyes," takes over (*T*, 234). In a memorable scene, this "devil," this "witch," pokes its "evil, orange, horridly whiskered" head out of the sofa in which it lives, flexes "its claws, which were as sharp as hatpins," and springs onto the head of an old lady who has the misfortune to wear a hat adorned with a golden pheasant (*T*, 232–34). The carnage is vividly described: the cat "rip[s] and claw[s] savagely at her headgear in an explosion of feathers" and then is brutally murdered by the tutor, who hurls it against the wall with a "savage rictus" on his face (*T*, 235). Even without their leader, the cats stay in control, terrorizing a remaining dog described as "wheezing and spent" (*T*, 281). In a last-ditch effort, the Major and Edward gun down the cats, who shriek as if "it were a massacre of infants" and "leave a dreadful mess: blood on the carpets, there forever, ineradicable, brains on the coverlets, vile splashes on the wall . . ." (*T*, 327). With regrettable inevitability, an invasion of rats follows the cat massacre.

Although the Majestic obviously does not provide a haven from violence, it does provide enough distractions from political issues to keep the Major from ever developing a clear sense of what is going on in Ireland. In spite of his personal experience of the horrors of the Great War, he arrives at the

Majestic convinced "that the cause had been a just one and that throughout the world the great civilizing power of the British Empire had been at stake" (*T*, 51). It is natural and above all necessary for the Major to believe that the British "presence" in Ireland "signified a moral authority" (*T*, 57), yet part of his Britishness is his belief in fair play and tolerance, which causes him to distrust the extreme anti-Catholicism of Edward and his landowning Protestant ilk: " 'Surely there's no need to abandon one's reason simply because one is in Ireland' " (*T*, 34). This sense that the world will correspond to the Major's illusory notion of his own rationality is invaded by Irish history; in the ungentle collision between his mind and the world resides much of the novel's historical consciousness.

History occasionally intrudes accidentally on the Major: a trip to Dublin exposes him to both the Victory Parade and the shooting of a suspected British intelligence agent by a man wearing a sandwich board displaying a verse of the Hail Mary (*T*, 100). Reading a newspaper account of the incident, the Major reflects on how such antiseptic stories, which make a "senseless act . . . both normal and inevitable," are like so many "poultices placed on sudden inflammations of violence" (*T*, 102). But these newspapers, whose interpretations he sees as questionable, make up a significant part of the Major's education about historical events. Throughout the novel, Farrell introduces, usually without transition, actual newspaper clippings from the period. Always managing to describe the wars and killings as much less horrible than the cat massacre at the Majestic, the stories often suggest parallels, which no character in the novel articulates, between unrest in Ireland and unrest in other trouble spots—India, Italy, Russia, Poland, South Africa, Mesopotamia, and Chicago. The specifically Irish stories provide points of orientation for the reader, who is becoming as mired in the bizarre decaying world of the Majestic as the Major. The story that Lloyd George has invited Eamon de Valéra to London for peace talks (*T*, 426), for example, reminds the reader with a shock that a political outcome is in sight. But the irrationality of life at the Majestic imparts something of itself to our perception of the most objective reporting. Edward Carson, the Ian Paisley of his day, speaks of the Sinn Féin "murder campaign directed from the U.S." and "fanned by Germans everywhere" (*T*, 174) and his words seem no more and no less grotesque than Edward Spencer's campaign to protect his hotel from "the vast and ruthless armies of the Pope" (*T*, 432). Lloyd George, in the outraged accents of Margaret Thatcher, denounces the "cowardly murder" of British soldiers, promises revenge ("we have murder by the throat") and offers Ireland "a partnership in . . . the Empire in the greatest day of its glory" (*T*, 280). The irony that the distance of more than sixty years lends to his statements is so intensified by the immediate context, which includes the description of old Rover beset by the cats that we have already seen, as to make them seem quite literally mad.

The Major's attempts to see Ireland are hampered by his increasing involvement with the running and maintenance of the Majestic, in which Edward seems to lose interest after his daughter's death. What news and interpretation he has time for often takes the form of rumor, such as the story, said to be widely believed, that both Maud Gonne and Con Markiewicz have been mistresses of the Kaiser. He is perennially subject to the commentary of the Anglo-Irish with whom he lives, one of the refrains of which Farrell presents in Tom Swift form: " 'In a lot of ways they're like children,' Boy O'Neill said" (*T*, 22). Moreover, every event is interpreted for him by Edward, who, to take a typical example, dismisses the Major's musings about what would happen if an Irish boy were sent to a "decent public school" with the comment that " 'You might just as well dress up a monkey in a suit of clothes' " (*T*, 187). The Major is conscious of the madness of Edward's refusal to compromise with his tenants, of his scientific experiments—in one of these he pretends to shoot a servant in order to measure the effects of fear on saliva production—and of his schemes to keep his statue of Queen Victoria safe from the Sinn Féin. Nonetheless, the Major cannot bring himself to leave the skewed world that these activities create.

The novel offers only ambiguous and finally unsatisfactory

alternatives to the strong misreadings of the Anglo-Irish. The only Irish Catholic characters of any consequence are relatively prosperous people with social ties to the Ascendancy. Of these the most sympathetic is Dr. Ryan, who warns the Major that Edward's stubbornness with the tenants can only lead to disaster and who refuses to sit down to eat with the Spencers because he would " 'not have fellow-Irishmen working to feed his stomach while they had nothing to put in their own!' " (T, 305). As a spokesman for the cause of Pearse and Maud Gonne, Dr. Ryan is undercut by his own senility—at one point, while the Major bleeds profusely, the doctor falls asleep hunting for a needle with which to stitch him up—and by the cavortings throughout the novel of his incipiently transvestite grandson, Padraic. The Irish Catholic with whom the Major has the longest and most consequential relationship is Sarah Devlin, who is occasionally crippled and spotty and always temperamental. His enchantment with her keeps the Major rooted to Irish soil, even when he realizes that she is sexually involved with Edward. Sarah advocates the Irish cause when its romanticism suits her; as she describes it to the Major, the predawn marriage of Grace Gifford and Joseph Plunkett becomes in his eyes, and perhaps in the reader's too, "the last act of an opera composed by a drunken Italian librettist" (T, 84). Sarah's romantic patriotism drops out of the novel abruptly when she elopes with an Auxie named Jackie Bolton, who regularly beats her. His view of the Irish is rather succinctly summarized in his observation that they are: " 'More like animals than human beings . . . used to make me sick sometimes, just watching them eat' " (T, 269).

The Major's common sense and good will occasionally surmount the obstacles to his understanding that are placed around him by everyone else's reading of Irish history. Seeing the Auxies terrorize members of the golf club makes him reflect that the "cure" they offer Anglo-Ireland "will be as bad as the disease" (T, 173). Unlike Edward, he can see hardship if it lies directly in front of his eyes: he is appalled by the horde of ragged men and boys who clamor for a chance to caddy for the club. The sight of old women going through the Majestic's garbage upsets him deeply and he takes to carrying chocolate for the "ragged, famished children he encountered on his walks" (*T*, 184). He is capable of arguing that it is more important to feed Edward's tenants than to protect his property rights: " 'Oh, hang law and order! Two miserable fields of corn which the beggars planted themselves anyway. You don't mind letting them go hungry so long as your own pious principles are satisfied' " (*T*, 195). But such moments are balanced by others when he is capable of thinking that "he hated the Irish" (*T*, 265), or that " 'They're all the same. . . . Even when they hold responsible jobs they're liable to go to pieces at the first sign of trouble' " (*T*, 369).

The bizarre violence of life at the Majestic is a disease that the Major, his psyche already damaged by the Great War, cannot escape. His moral and mental collapse is precipitated by an incident that sums up the whole struggle: Edward's killing of the young Irishman trying to blow up the life size equestrian statue of Queen Victoria that adorns the front lawn of the Majestic. Fresh from a night of listening to the high-minded liberal sentiments of a group of visiting students from Oxford, the Major is stunned to realize that neither Edward nor his victim could have imagined the other was human, that Edward had used the statue "like a salt lick in the jungle" to bait his prey: "For an instant the dreadful thought occurred to the Major that Edward had now gone completely insane and was looking for a place on the wall to mount the Sinn Feiner" (*T*, 416).

Actually, the blood-letting seems to release some of Edward's madness and it is the Major who is pushed over the edge. Trying to forestall Irish vengeance, he goes to the local priest to explain Edward's state of mind. The priest is unsympathetic and the Major is "fascinated by . . . the hatred in his eyes" and his "fanatical" gaze at the crucifix on his wall. The actual horrors the Major has experienced and everything he has heard about the Pope's religion converge in this crucifix: "The yellowish naked body, the straining ribs, the rolling eyes and parted lips, the languorously draped arms and long trailing fingers, the feet crossed to economize on nails, the cherry splash of blood from the side (*T*, 420). The Major barks out that the "Sinn Feiner" deserved his fate: " 'I only hope it may serve as an example to some of the other young cut-throats who are laying Ireland to waste!' " (*T*, 421).

In this grotesquely tortured image of Christ, the Major, not a religious man, discovers the truth of Sarah's assertion that, in Ireland, rationality is irrelevant: " 'You have to choose your tribe' " (*T*, 34). From that moment, the Major wishes to hold out at all costs until even Edward tells him to "face reality" (*T*, 428). The Major's capture by the IRA, which buries him up to his neck on the beach amid the shrieks of Yeatsian peacocks, his rescue by a party of old ladies, even the burning of the Majestic by its one remaining servant, are all anticlimactic.

For Farrell, the real history of Ireland is not found in the names of its leaders or in accounts of its politics but in the moment when a decent man assents to its fanatic hatreds. The history of 1919–1921, as he sees it, is the story of the dissolution of objectivity and kindness, of the willingness to identify with the oppressor when one realizes the depth of one's alienation from the victim. Like Bowen, Farrell takes the risk of portraying history marginally in the view from the Big House. Unlike Bowen, he avoids the suggestion that the patricians embodied civilization: Edward Spencer and Boy O'Neill are not the people of Grattan and Burke. Remarkably defamiliarized, the native Irish become one with the dirty hungry mobs of India and Singapore that Farrell describes in the other novels of his trilogy. This resemblance is no matter of chance. Farrell has written that:

> the Irish troubles of 1919–1921 were chosen partly because they appeared to be safely lodged in the past; most of the book was written before the current Irish difficulties broke out, giving it an unintended topicality. What I wanted to do was to use this period of the past as a metaphor for today, because I believe that however much the superficial details and customs of life may change over the years, basically life itself does not change very much. Indeed, all literature that survives must depend on this assumption.[14]

[14] From Bridget O'Toole, "J. G. Farrell," in *Contemporary Novelists*, ed. James Vinson (London: St. James, 1976), 426.

Farrell's newspaper clippings, palm trees, and wild cats urge us to draw parallels between Ireland and the more far-flung reaches of the British Empire. So do more explicit metaphors: toward the end of the novel, the servants who abandon the Majestic are said to have "gradually melted away, as native bearers on safaris are reputed to melt, one by one, into the jungle" (*T*, 424). Edward had lived in India before buying the Majestic; the club bar is full of colonials who primarily differ from the Anglo-Irish in "being more used to a division of people by race than by religion" (*T*, 387). Dispersed from the Majestic, the old ladies who had been its last guests go out to "Egypt, India, and other places (remote, certainly, but where the natives were better behaved than the Irish)" (*T*, 423).

Farrell's remarkable success in portraying the colonial mentality and, in particular, the corruption of well-meaning people who believe they are acting in behalf of a benign system is achieved at a price. As in *The Last September*, a restricted narrative point of view shuts out the Catholic Irish and, thereby, becomes complicit in their dehumanization by the British. With Farrell's brilliant irony, a people with whom he personally felt close ties, on whose behalf has been written some of the most eloquent literature of the century, become as voiceless and alien as the Haitians who have besieged Miami. Closed to certain elements of the real historical record, Farrell's Irish past is, as he had hoped, a metaphor open to the present. No one who reads *Troubles* can fail to detect his distinctive tone in the actions of the city of Phoenix, Arizona, which, having been disturbed by the growing numbers of hungry transients caught foraging in trash barrels, voted to declare garbage municipal property.[15]

Like *The Last September*, *Troubles* is splendidly effective in its enactment of a certain kind of historical consciousness

[15] Alder, Jerry, et al. "The Hard-Luck Christmas of '82," 100 *Newsweek*, 27 December 1982, 12–16. Watching old women foraging in the Majestic's garbage, the carbuncular tutor comments: "If you ask me, the cook sometimes throws away perfectly good food on purpose. They can get away with murder if no one keeps an eye on them" (*T*, 278).

that both authors seem to consider normative: the slow erosion of every defense against the acknowledgment of change and violence. Yeats from his tower looked down at the civil war that followed the Treaty of 1921 and could see "Nothing but grip of claw, and the eye's complacency" ("Meditations in Time of Civil War," CP, 204). To show how and in what conditions the complacent eye comes to see the gripping claw was the achievement of both Farrell and Bowen.

CHAPTER THREE

Northern Ireland in Four Contemporary Novels

IRIS MURDOCH's indictment in *The Red and the Green* of the complicity of literature in public violence and the dangerous obsession of the Irish with their mythicized past preceded the renewed outbreak of sectarian violence in Northern Ireland by only four years. Like Farrell, who had chosen the troubles of 1919–1921 as subject matter because they were "safely in the past"[1] and then discovered an "uncanny" resemblance between the *Irish Times* for 1920 and his daily newspaper,[2] Murdoch might well feel the discomforts of "unintended topicality."[3] Yet the topicality of historical fiction is not necessarily an accident. Lion Feuchtwanger's claim that "creative writers desire only to treat contemporary matters even in those of their creations which have history as their subject" may be too sweeping, but for the study of contemporary Northern Ireland, it is highly suggestive.[4] Although traditional realistic fiction seems sharply limited in its ability to analyze the current troubles, Thomas Kilroy's *The Big Chapel*, an experimental historical novel, illustrates how a fiction set in the past can open up a present that is its most compelling concern.

As we have seen, for Bowen and Farrell the mental processes of the Anglo-Irish often seem to consist almost exclusively of attempts to defer awareness of the Irish Indepen-

---

[1] O'Toole, "J. G. Farrell," 427.

[2] Binns, *J. G. Farrell*, 27.

[3] O'Toole, "J. G. Farrell," 427.

[4] *The House of Desdemona, or the Laurels and Limitations of Historical Fiction*, trans. Harold A. Basilius (Detroit: Wayne State University Press, 1963), 129.

dence War being waged around them. Since 1969, when the troubles that earlier war failed to resolve were renewed in an urban, Northern setting, most current British fiction has evaded them even more successfully than Bowen and Farrell's protagonists do. Mainstream, internationally famous British writers mention the conflict in Northern Ireland only in passing, if at all; the observation is as true for realistic writers, such as Alan Sillitoe, John Braine, and Margaret Drabble as it is for experimental writers, such as Anthony Burgess, D. M. Thomas, and Muriel Spark. The silences are sometimes significant, as in Iris Murdoch's *Nuns and Soldiers*, when the Count, temporarily suicidal, contemplates having himself transferred to Belfast; more often they seem to reflect either a becoming diffidence about the writer's competence to analyze that foreign territory or a reluctance to admit its horrors. The occasional thriller aside, fiction in any sense, however oblique, about Northern Ireland seems to be written largely by its inhabitants and by a handful of writers from the Irish republic.

Surveying the fiction produced by the current troubles, one can begin to sympathize with those writers who avoid them altogether. The intractability of Northern violence, the seemingly random way in which it selects its victims, the brutalization of public attitudes and discourse, even the desolation of what has surely become, in Belfast and Derry, one of the world's ugliest urban landscapes: all of these aspects seem at odds with much on which even twentieth-century fiction usually depends. The aesthetic impulse is as alien to the Shankill Road as the well-shaped plot is to the erratic behavior of homemade bombs; a private life, in the face of repeated violations, becomes almost as inconceivable as a simple moral judgment or a happy ending.

Moreover, Northern Ireland itself does not have a long tradition of political fiction; indeed the standard work, John Foster Wilson's *Forces and Themes in Ulster Fiction* (1974) does not grant significance to the history of political and religious conflict in that province either as theme or force. Pre-1969 Belfast emerges, whether in the Catholic Brian Moore or the

Protestant Janet O'Neill, as the archetypal place where nothing happens, a repressive backwater threatening, too often successfully, to destroy the hero or heroine's psychic vitality. In Maurice Leitch's *Liberty Lad* (1965), Northern Ireland produced an urban realistic novel reminiscent, in its concerns and techniques, of its English proletarian counterparts. Perhaps only in the fiction of Benedict Kiely, whose closest affinities are with fellow Irish Catholic writers to the South— Frank O'Connor and Sean O'Faolain, as well as James Joyce— is there a persistent sense of a political context, even where the theme is not overtly political. Since 1969, Northern Ireland—the Civil Rights movement and Bloody Sunday; power-sharing and direct rule and British troops; bombings, assassinations, and kneecappings; internments and hunger strikes— is no longer a place where nothing happens. On the contrary, it has lurched into the dubious company of Lebanon, Afghanistan, and Nicaragua as a place in which the frequency of violent events has rendered them unassimilable, incomprehensible.

Contemporary events are always a problem for fiction, says Feuchtwanger, who sees the present as a "brutal actuality" that resists attempts to discern outlines or define perspectives.[5] That resistance to perspective is more intense where— as in Feuchtwanger's Germany or contemporary Northern Ireland—changes have been radical and the brutality of the present is more than a metaphor. Realistic fiction about the contemporary conflict in the North is well-equipped to convey the confusion and despair of people living through that conflict, but it is limited in its ability to define causes or suggest solutions, if only by its need to be faithful to the discouraging experience of daily life. Feuchtwanger sees the historical novel as offering the writer a means of establishing perspective not only about its ostensible subjects but about the present. The validity of his observation becomes clear when we examine three recent novels with contemporary Northern settings and compare them with a fourth work,

[5] Ibid., 135.

Thomas Kilroy's *The Big Chapel*, which is set in an imaginary nineteenth-century village in what is now the Republic of Ireland.

·   ·   ·

Some features of life in Northern Ireland are well known. Newspaper photographs of grimy-faced children throwing stones at British troops or of blasted walls on which "No Pope Here" is inscribed in dripping paint have taken their place in the world's conscience. Nonetheless, others are less well understood by outsiders, and before beginning to analyze some of the contemporary fiction about the North it is useful to review the public record. Between 1969 and 1985, 2,429 people died as a result of the troubles.[6] Both terrorism itself, and government responses to it, impose themselves on daily urban life in small and large ways. Some twelve thousand British troops, seven thousand policemen, forty-five hundred police reservists, and eight thousand members of the Ulster Defence Regiment (a locally recruited unit of the British army, 98 percent Protestant in 1980) patrol a province of 1.5 million people, giving some city areas the look of a country under military occupation.[7] Habeas corpus was revoked in 1973, when a Northern Ireland Emergency Provisions Act allowed authorities to arrest without a warrant and hold suspects for up to seventy-two hours; homes may be searched and property seized without a warrant. The Prevention of Terrorism Act (1974) allows authorities to hold a suspect for up to seven days without charge; this law, unlike the 1973 Act, applies to all of the United Kingdom.[8] This curtailment of civil liberties has been inevitably accompanied by numerous small invasions of privacy—for example, shoppers are rou-

---

[6] *Detroit Free Press*, 1 March 1985, 10A.

[7] Jack Holland, *Too Long a Sacrifice: Life and Death in Northern Ireland since 1969* (Harmondsworth: Penguin, 1982), 196; and Katherine Sullivan See, *First World Nationalisms: Class and Ethnic Politics in Northern Ireland and Quebec* (Chicago: University of Chicago Press, 1986), 128.

[8] Holland, *Too Long a Sacrifice*, 196.

tinely searched in central Belfast, where it has long been illegal to leave a parked car. Constant violence has severely damaged an economy that was virtually always at a disadvantage vis-a-vis the rest of the United Kingdom, to the point where one writer speaks of the North as "de-industrialised"; "between 1974 and 1984, Northern Ireland lost one-third of its industrial jobs."[9] All of the employment statistics are chilling: in 1982, real unemployment approached 28 percent, with only 96,000 workers holding jobs in manufacturing;[10] Catholic male unemployment in some areas was 49.2 percent.[11] Meanwhile, the religious segregation that contributes to the conflict has hardened, as terrorists on both sides have forced the group in the minority to leave low-income housing; to take one example, perhaps one-fifth of the population of Belfast has moved out of mixed areas.[12] Moreover, no progress has been made in education, where segregation is almost absolute at all income levels: 98 percent of Catholic children go to Catholic schools.[13] Northern Ireland is a profoundly divided country where civilians die in pubs and grocery stores, where Christmas shoppers take risks formerly associated with commando raids.

As exemplary of both the successes and failures of realistic fiction with a contemporary Northern setting, we can look briefly at Leitch's *Silver's City*, Kiely's *Proxopera*, and Bernard MacLaverty's *Cal*. *Silver's City* is the story of Silver Steele, the jailed leader of an unnamed Protestant terrorist organization. Suspecting him of disloyalty, Silver's fellow terrorists engineer his escape from a hospital. The plot follows Silver through his interrogation by them, his escape, a brief relationship with a notably golden-hearted prostitute, and his eventual recapture by the police. Like Gerald Seymour's Brit-

---

[9] James Downey, *Them and Us: Britain-Ireland and the Northern Question, 1969–1982* (Dublin: Ward River Press, 1983), 223; See, *First World Nationalisms*, 129.

[10] Ibid., 216.

[11] Holland, *Too Long*, 203.

[12] Downey, *Them and Us*, 121.

[13] Dominic Murray, "School and Conflict," in *Northern Ireland: The Background to the Conflict* (Syracuse: Syracuse University Press, 1983), 141.

ish thriller with a Belfast setting, *Harry's Game*, and Shaun Herron's *The Whore-Mother*, the novel evokes an urban landscape of violence, of concrete, barricades, and bomb craters occasionally relieved by a visit to lower-middle-class interiors in which the world of childhood survives: "It was another era . . . framed Bible texts on the wall and feminine toilet articles on the dressing table" (*SC*, 82). The strengths of the book are those of the tradition in which it is written: immediacy of description, a feeling for what it would be like to live in the midst of guerilla war and for its brutalizing effects on people like Young Terry, whose voracious appetite for fries of eggs, chips, and sausage drowned in revolting gouts of sauce aptly suggests his vocation as a hired gun. In Silver's doomed attempts to have a love idyll with Nan, we see a theme found in most recent Northern Irish fiction, the impossibility of personal life.

Yet, in spite of its successes, in the end the urban proletarian genre does not offer enough scope for the novel's subject matter. Silver is presented as a sympathetic character who, quite out of keeping with the stereotype of the Protestant militant, is first seen reading a book by Che Guevara. What are his motives? Had he really intended to betray his group? What outcome might he, or the reader, wish for his country? The novel's narrow focus on this slice of urban, Protestant, working-class Belfast—significantly, the city is never named, although its landmarks are—excludes any attention to larger issues. Just as abstract questions about the hero and his motives are left unasked, so similar questions about Northern Ireland as a political entity are ignored, as is a larger social context: the novel's only Catholic is gunned down in the first chapter. And although the deep pessimism that such failure to discuss solutions or even causes inevitably produces may well be justified, it has the side effect that Chesterton saw in nineteenth-century naturalism: the suggestion that the victimized are unredeemable brutes whose horrible conditions, from which the middle-class reader is comfortably excluded, represent "a kind of cruelty to animals" rather than "injustice to equals." The "brutal pity" of such novels, said Chesterton aptly, "has an elemental sincerity of its own, but it is entirely useless for all ends of social reform."[14]

The impact of the recent troubles on more fully conceived characters is the theme of Kiely's *Proxopera* and MacLaverty's *Cal*. Like Bowen, Kiely chooses as his protagonist a civilian, a retired teacher of history and classics named Mr. Binchey. The IRA takes his family hostage to force him to drive a bomb into the center of his hometown; Binchey instead drives the bomb to a British checkpoint; the terrorists retaliate by burning his house and shooting his son through the knee. For Binchey, the destruction of his lake house is the destruction of a "living dream" that goes back to childhood; that loss becomes a lens focusing all of the civilian deaths, all of the bombing and burning of nonmilitary targets that have made up daily newspaper fare for the past eight years of his life (*P*, 91). As Joseph McMinn points out, *Proxopera* is essentially apolitical, a "version of pastoral lost" in which the IRA replaces industrialization as the chief threat to "the hard-won contentment of the rural bourgeoisie."[15] Nevertheless, Kiely's novel, unlike Leitch's, explicitly acknowledges a larger context. That terrorism is perpetuated by both sides is much of the point: Kiely's country is caught in a chain of irrational acts intended to avenge others, equally irrational. All the same, dry public issues—discrimination in housing, hiring, and access to political power, for example—go unmentioned, although they may well be assumed. What dominates *Proxopera* is some dark human need for violence. Noting a story about a Glasgow immigrant's child beaten to death in Australia, Binchey thinks, "thus the whole round earth is every way bound by gold chains about the feet of God" (*P*, 85). This need is fed, in Ireland, by a mythicized history—King William and the Battle of the Boyne (*P*, 13), Patrick Pearse, Cuchulain, Edward Fitzgerald, Robert Emmett, and Wolfe Tone (*P*, 58). Asked who "guided or misguided" Ulster youth, Mr. Binchey replies, "Ireland. A long history. England. Empire. King Wil-

---

[14] *Charles Dickens: The Last of the Great Men* (1906; New York: Readers Club, 1946), 197.

[15] "Contemporary Novels of the 'Troubles,' " *Études Irlandaises* 5 (1980): 117.

liam. The Pope. Ian Paisley. Myself. I was a teacher of history" (P, 84). Such dark historical myths must indeed seem
more intractable than even the worst sociological phenomena,
than even, for example, James Downey's grim assertion that
"for much of West Belfast especially, such a thing as employment hardly exists: in the worst areas, unemployment among
male school leavers approaches 100 per cent."[16] For although
it is deeply critical of Irish historical myths, the novella's commitment to them hardly suggests how they might be replaced,
and in the last line Binchey, despairing of civic peace, returns
to a private dream: "To have your own stream in your own
lawn is the height of everything" (P, 93).

Like *Proxopera, Cal* focuses on a single character destroyed
by overwhelming political forces. Yet the relationship of
MacLaverty's hero to his world is not the same as that of Mr.
Binchey. In his 1980 survey of novels about the Troubles,
McMinn notes that the choice of outsiders (journalists, British
agents, psychopathic terrorists) or radically detached people
like Mr. Binchey as heroes contributes to their essentially
apolitical and despairing tone. To such characters, the Troubles are a "separate but proximate world which impinges on
the preference for private order"; their social and political dimension is "incomprehensible from the point of view of characters who are naturally solitary."[17]

Like the characters McMinn indicts, Cal lacks political so-
phistication and imagination, but, unlike them, he is deeply
imbedded in Irish working-class life. The kind of private life—
marriage, a job—for which he yearns reflects no preferences
for a private, solitary order but only for an ordinarily peaceful
social one. Cal McCrystal, the unemployed son of a meat cut-
ter, is drawn into the IRA by an old school friend. Accepting
an assignment as a driver, he finds himself an accomplice to
the murder of a Protestant farmer, Robert Martin. In the
course of the novel, he comes to work for the dead man's
mother and have an affair with his widow, Marcella. After
Cal's council house is burned down by Protestant terrorists,

[16] *Them and Us,* 123.
[17] "Contemporary Novels," 119–120.

he hides from the IRA in an abandoned cottage on the Martin's farm. But his idyll in the countryside ends abruptly when he spots Crilly, an IRA acquaintance, planting a bomb in the library where Marcella works. The climax is sudden: Crilly forces Cal to accompany him to an IRA gathering, which is raided; Cal escapes only long enough to inform the police of the bomb's location. The next day they arrive to arrest him.

The story of Cal and Marcella's impossible love affair is set within an almost flatly realistic social context. From teenage unemployment and the dole, segregated housing and education, to the unimaginative Belfast diet and the Protestant penchant for tea cozies decorated with equestrian Queen Elizabeths (which is matched by the Catholic enthusiasm for ugly plaques made in "Long Kesh Concentration Camp"), life in contemporary Northern Ireland is meticulously detailed. While the old bigotries and myths make themselves felt, as when an IRA gunman quotes Pearse's "Mother," MacLaverty emphasizes unemployment as a catalyst to violence. Although his education has taught him that Catholics have too long been "the hewers of wood and the drawers of water" in Northern Ireland, for Cal, physical labor is "cleansing" and only his job offers a way of deferring involvement in the IRA (*C*, 10). *Cal* depicts good will and hatred alike as evenly distributed between religious factions and this balance, along with a well-described social context, goes a long way toward giving Northern Ireland the human face it lacks in *Silver's City*. However, given the de-industrialization of the North, unemployment there may easily be seen as a problem only slightly less intractable than the secular version of original sin and the mythic glorification of violence that we saw in *Proxopera*. In *Cal*, as in the other works we have examined, public life intersects with private life only to destroy it. The novel itself is threatened when the contest between private and social life, one of its oldest themes, is so manifestly unequal. The present is indeed unbearable, and the realistic novelist does not imagine solutions.

. . .

Thomas Kilroy's *The Big Chapel* offers a different approach. In a 1972 interview with the *Irish Times*, Kilroy signaled his intention for the novel, which is set one hundred years earlier, "to relate to recent events in Northern Ireland"; the signals of that intention are not at all difficult to discern in the novel itself.[18] *The Big Chapel* is one of those historical novels in which history functions, in Feuchtwanger's language, as a "disguise." Feuchtwanger further argues that "historical disguise often enables an author to express truths, notably those of a political or daringly erotic kind, he would fear or be incapable of stating in a contemporary setting."[19] To use examples more contemporary than his, it is certain that Stalin is more central to Stefan Heym's *The King David Report* than David himself, or that Christa Wolf's *No Place on Earth* is at least as interesting for what it has to say about the German Democratic Republic at the present time as for what it has to say about Winkel on the Rhine in June 1804. Yet even when censorship is not an issue, an author may wish to "make . . . the reader feel the peculiar and essential quality of his own time . . . by removing himself from his own time, and by regarding it as something foreign, in short, by assuming an historical point of view." This "perspective of the past" enables the reader to see the "grand outline" of contemporary problems.[20] Moreover, as an experimental historical novel, *The Big Chapel* resists the closure of naturalistic novels such as *Silver's City*, suggesting that, since the past is open to many interpretations, the present need not be seen as doomed to follow a predetermined course. But before we look further into Kilroy's techniques and conceptions, it is first necessary to look closely at his historical subject.

The Big Chapel is the story of a small Irish town that becomes bitterly divided over the decision of its Catholic pastor, Father William Lannigan, to oppose his bishop about the question of Catholic education. The priest, as overseer of a

[18] Brian Cosgrove, "Ego Contra Mundum: Thomas Kilroy's *The Big Chapel*," *Cahiers Irlandaises* 4–5 (1975): 298.

[19] *House of Desdemona*, 129, 133.

[20] Feuchtwanger, *House of Desdemona*, 141.

National School, refuses to close it down in favor of a new Christian Brothers' school. He is dismissed and the town erupts into civil violence; after a pyrrhic legal victory, the priest submits to his bishop and dies in a county home. Closely interwoven with his story is that of Master Scully, the headmaster of the National School, and his family, whose loyalties and rivalries comment on the historical theme.

Kilroy's subject is double-edged. It is obvious, even without the author's word, that the novel is about "lunacy, about rigid orthodoxy . . . in a community."[21] The irony of Christians warring with each other is everywhere apparent: "It said a lot about the nature of men that such pain, such fear, such hatred could be made out of so simple a start as that, shepherds and stars" (*BC*, 91). At the same time, the subject matter, grounded in historical fact, does more than illustrate the pointless, Big Endian versus Little Endian side of religious disputation. Throughout the latter half of the nineteenth century, Catholic education in Ireland was a subject of struggle and debate. Although most National Schools were, like Father Lannigan's, under sectarian control, they were often bitterly resented because of a standard curriculum set in London that included the King James Bible and excluded the Irish language.[22] During his long episcopacy, Archbishop Paul Cullen urged, at a minimum, the reform of these schools and the creation of a Catholic secondary system and a Catholic university. His was a popular cause; as Peter Paul MacSwiney said in January, 1872: "Every Catholic in Ireland was for denominationalism, excepting for only a few impatient and ungovernable agitators."[23] Actuating the impatient and the ungovernable was likely to be resentment against Cullen himself, one of the "apples of God's eye" against whom Mr. Casey and Simon Dedalus fulminate at Joyce's famous Christmas dinner. Cullen's ambitions for Catholic education were inextricably

[21] Cosgrove, "Ego Contra Mundum," 298.

[22] Joseph Lee, *The Modernization of Irish Society, 1848–1918* (Dublin: Gill and Macmillan, 1973), 27.

[23] E. R. Norman, *The Catholic Church and Ireland in the Age of Rebellion, 1859–1873* (Ithaca: Cornell University Press, 1965), 442.

tied to a larger policy of disciplining, centralizing, and romanizing the Irish church—down to the imposition of clerical dress—that came to be known as ultramontanism. Since the church at Rome was in one of its more reactionary phases—the Syllabus of Errors, the doctrines of papal infallibility, and the Immaculate Conception all date from the second half of the nineteenth century—romanizing the church was not universally acceptable. In E. R. Norman's words, "throughout the 1860s, and before and afterwards, Protestants in England and Ireland argued that concession of the bishop's educational demands would only lead to greater ignorance and subjugation of the Catholic laity, and some Catholics were found to agree with them."[24] More tellingly perhaps, Cullen's persistent opposition to revolutionary violence, which made him an anathema to Mr. Casey, was seen as a related betrayal of local interests in favor of the universal church.

Thus, the fictional dispute at Kyle imbeds itself in the major issues of the 1870s. But these again are of more than antiquarian interest. Joseph Lee debates Mr. Casey's myth, noting that "the centralising policy of Cullen . . . did more to . . . accustom the faithful to think in national terms than did the attitude of his Gallican opponents."[25] This identification of the church with nationalism, when combined with denominational education, is frequently cited as a serious obstacle to the liberalizing and integration of Northern Irish society today. There are those who disagree: Dominic Murray, in a 1983 study, concludes that "at the levels of religion and culture, the influence of the school seems to have been grossly exaggerated" although even he concluded that some Catholic schools "can validly be said to perpetuate community division by directing their pupils either towards, or away from, certain sectors of their community."[26] But even if, as Murray and Lee argue, the schools merely reflect intransigence "lovingly inculcated in the bosom of the Christian family,"[27] they remain

[24] Ibid., 20.
[25] *Modernization*, 44–45.
[26] "Schools and Conflict," 149.
[27] *Modernization*, 27.

a powerful instance and symbol of religious segregation in Northern Ireland.

The major characters in *The Big Chapel* embody ways of responding to public life, and the undecidability found elsewhere in the novel is manifest in its hesitations about turning any one of them into a model. The one who comes closest to being a hero is the man at the center of the controversy in Kyle, Father Lannigan. Father Lannigan is physically imposing in the Gothic style: his parish is in awe of "that severe, huge head with its black locks, black brows, the paleness of its anger, the gathering of muscles of its strength" (*BC*, 11). The child of peasants, he has a "lineage of poverty, ignorance, disease" (*BC*, 112); his rise to the priesthood has left him perennially divided, "a victim of . . . two styles," one coarse, one elegant, neither fitting "the needs of his own heart" (*BC*, 112). His initial defiance of the bishop is based on a liberal view "that education was positive and the pursuit of knowledge and not negative and the limitation of knowledge" (*BC*, 14). He sees how inextricably linked the question of religious education is to other ultramontane concerns, which he characterizes as "episcopacy and dictatorship instead of freedom and local tradition" (*BC*, 17). Yet Lannigan's personal courage is accompanied by a "blindness to the sufferings of others," including his most fervent supporters (*BC*, 111). His intransigence, as much as the bishop's, leads to death and destruction. Setting out to oppose bigotry, he becomes a fanatic who "never forgave what he called a betrayal" (*BC*, 113), who, only able "to live and be himself at an extremity . . . craved the attention of those that hated him with a passion" (*BC*, 203). Caught up in the public role of a man of conscience, the priest eventually discovers "that he had become a hollow man, sounding forth as resonantly as before, but in the end without as much as a scrap of conviction" (*BC*, 113).

If Father Lannigan is in the end reduced to a Yeatsian "image of such politics" whose collapse warns of the danger of passionate commitment to a "common right or wrong," his counterpart in the novel, Horace Percy Butler of Whytescourt, is no more attractive as a model. Butler is the last descendant of a prominent Anglo-Irish family. In his old age nearly deaf, he spends his days in a "monkish room at the top of the house," the Observatory. He is detached, cynical, Olympian: "The essential for sanity was to avoid traffic: in some easeful, minimal investment of attention to preserve life in the flesh: it would all end someday" (BC, 59). Knowing that the Anglo-Irish are doomed "as a class" (BC, 95) and persuaded that their heritage is "all loot" (BC, 59), he is nonetheless incapable of forming bonds with the "ragged wretches" (BC, 59) they oppress. His Irish Protestant bigotry and his attachment to the principles of "scientific" progress similarly limit his friendships with educated Catholics such as Father Lannigan and the Scullys.

Butler characteristically defines for himself only the role of observer during the troubles at Kyle. In the same journal that records his notes about local flora and fauna, he describes, without transition, events and personalities and his conversations with other members of the gentry. Butler's interests include the new science and technology as well as current social thought, Bianconi cars as well as Saint-Simon and Robert Owen. He considers religion in all its forms a degrading superstition, its factions the most savage of all "because its hatreds are based on mindlessness" (BC, 166). Mr. Butler "believe[s] in progress" (BC, 166). "Our evolution," he claims, "is only just begun" (BC, 69); someday human beings "will be able to accomplish [their] intentions" (BC, 244). Yet his radical isolation and the gap between what he can see of human behavior and his rational aspirations for it prove an impossible strain. By the end of the novel he appears to have collapsed into the insanity his theories had been designed to keep at bay. When he invites a French balloonist to give a demonstration at Whytescourt, it is obvious that he invests this latest technological development with quasi-religious significance. To Nicholas Scully, who is frightened by his soot-blackened face and "sulphurous, infernal air," he shouts: "I like the balloon! . . . It has aspirations in the other direction . . . which is the only direction that counts. I'll assist anyone . . . who wishes to flaunt Newton!" (BC, 248–49). Just as a crusading

liberalism ends for Father Lannigan in intolerance and fanaticism, so a "belief in science" ends for Mr. Butler in superstition and lunacy.

Between the extremes that Father Lannigan and Mr. Butler finally become lies Master Scully, a Catholic married to a
Protestant who for years struggles to maintain the only reli-
giously integrated school at Kyle. His argument that "there's
nothing that's simply right or wrong" (*BC*, 75) fails to convince his sons; he dies trying to rescue one of them from a
rioting mob. Nicholas, the most likely by temperament and
intelligence to follow his father, becomes torn between the
priest and Mr. Butler as "the only possible convert either of
them was ever likely to make" (*BC*, 242). In the end, although
he has lost his faith in God, Nicholas chooses the priest "as a
man" and Catholicism because it sees human beings "as they
are" (*BC*, 244).

Not only does a tolerant humanism fail in a situation that
provokes irrational loyalties, but the only character in the
novel who seems consistently to have the emotional strength
to oppose fanaticism dies in exile. Emerine, Master Scully's
illegitimate niece and adopted daughter, is passionately loved
by Nicholas and his brother Marcus. Unafraid of nature, of
what people think (*BC*, 228), she is horrified when Nicholas
becomes the priest's only companion, reminding her of "what
she feared and hated in the town, the poisoning of everything
that was trying to live naturally" (*BC*, 225). When Emerine
finally marries Marcus, the incestuous overtones are unmistakable. Seeing herself as a mythic force striving to unify the
warring sides, she decides to be married in Kyle rather than
avert scandal by going elsewhere because "it might be the
only salvation of all of them" (*BC*, 213), presumably because
the town can use an example of an unthinkable union. After
her husband is convicted of the equally mythic act of murder-
ing his brother, she leaves for England, "driven . . . by the
conviction that she had to get out and go on living free because she seemed to know that what was being trampled on
here wasn't . . . a few people but some part of life itself" (*BC*,
213). Yet, Emerine, like all the others, is defeated: she dies a

suicide and her son, a "butcher's help with a harelip . . . was frequently pointed out as an example of the priest-curse that was said to affect with deformity all those families who had sided with the Red Priest, years before" (BC, 254).

If this dismal record of murder, suicide, and madness proves nothing else, it surely demonstrates that facile optimism and schematic solutions are no more of a temptation for Kilroy than for writers who portray contemporary events in Northern Ireland. In fact, the very existence of Belfast 1971 makes such optimism unthinkable in an Irish historical novel. All the same, as Feuchtwanger argues, an eponymous historical perspective seems to allow more interest in causes, and to suggest more solutions, than a novel with a contemporary setting is likely to. In the simplest sense, Kilroy demonstrates the centrality of education. Listening to his fellow train passengers airing their fixed views on the troubles at Kyle, Nicholas Scully reflects that "our ignorance is a more exacting master than the English and their landlords and their peelers. If we knew better we would do more" (BC, 30). Yet the experimental form Kilroy uses is more crucial. His subject belongs both to the past and the present, and his narrative techniques keep this double theme before the reader's eyes. Those readers drawn to historical fiction for the reasons that Mr. Scully is drawn to local antiquities—"I will take the past over the present any time—it's all ended there" (BC, 77)—must be continually discomfited by reminders of the present. Yet the interchange between past and present that the novel promotes is the major source of its limited optimism that contemporary Northern Ireland can be liberated from an imprisoning history.

In spite of its interest in the present, the novel never reduces the past simply to an allegory. The Big Chapel is steeped in references to the famous men and issues of 1871: to Matthew Arnold, John Stuart Mill, Thomas Carlyle, Bismarck, and Pius IX; to Darwinism, the Paris Commune, Ultramontism, and the Syllabus of Errors. References to Irish figures such as Judge Keogh and John McHale and to real events, such as the arrest of Arthur O'Connor for attempting to present Queen Victoria with a Fenian petition, are of course also to be found. These, however, are less frequent, and some omissions, such as that of any specific reference to Paul Cullen, are remarkable. Still the ambience of a particular time and place is scrupulously created. Note, for example, the care with which Kilroy creates Nicholas's long train ride from Kildare Station to Kyle. The reader sees the desolate landscape of the Midlands through a "streaming window," and cringes with him from the poverty of the other passengers, like the silent one-eyed boy whose mother feeds him "yellow meal that she had dampened with sugared water and . . . kneaded with her fingers into small pellets" (*BC*, 42).

Yet even as he evokes a specific past, Kilroy emphasizes those features of 1871 that persist one hundred years later. As in 1971, both religious factions burn down houses and shops; the savage breaking of a child's arms because his father opposes the Bishop (*BC*, 68) anticipates the civilian reprisals and kneecappings of the present; barricades are built and chapels desecrated. Events in Kyle are repeatedly called "the Troubles," a phrase that links them to the 1920s as well as to the present. References to "Prods" and to "tribalism" have a contemporary flavor, as does the claim that "outside agitators" cause most of the problems (*BC*, 66). An Anglo-Irish doctor cites a still familiar problem: "The country is not at war . . . and still one fifth of our army is quartered here" (*BC*, 97). References to Lannigan's faction as the "Reds" not only remind us of modern Unionist exaggerations of Marxist influence in the various Catholic militant groups, but serve to link Kyle and its rebels to "the worst excesses of the Paris Commune" (*BC*, 49).

The novelist constantly reminds the readers in other ways that the past is not self-contained. When Miss Joyce makes her Easter duty outside Father Lannigan's parish (*BC*, 154), the nearly inevitable association with Stephen Dedalus's crisis compels the reader to recognize that Kilroy's characters are faced with some of the same characteristic choices that James Joyce described. The persistence of themes in history, and the difficulties of resolving them, are also signaled internally in the novel. Kilroy does not content himself with a simple sequential account of "what happened"; instead, he intersperses his narrative with references to future interpretations of events in Kyle, to "how the children will tell it to their children," to "stories told a hundred years later" (BC, 175; 177). Events within the narrative are foretold long before they occur; for example, the manner of Mrs. Scully's death and her adoptive daughter's suicide are almost the first things we learn about them (BC, 20). Master Scully's death is noted in Butler's journal (BC, 191) before it occurs, on-stage as it were, in a mob scene (BC, 205). This death explicitly carries with it a sense of an ending: "Something at least had come to an end with the Master's death . . . it was the people themselves who suggested an end by the way they went out of their way to show to the Scullys that all was forgotten now, that it was all over now with the priest and wouldn't it be better, in God's peace, to make the town a fit place again for Christians?" (BC, 209). Yet, the promised conclusion is a chimera. The novel goes on for another forty-two pages, ending apparently inconclusively with a French balloonist's demonstration and Nicholas's return to the Presbytery where "the priest would be dozing, labouring each breath, in a parlour chair" (BC, 251). Only in the appendix do we learn, briefly and generally, about Nicholas's violent death, which certainly would have provided a more dramatic climax. Kilroy, however, prefers to suggest that even the lives of fictional characters continue beyond the end of the novel.

Unable to find the past comfortably finished, readers are also denied certainty about what it is. The view that the problems of Northern Ireland stem from a fatal preoccupation with the past, in the form of the Battle of the Boyne and the Penal Laws, is commonplace. As A.T.Q. Stewart points out, however, the real preoccupation is not with the actual past but with "a garment of myth and legend which they call Irish history."[28] Like Kiely, Kilroy suggests how a fixed, unproblem-

[28] The Narrow Ground: Aspects of Ulster, 1609–1969 (London: Faber, 1977), 15.

atic version of history leads to violence. His historical setting, however, allows for a different emphasis; throughout *The Big Chapel*, we see the difficulty of ever knowing the truth about a past event. The novel begins in uncertainty: "As the years passed details . . . became vague and unsettled. The story turned and twisted with each telling and this is a problem" (*BC*, 9). Oral history of the crisis of 1871 is represented in the form of local legends—one involving a hermaphroditic dancing ghost—"as the town still preserved them, nearly one hundred years after the event" (*BC*, 177), without any comment as to their origins or truth. Interspersed throughout the novel, also without comment, are excerpts from Butler's journal and items from Dublin newspapers and *The Times* of London. The biases of all of these versions of the past are as obvious as one might expect. The patronizing tone, for example, that *The Times* maintained toward its Irish cousins, even during the Famine, is faithfully mimicked: "We would simply offer to all those concerned in the treatment of civil and religious strife in Ireland the principle, well-founded, well-tried and acceptable to all men of good-will, of 'a stout constable, an honest justice, a clear highway and a free chapel!' " (*BC*, 49). Such accounts, in which the social class, temperament, and interests of the teller are everywhere visible, call the objective verifiability of all of the novel's historical assertions into question.

Uncertainty even about dates also crops up; Henrietta Scully "died in a home for indigent Christians in Dublin, in 1888 or 1889, it is said" (*BC*, 20); her son Marcus "dies of pneumonia on the Farm Prison at Lusk, County Dublin, in 1878 or 1879" (*BC*, 252). Not only are the narratives and records that make up history difficult to verify objectively, but even history's medium, time, is subjective and elusive. As in a modernist novel, time is experienced in terms of strongly felt emotional moments; the novel's second sentence makes the point explicit: "This was the time from which people would measure its [the town's] age, not with the simple measurement of years" (*BC*, 9). Eventually "this energy died . . . and the town relapsed into timelessness" (*BC*, 9). Much fur ther on, Emerine Scully tries to "put a shape on those last, nearly five years in the town" and finds that "they resisted her like softly dissolving butter . . . and all she was left with was this blend, this running together of everything into the one, drawn-out moment" (*BC*, 211).

"It is difficult," remarks the narrator, "to decide between truth and lie . . . each side claimed to have acted in extravagant contradiction to what the others represented as the true account" (*BC*, 17); clearly the novelist cares more about reinforcing our sense of this undecidability than about displacing *The Times* or local legend as a reliable historical narrator. Thus he shows us, through Mrs. Dawson's incredulous gossip about the Royal Family, how even the most noncontroversial public figures are mythicized by their contemporaries (*BC*, 82). Even the private lives of his characters, matters over which we might assume the writer to have the greatest authority, are finally unknowable. Was Nicholas murdered by his brother Marcus? If so, is it true that Marcus acted only in self-defense? Or was the death a suicide, for which Marcus felt some bizarre compulsion to take responsibility? Lacking answers to these questions, we are unable to adopt the black and white simplicities about the past on which contemporary passion depends.

A fiction's refusal to answer historical questions decisively may well dismay those who, like Neil McEwan, seem to equate "contemporary scepticism" with the "Orwellian" position that when we turn to the past "there is nowhere to look and nothing to see."[29] For McEwan, "the opponents of historical objectivity depreciate the first motive for reading historical fiction, which is to find that sense [of the past] given more powerful imaginative truth than we give it ourselves."[30] But in a place like Northern Ireland, where the dead hand of historical myth seems to hold the present in an icy grip, determined that it too shall run its course of bigotry and terrorism,

[29] *Perspective in British Historical Fiction Today* (Wolfeboro, N.H.: Longwood Academic, 1987), 3, 13.
[30] Ibid., 13.

a degree of indeterminacy is welcome. By problematizing historical perception and denying the reader a finished narrative, Kilroy refuses to imprison the past in a fixed mythology. The act of reading becomes a model for historical and political interpretation, conceived as a liberating movement of consciousness among alternative versions of events.[31] If even the past is thoroughly open to interpretation, the course of the present is not rigidly determined by ancient injustices. To encourage those acts of interpretation that might break the pattern of sectarian violence about which he himself writes (as do Kiely, MacLaverty, Leitch, and the daily newspaper), is for Kilroy a political outcome to which an experimental historical fiction may well aspire.

[31] Dominick La Capra provides an illuminating comment on this novelistic strategy: "one way a novel makes challenging contact with 'reality' and 'history' is precisely by resisting fully concordant narrative closure (prominently including that provided by the conventional well-made plot), for this mode of resistance inhibits compensatory catharsis and satisfying 'meaning' on the level of the imagination and throws the reader back upon the need to come to terms with the unresolved problems the novel helps to disclose" (*History, Politics, and the Novel* [Ithaca: Cornell University Press, 1987], 14).

PART TWO

Losing Confidence: Spies and Other Aliens

CHAPTER FOUR

Philby and His Fictions

TO MAKE SENSE of history is one of the fundamental impulses behind historical fiction; an accompanying danger, that the novelist will simplify a dense and contradictory experience in the interests of meeting conventional expectations about finished plots, symbolic patterns, and authorial omniscience, is not easily avoided. In an essay debating John Searle's "The Logical Status of Fictional Discourse," Thomas Leitch argues that, "In order to escape the charge of proposing a hypothetical explanation of public history in terms of private motives and then inventing private motives in order to support that hypothesis, historical novels incur the . . . commitment of making their fictional characters typical or representative. . . . The leading characters in historical novels, although nonexistent as actual individuals, are intended as representatives of general social, cultural, intellectual, or political types which do exist or have existed."[1] When the novelist looks to real figures as subjects for fiction, his or her temptation is to turn them into such representative figures, to make their life stories into myths that will explain the events of their time. One measure of the distance between the nineteenth century and our own is that, although earlier generations seemed preoccupied with heroic figures like Napoleon, Joan of Arc, and Bonny Prince Charlie, the figure who recurs in contemporary English fiction is Harold Adrian Philby. The story of this Anglo-Indian Cambridge graduate who defected to Moscow after several years as head of the Soviet section of the Secret Intelligence Service seems to embody and explain the changed social order of postwar England, the loss of her Empire, prestige, and influence. Yet attempts to understand the postwar

---

[1] "To What Is Fiction Committed?" *Prose Studies* 6, no. 2 (1983): 171.

period in terms of Philby's career have been only partially successful. In the hands of the novelists, the Philby story, variously assimilated to the conventions of the boys' adventure story, the spy novel, English Catholic fiction, light comedy, and the Oedipal narrative, becomes a myth, however ironic and deflating, behind which the historical personage disappears.

Perhaps one reason that Philby has appealed to novelists so much is that in his life itself the usual distinctions between fiction and history seem to blur. Known from early childhood by the name of Kipling's fictional spy, Kim Philby lived in a world that really exists but that takes shape for most of us in the fantasies of the thriller and, since his defection in 1963, he has been the property not so much of sober historians as of novelists, both serious and popular. The British edition of Philby's autobiography has an introduction by Graham Greene; the most convincing biography, Page, Leitch, and Knightley's *The Philby Conspiracy*, is introduced by John le Carré. The figure of the well-bred British defector appears again in Greene's *The Human Factor* and le Carré's *Tinker, Tailor, Soldier, Spy*; in Reginald Hill's *The Spy's Wife*, and in Joseph Hone's *The Private Sector*; a more distant avatar, perhaps owing more to Alan Nunn May than to Philby, appears in Anthony Burgess's *Tremor of Intent*. The dramatist Alan Bennett has contributed a two-act play, *The Old Country*, which treats an aging British defector on the verge of returning to England; a close variant of that theme animates Alan Williams's *Gentleman Traitor*. Several historical works, on the other hand, draw on a Philby numerology that derives from a well-known Graham Greene story and film: there is *The Third Man*, *The Fourth Man*, and finally, *Was There a Fifth Man?* Several of the writers appear to suggest, as Alan Williams does overtly, that the purpose of their novels is partly to relay information that the Official Secrets Act and the British libel laws, far stricter than their American counterparts, would suppress. Novelists like le Carré and Williams hinted at Anthony Blunt's identity as the "fourth man" several years before the British government confirmed it. Andrew

Boyle, author of *The Fourth Man*, gets around the same laws by constructing fictional names for Blunt and Wilfred Mann (the "fifth man," in his view); Blunt is called "Maurice," presumably to evoke his friend E. M. Forster.

The Philby story of course appeals to novelists because it contains so many of the elements of the popular thriller. The search for the spy's identity—who tipped off Moscow?—is after all a staple of the genre. Put identity in italics and we see how readily that convention lends itself to deeper questions of motive and psychological, as well as moral, integrity. Spies are congenial to the age, says Jacques Barzun, because psychoanalysis has told us we are all impostors.[2] Thus, when Kim Philby, to all appearances an efficient member of the Secret Intelligence Service (SIS), was revealed as a KGB agent of a thirty year standing, there was a powerful impulse to produce psychological explanations, an impulse reflected even in the titles of Hone's *Private Sector* and Greene's *The Human Factor*. Yet the double agent is not just any betrayer, cannot be equated with, say, the successful adulterer; his actions are determined by, and themselves determine, the course of public events. Thus the attempt to find his identity has a public dimension: one also asks of Philby if Ramsey MacDonald's National Government or the suppression of the Viennese workers in 1934 drove him into the KGB. Thus, too, the spy can easily become not only a metaphor for our own divided, deceptive selves but for the failures and "betrayals" of liberal parliamentary government in England or in the West more generally. John le Carré, stressing the public issues, says that the public is drawn to spy novels because: "We have learned in recent years to translate almost all of political life in terms of conspiracy. . . . There is so much cynicism about the orthodox forms of government as they are offered to the public that we believe almost nothing at face value."[3]

Yet the spy not only acts to influence public events; he or

[2] "Meditations on the Literature of Spying," *American Scholar* 34 (Spring 1965): 177.

[3] "John le Carré: An Interrogation," *New York Times Book Review*, 25 September 1977, 9.

she also represents a particular part of the public. People in the West are all too willing to believe in the guilt of Jewish people accused of spying—Dreyfus, the Rosenbergs, David Greenglass. Spies are readily conceived of as beautiful women like Mata Hari or as the plumpish men in ill-fitting shiny blue suits with foreign accents and nasty sexual vices who, as Bruce Merry says, almost always turn out to be spies in novels.[4] But Philby's suits fit, he had the right accent; he was certainly not Jewish and even the imputation of homosexual leanings has never been proved.[5] He was, as George Steiner rather oddly remarks, considering that the same might be said of the original, a "Judas" who "belonged to the right club."[6] He did not betray his country for money, nor did he strike his acquaintances as a man capable of deep political convictions. Thus, Philby raises questions about the English class system that he both represents and betrays.

Philby's identity is sought then by those who wish to understand his psyche, his politics, and his social class. It is an elusive identity, one that by a fatally easy movement becomes a symbol, a metaphor, something other and less than a human being. As representative of those who have searched for his identity we can look to three novelists: John le Carré, who emphasizes the public origins and consequences of his behavior; Graham Greene, who is intensely interested in the questions of psychology and private morality that associate themselves with his case; and Joseph Hone, who interests himself in both. At least as fascinating as these novels, and in some sense as "fictional," is Philby's own contribution, *My Silent*

[4] *Anatomy of the Spy Thriller* (Dublin: Gill and Macmillan, 1977), 127.
[5] Philby was "not at any stage of his life a homosexual" (Patrick Seale and Maureen McConville, *Philby: The Long Road to Moscow* [London: Hamish Hamilton, 1973], 12). An incident in which Dr. Wilfrid Mann, sent upstairs by Philby's wife, finds him in bed drinking champagne with Burgess (Andrew Boyle, *The Fourth Man* [New York: Dial-James Wade, 1979], 361; and Wilfred Basil Mann, *Was There a Fifth Man?* [Oxford: Pergamon, 1982], 84) may or may not cast doubts on Seale and McConville's statement; it seems to be the strongest evidence for Philby's alleged bisexuality that anyone has yet been willing to make public.
[6] "God's Spies," *New Yorker* 54 (8 May 1978): 150.

War, a strangely literary autobiography that is obviously a major source for his portrayal in English fiction.

Before turning to these carefully shaped visions of Philby's story—not one of which corresponds fully to the known facts—it is useful to have an idea of the public record. Philby was born in India in 1912, and educated at the best schools: Westminster, and then Trinity College, Cambridge, where he knew Guy Burgess, Donald Maclean, and Anthony Blunt. He was in Vienna in February 1934 during the shelling of the workers' flats and married a young Jewish Communist woman there. By 1936, when he had become a *Times* correspondent in Spain and an outspoken proponent of what was euphemistically referred to as Anglo-German fellowship, he was already a Soviet agent. Recruited to SIS in 1940, Philby, on all accounts a brilliant agent and administrator, rose to become head of the newly formed anti-Soviet section in 1946. Philby was transferred to Washington in 1949 as SIS liaison man with the CIA. There, he came under CIA suspicion and was finally expelled when Guy Burgess and Donald Maclean turned up in Moscow. The British interrogated and suspended Philby in 1953, but lacked the evidence to convict him of spying. After a period of disgrace, Philby became a newspaper correspondent in Beirut, where he also apparently worked again for SIS; in 1963, when he had been definitively identified by a defecting Soviet agent, Philby disappeared from Beirut and reappeared four months later in Moscow. His four wives, his affair with Melinda Maclean, wife of his fellow defector, his heavy drinking, his pronounced stutter, and his unfailing charm are all part of the public story.

Many other points remain unclear and they too are part of the story's fascination. Common sense says that a Soviet agent at the head of the anti-Soviet section of British intelligence who has close contacts with U.S. intelligence must do immense damage—but what was it? Some specific details are attested to by both Philby and his biographers—the betrayal, for example, of successive groups of anti-Communist Albanians who attempted to overthrow their country's government between 1950 and 1952. The penetration of British intelligence by Soviet agents clearly helped to break down Anglo-American cooperation in intelligence. But obviously there is much more that has never met the public eye, and the novelistic imagination is free to run riot. Questions remain about why Philby was not detected earlier, about what he was doing in Beirut in the early sixties, and about why he was permitted to escape. There are, to take a relatively small matter, almost as many accounts of Philby's escape route as there are books about him. Speculation about the "fourth man," rampant for years, has been calmed by public identification of Anthony Blunt, but speculation about a "fifth man" has recently been fueled by the publication of Peter Wright's *Spycatcher: The Candid Autobiography of a Senior Intelligence Officer* (1988), which identifies Roger Hollis, former Director-General of M15, as a Soviet agent. The British government's willingness to spend "millions of pounds" in "the courts of Australia, New Zealand, Hong Kong, Canada, and Britain" to halt the book's publication seems only to confirm the work's allegations or, at the very least, the enormous sensitivity of Margaret Thatcher's government to an old spy scandal still felt as immensely damaging to the national image.[7] The specter of an infinitely receding chain of British Communists in high places haunts the imagination; Joseph Hone's Peter Marlow, both in *The Private Sector* and *The Sixth Directorate*, discovers the hidden Communist identities of his colleagues in the sis at about the same rate at which Proust's narrator discovers the concealed homosexuality of the people in his milieu.

Not the least interesting of the Philby myths, as we have said, is Philby's own 1968 autobiography, *My Silent War*. In his preface, Philby claims that he had worked on the book for five years before finishing it in the summer of 1967, when he decided against publication "after consulting a few friends whose views might be helpful" (*MSW*, xi). Fears of "international complications" were alleviated in October of that year when *The Sunday Times* and *The Observer* published the series of articles later collected in Page, Leitch, and Knightley's *The Philby Conspiracy*, which Philby characterizes as "a substantially true picture of my career" (*MSW*, xii). With much of the potential damage already done, the former spy claimed that it was time for him to correct the "factual inaccuracies and errors of interpretation" (*MSW*, xii) in Page, Leitch, and Knightley; if such capitalist motives as a desire to cash in on the publicity their work generated also played a part will probably never be known. We must contemplate the paradox of a "true" story written by a man who deceived everyone around him for thirty years and was compelled by circumstances to clear every sentence with the KGB. Yet no one who searches for Philby's identity can ignore this book. *My Silent War* is not a crude piece of propaganda filled with obvious big lies, although there is disagreement about how many smaller ones it contains. Graham Greene professes to detect none and points to the truthfulness of many of Philby's unflattering sketches of his British colleagues. Robert Cecil, who was appointed personal assistant to the head of SIS in 1943 and had been at Cambridge in the middle thirties, finds, on the other hand, that the "measure of credence" Philby's book has been given is "astonishing" and adds that: "Among his sparse pleasures in Moscow these days must be that of noting how well his fictions have gone down in the West."[8] Yet Cecil's rather searching claims amount in the end to the statement that two deaths that Philby attributes to suicide or the CIA were in fact KGB assassinations, and a refutation of Philby's story that Guy Burgess, in the last days before his defection, engineered his deportation from the United States by deliberately piling up four speeding tickets in a single day. The inference that, as Cecil believes, Philby fingered Maclean, is rather too easily drawn from the autobiography itself to constitute a serious distortion.

Philby's autobiography is more usefully regarded as fiction in terms of the artful selection of material, the skillful use of

[8] "Legends Spies Tell: A Reappraisal of the Absconding Diplomats," *Encounter* 50 (April 1978): 9.

irony and epigraph, and the evident dependence on literary models that it displays. Selectivity is obvious and goes beyond that needed for the security of KGB networks. Philby the persona is a man without women, although his creator had had at the time of writing three wives. Five children go unmentioned; a colorful father and a mother on whom he was so dependent that he moved in with her after his fall in 1953 receive only one mention each. Thus, "Philby" is a creature of intelligence in a second sense, a hero of the mind who makes free rational choices unencumbered by the flesh. Alcoholic debauches that caused a reviewer to remark that two biographies of him read like temperance tracts are similarly excised. Creature of intelligence, this existential Philby is a man of irony who characteristically remarks of David Boyle, a friend of the wartime chief of SIS, "I was increasingly drawn to him for his inability to assess the intelligence that passed through his hands" (*MSW*, 79). Verbal wit dominates his perception of the world, to the exclusion of other values. Philby describes a ten day wait for a plane to Turkey in the company of "a group of nuns bound for Bulawayo. Their departure was finally announced one perishing morning—and perish they did, every one of them" (*MSW*, 164).

Of the literary influences at work in *My Silent War* the most obvious are P. G. Wodehouse, Compton MacKenzie, and Graham Greene. The Wodehouse opus, MacKenzie's *Water on the Brain* (which Philby footnotes, *MSW*, 69), and Greene's *Our Man in Havana* come into play as he draws his caricature of the SIS. In the allusive style of Bertie Wooster he remarks of the failure of the British to identify correctly the Soviet units near the Turkish border that "the *tabula* was depressingly *rasa*" (*MSW*, 175). Life in the SIS under Cowgill was excessively cozy: "It felt as if the office might at any moment burst into wholesome round games" (*MSW*, 77). The absurd pretentiousness and incompetence of British intelligence as portrayed in *Water on the Brain* and *Our Man in Havana* are constant topics. Both Philby and his Soviet contacts are afraid in 1940 that Philby has not managed to get into the right service: there must be another, they reason, "really secret and really powerful" (*MSW*, 11). Philby seems never to miss a detail, however trivial, that makes British Intelligence appear ridiculous, be it his own secret initials, DUD (*MSW*, 14) or the epistolary attainments of Stewart Menzies, his chief: "His stationery was a vivid blue, his ink green. He wrote an execrable hand" (*MSW*, 78). The wartime work of the famous is ridiculed: "More corrosive imports, such as Graham Greene and Malcolm Muggeridge . . . merely added to the gaiety of the service" (*MSW*, 48). Only by an effort of the will can the reader keep in mind that the enemy is not Wodehouse's British fascist, Roderick Spode, and his Saviours of Britain (the Black Shorts), but Hitler's Germany. Even when Philby is directly at risk the irony continues. In 1945 a Soviet vice-consul in Istanbul named Volkov planned to defect to the West, bringing with him information about two Soviet agents in the Foreign Office. Philby narrowly escaped detection when he tipped off the KGB and had Volkov kidnapped and returned home. Only a series of fortuitous delays kept Philby safe: these, and his willingness to fly to Turkey to take charge of the case. The original choice for that job, Douglas Roberts, "though doubtless as lion-hearted as the next man, had an unconquerable distaste for flying" (*MSW*, 152).

It would be hard to disagree with the reviewer in the *Times Literary Supplement* who saw Philby's intention to publish his autobiography as an attempt to discredit the SIS, possibly in order to prevent fuller cooperation between British and American intelligence.[9] In carrying out this intention, Philby is assisted not only by extreme selectivity but by a literary subgenre that insists on a ludic, even farcical element in espionage. What he did not wish to borrow from that genre was its underlying seriousness. We should note that MacKenzie's introduction to *Water on the Brain* claims that he wrote that book because "recently on one or two occasions the farcical has been mixed with the tragic in a way that might encourage even the sophisticated to accept farce as history" (8). John le Carré's *The Looking-Glass War* is a continuation of the

[9] "In His Master's Service," 26 September 1968, 1087.

MacKenzie tradition that bears comparison with Philby's book; in that novel the pathetic pretensions of an outmoded intelligence agency to carrying on World War II espionage in the mid-sixties (even to the direct imitation of MacKenzie's running joke about agents who insist on using code names among themselves) end in disaster for a man who has given the agency his trust. In Philby's world there are no real consequences, no disasters, and certainly no social context—in this last respect his autobiography is surely the least Marxist of books. Of an ambush of Albanian nationalists for which he was responsible Philby remarks archly: "I do not know what happened to the parties concerned. But I can make an informed guess" (*MSW*, 202). A reader of Philby with no access to other information about mid-twentieth-century history would learn that there was a "Los Alamos group" and that it included the Rosenbergs, but would remain unenlightened about what it was they were accused of doing.

Philby's debt to Greene goes deeper. If Greene is, in Hugh Trevor-Roper's phrase, "Philby's chief English apologist,"[10] Philby seems to derive from him the only serious apology he makes for himself. Many other people had been attracted to Communism in the thirties, but, Philby concedes, they gave it up after the purges or, at the very latest, at the time of the Nazi-Soviet Non-Aggression Pact. Why did Philby, in a phrase that makes a virtue of ignoring evidence, "stay the course" (*MSW*, xix)? His answer is a quotation from *The Confidential Agent*. The heroine has asked "D" if his leaders are better than the enemy's. " 'No. Of course not,' he replies. 'But I still prefer the people they lead—even if they lead them all wrong.' " She responds that that is not very different from " 'my country right or wrong' ": " 'You choose your side once and for all—of course, it may be the wrong side. Only history can tell that' " (*MSW*, xx). Through this quotation, which is surely not entirely representative of Greene, Philby links himself emphatically with the hero of the "crystalline" novel whose exaltation of the lonely choosing will at the ex-

---

[10] *The Philby Affair* (London: William Kimber, 1968), 100n.

pense of social reality Iris Murdoch has so ably dissected.[11]
The present may be safely ignored: value for Philby lies in
fidelity to a past choice and the future that will flow from it
even if: "Advances which, thirty years ago, I hoped to see in
my lifetime, may have to wait a generation or two" (*MSW*, xx).
Having offered this moral explanation, Philby ends with a
stranger one. Speaking of the KGB as if it were the Blades or
possibly a fellowship at Kings College, Philby says: "One does
not look twice at an offer of enrolment in an elite force"
(*MSW*, xxi).

If *My Silent War* is the least Marxist of autobiographies,
unconcerned with representing or analyzing the working
class, too aloof and ironic to evince or evoke concern with social welfare or day-to-day politics or even the "verdict of history" in which the author professes belief, Philby's life—a different matter—can be read, according to John le Carré, as "a
Marxian novel; a novel without humanity; a novel rich in
scenes of social decay" (*PC*, 35). "Like a great novel, and an
unfinished one at that," says le Carré, "the story of Kim
Philby lives on in us: it conveys not merely a sense of participation but of authorship" (*PC*, 23). Le Carré discusses Philby's father, St. John, in social rather than psychological terms:
"Through his father, and the education which his father gave
him, he experienced both as a victim and as a practitioner the
capacity of the British ruling class for reluctant betrayal and
polite self-preservation" (*PC*, 26). Le Carré's uncharacteristi-
cally Marxist analysis sees Philby as the embodiment of the
prewar upper class whose continued presence in the SIS after
1945 can only be explained in terms of its having become a
bastion of reaction: "Within its own walls, its clubs and country houses . . . it would enshrine the mystical entity of a van-
ishing England" (*PC*, 30). Because the SIS "identified class
with loyalty" (*PC* 30) it found Philby's treachery unthinkable.
Thus Philby's story is the story of the evils and decay of a class
system. And more: since "the British secret services . . . are

[11] "Against Dryness: A Polemical Sketch," *The Novel Today*, ed. Malcolm
Bradbury (Manchester: Manchester University Press, 1977), 23–31.

. . . microcosms of the British condition, of our social attitudes and vanities" (PC, 28), Philby's success reflects "the prevailing nature of our society, and our predicament as a fading world power" (PC, 34).

This fascination with Philby is evident in several of le Carré's novels, but it is at the center of *Tinker, Tailor, Soldier, Spy*. The many links between that novel and Philby's story have been closely argued by John Halperin.[12] To cite only the most important, Halperin finds the "mole," Bill Haydon, to have been based on Philby, and George Smiley on Dick White, the SIS man in his opinion most responsible for identifying Philby; Halperin points out that these resemblances include details of the characters' physical appearance and personal tastes. Numerous plot elements have been borrowed from history: the Volkov incident, described above, is the source of the Irina-Ricki Tarr subplot; the betrayal of Jim Prideaux's Czech network is based on Philby's betrayal of anti-Communist groups in Albania and the Ukraine. Yet it must be said that, when it comes to exploring Haydon's identity, the novel, distinguished as it is by its Byzantine plot, does not go beyond le Carré's earlier essay on Philby. Haydon has few lines and there is no attempt to reveal his mental processes. He is protected by a KGB plot known as Merlin, by extremely elaborate precautions surrounding his contacts with his London control, by his charm and breeding and not at all, incidentally, by his seduction of Ann Smiley, an act that is itself a KGB ploy to distract her *sympathique* husband, the most clear-sighted member of the Circus. Unlike Philby, Haydon is bisexual as well as a philanderer; unlike Philby, he is captured by his own agency and then murdered by Jim Prideaux, his former lover. The Jim Prideaux subplot, with which the novel begins and ends, serves the important function of displaying the personal and political consequences of Haydon's betrayals; Prideaux, tortured and then sent to a special KGB gulag after the exposure of his network, still suffers

---

[12] "Between Two Worlds: The Novels of John le Carré," *South Atlantic Quarterly* 79 (Winter 1980): 27–37.

from an unhealed back wound. Yet most of the details of plot and characterization have the effect of conventionalizing the Philby story. Sexual deviance, whatever its role in the Guy Burgess and Donald Maclean cases, is a dead giveaway for fictional spies, as we have noted. The better to display Smiley's power of induction, le Carré has provided more satisfactory reasons for the mole's success than he himself found in the Philby case. Haydon's death provides the rough justice desired by readers of thrillers, while leaving most of the real questions unanswered; a strong suggestion that Haydon's Oxford tutor, "Fanshaw of the Christ Church Optimates," had recruited him for the Soviets will never be followed up.

What complexity there is, beyond the complications of excellent plotting, resides in George Smiley and his meditations on Haydon's treachery. Smiley, as Richard Locke says, is an anti-Bond figure;[13] overweight and giving the impression of clumsiness, he must rely on intelligence rather than physical prowess or gadgets; sexually he seems a failure, unable to keep his wife faithful, let alone convert a lesbian like Bond's Pussy Galore to heterosexuality. Moreover, unlike Bond, whose contributions to the British collective ego Kingsley Amis analyzes with wit and perception, Smiley is well aware that the sun has set on the British Empire.[14] Trying to understand Haydon, Smiley entertains many notions: that there is "mindless treason" as there is "supposedly . . . mindless violence" (*TTSS*, 340), or that Haydon's father, the Monster, is to blame. Using Philby's language, Smiley wonders if it was simply that Haydon, a "romantic and a snob" had "wanted to join an elitist vanguard and lead the masses out of darkness" (*TTSS*, 367). It occurs to him that what had appealed to Hay-

---

[13] "The Spy Who Spied on Spies," review of John le Carré's *Tinker, Tailor, Soldier, Spy, New York Times Book Review*, 30 June 1974, 1.

[14] Kingsley Amis, "We May Be Slow, But . . ." in *The James Bond Dossier* (New York: New American Library, 1965), 73–83. "When the frogman's suit arrives for Bond in *Live and Let Die*, I can join him in blessing the efficiency of M's "Q" branch, whereas I know full well that given the postwar standards of British workmanship, the thing would either choke him or take him straight to the bottom" (83).

don was the "symmetry of an historical and economic solution" (*TTSS*, 367) and finally that Bill had been like a Russian doll containing many smaller dolls: only Karla, the head of KGB, "had seen the last little doll inside Bill Haydon" (*TTSS*, 367). But the most dangerous explanation is so close to Smiley himself that it almost induces him to defend his former friend—the notion that Bill himself had been betrayed by postwar England: "He saw with painful clarity an ambitious man born to the big canvas, brought up to rule, divide and conquer, whose visions and vanities all were fixed . . . upon the world's game; for whom the reality was a poor island with scarcely a voice that would carry across the water" (*TTSS*, 345). As the faithful Smiley mediates it, Haydon's treachery is not only the failure of a class but, in George Grella's phrase, "a failure of love," the act of a man who has no other word for love than "illusion."[15] Any idea that Haydon has made a defensible political choice is effaced.

Whereas le Carré has declared his distaste for Philby and sought both in fiction and elsewhere to emphasize the damage he did in turning the SIS, for at least ten years, into an "appalling liability" (*PC*, 34), Graham Greene has expressed affection for the man and minimized the amount of harm he did. In an essay originally published as an introduction to the British edition of *My Silent War*, Greene insists that the most significant damage was caused by MI5's "forc[ing] him into the open," for "a spy allowed to continue his work without interference is far less dangerous than the spy who is caught" (*CE*, 414). Greene dismisses the charge that Philby sent men to their deaths with the comment, "so does any military commander, but at least the cannon fodder of the espionage war are all volunteers" (*CE*, 415). A similar two-wrongs-almost-make-a-right argument in more portentous language asks, "Who among us has not committed treason to something or someone more important than a country" (*CE*, 415)? Philby's arguments for "staying the course" in spite of Stalin seem congenial to Greene, who compares him to a Catholic at the time

[15] "Murder and Loyalty," *New Republic* 31 July 1976, 24.

of the Inquisition. The content of Philby's convictions is clearly irrelevant to Greene; a "disagreeable" "drive to power" Philby had manifested in office politics has shown itself acceptable in light of the requirements of being a KGB agent: "He was serving a cause and not himself, and so my old liking for him comes back" (*CE*, 418). One must consider the stresses of being a double agent: "After thirty years in the underground, surely he had earned his right to a rest" (*CE*, 419).

For these views Greene has frequently been criticized, most notably by Hugh Trevor-Roper. At first reading, *The Human Factor* might well be seen as a fuller defense, if not of Philby, then of political betrayal in general. In the same issue of the *New York Times* in which Denis Donoghue proposed his "little theory" that the novel "is a book about Kim Philby . . . or rather, a book which rose from Greene's feeling that he could not, in his heart, condemn Philby, or judge a traitor merely by his actions," V.S. Pritchett provides evidence for that theory[16] that we must take seriously, notwithstanding Greene's protestations elsewhere that "there's no connection" between Philby and his own novel.[17] In an interview with Greene, Pritchett discovered that Greene had written "the first 25,000 words of *The Human Factor* about 1967, but when Philby wrote his defense of his defection in 1968, Greene put the book aside and wrote *The Honorary Consul* instead."[18] Quite properly Pritchett links Greene's response to an old interest in what he has called the "virtue of disloyalty" and quotes from a letter to Elizabeth Bowen in which Greene asks rhetorically if it is not "the storyteller's task . . . to elicit sympathy and understanding for those outside state sympathy."[19] Even the most cursory glances back at Greene's novels of the thirties and forties reveal that traitors, whether adulterers or double agents, have long fascinated him. The notion of a dou-

---

[16] "The Human Factor in Greene," *New York Times Magazine*, 26 February 1978, 33–36, 38, 40–42, 44, 46.

[17] Cited in Judie Newman, "Games in Greeneland: *The Human Factor*," *Dutch Quarterly Review of Anglo-American Letters* 14, no. 4 (1984): 25.

[18] Pritchett, "The Human Factor in Greene," 38.

[19] Ibid.

ble self is an assumption of the modern world, as Barzun says; it is equally part of a Christian ethic that emphasizes the deceptions of appearance and the value of the inner motive. Moreover, as Judie Newman points out, the spy motif seems to have figured prominently in Greene's psyche from early childhood: he felt "betrayed" when his father sent him to Berkhamsted, where as the headmaster's son, he believed that other boys treated him like a spy; later, at Oxford, he agreed to spy for the Germans, long before his more publicized stint in SIS under Philby; still later, he wrote in his autobiography that "every novelist has something in common with a spy: he watches, he overhears, he seeks motives and analyzes character and in his attempt to serve literature he is unscrupulous."[20] Thus, Philby, whose ideas about himself seem curiously shaped by Greene, comes into that author's work as an element not wholly new.[21]

Greene's novel is by no means a simple transcription of political and biographical facts. Set at an unspecified time in the seventies, when the Vietnam war has ended and the Russian invasion of Czechoslovakia can be regarded, at least by the novel's protagonist, Maurice Castle, as safely past, *The Human Factor* evokes a London plagued by strikes, inflation, and a moral breakdown in the form of visible pornography and the casual sexual habits of the young. There are anachronisms—most jarringly the failure of the Castles to have seven-year-old Sam vaccinated against measles or whooping cough—but, in general, Greene, like le Carré, has moved his story out of the World War II and Cold War era in which Philby operated into a time when disillusion with the West has become more widespread, even popular. Like le Carré, Greene ascribes to his hero upper-class origins that protect him from suspicion; Castle took "a third class in history at the

---

[20] Newman, "Games," 253–54.

[21] According to Phillip Knightley, Greene sent the manuscript of *The Human Factor* to Philby "to check it for authenticity. Philby, no doubt looking around his own pleasant apartment, said that the man's flat was too drab, but Greene stuck to his description." *The Master Spy: The Story of Kim Philby.* (New York: Knopf, 1989), 245.

House. . . . Roger Castle in the Treasury is his cousin" (*HF*, 44). When a leak is discovered, suspicion automatically falls on his officemate, Arthur Davis, a Reading University man who votes Labour.

Yet, unlike le Carré, who keeps the Russian spy at arm's length and structures his plot around the conventional search for the spy's identity, Greene makes the spy the novel's central consciousness and suggests his guilt from the very first paragraph; at the beginning, Castle is described as "always prepared to account for his actions, even the most innocent" (*HF*, 15). Minimizing suspense, Greene makes the discovery and evaluation of the spy's motives the central interest of the novel and adds to the whole story a metaphysical dimension that neither Philby nor le Carré consider. In the process of "eliciting sympathy" for a man who is "outside state sympathy," Greene moves away from Philby the man to create a character who is much easier to understand.

Unlike history's Philby or le Carré's Haydon, Maurice Castle is strictly limited in his ability to damage the West. Assigned to a small section dealing with Africa, he is comforted from the beginning by the knowledge that "the fate of the world . . . would never be decided on their continent" (*HF*, 16). In its portrait of the SIS, *The Human Factor* follows the *Water on the Brain* / *Our Man in Havana* strain that we noted in Philby's autobiography. The activities of the secret service are occasionally ridiculous, almost always schoolboyish. Sympathetic Arthur Davis complains of the "silliness" of intelligence work and yearns for excitement in the form of microdots and invisible ink. " 'What was the most secret information you ever possessed, Castle?' 'I once knew the approximate date of an invasion.' 'Normandy?' 'No, no. Only the Azores' " (*HF*, 61). The scene where Davis plays at spies with Sam Castle seems scarcely more childish than the scene in which "C" and Colonel Daintry discuss catching the double in their midst while the colonel agonizes over the humiliations of having brought his hostess three pounds of Maltesars and then having chipped her crystal. The personal quirks of Castle's colleagues—Daintry's grouse-hunting affectations, Emmanuel Percival's obsession with trout fishing, which he much prefers to sex with anyone—obviously justify the habit, which Castle shares with Philby and Guy Burgess, of "making lightning sketches of his colleagues: there were times when he even put them on paper" (*HF*, 19). The kind of stupidity that leads to the assumption that Davis's racing form is in code (" 'Kalamazoo sounds like a town in Africa' " [*HF*, 183]) is perennially evident. It is true, however, that these rather harmless, seemingly overgrown schoolboys are capable of doing real damage; Greene makes the actual consequences of espionage farce, to which MacKenzie alludes, a part of his novel. The murder of Arthur Davis for Castle's crime finally links him in death with the dangerous world of spies he had dreamed of joining.

The political context, nonetheless, remains sufficiently blurred for Greene to develop Castle's dilemma as a matter mainly of private conscience—something that would be difficult to do if he were made responsible for actions with recognizable historical consequences such as, for example, the rise of Idi Amin or the outbreak of a civil war in Rhodesia. A literary self-consciousness in the novel evokes comparisons with other novels rather than with the historical world: Arthur Davis, when he contemplates adding an *e* to his last name, recalls Arthur Davies, the earnest middle-class hero of Erskine Childers's *The Riddle of the Sands*. Maurice's name evokes Forster, but we also recall that the two lovers in *The End of the Affair* were named Maurice and Sarah and are not particularly surprised when we discover that the Castle's doctor has a large strawberry mark on his left cheek. The omission of precise dates prevents identification of real events, although the one public issue with which the novel deals biases the reader in Castle's favor. We learn early on that Castle had decided to spy for the Soviet Union out of gratitude to a Communist agent named Carson who had helped Sarah, who is black, escape from South Africa. Castle takes the final risk that makes his escape to Moscow inevitable out of a moral conviction that he must betray the details of plans for the British, American, and West Germans to enter into a secret agreement with the government of South Africa that will permit it to use tactical ("a reassuring word" [*HF*, 206]) nuclear weapons to defend itself against black revolutionaries. This all too credible agreement—its real-life counterpart, as Leopoldo Duran points out, is the subject of a book published four months after *The Human Factor*[22]—reminds the reader of the willingness of the West to blinker itself to repression in the Free World.[23] Any similar excesses of the Soviets are only fleetingly suggested. For the martyred Carson, Greene borrows the phrase he had used to excuse Philby: Castle tells Sarah, " 'He survived Stalin like Roman Catholics survived the Borgias' " (*HF*, 140). Speaking of the Russian invasions of Czechoslovakia and Hungary, Castle says " 'Your worst crimes, Boris, are always in the past' " (*HF*, 158) and when he raises these "crimes" with Halliday, the old Communist reminds him of "Hamburg, Dresden, Hiroshima" (*HF*, 288). It must be noted that cynicism about the methods of the West is stock and trade of the better run of post-Bond spy novels: le Carré's Leamas, Adam Hall's Quiller, Hone's Marlow, and Len Deighton's Bernard Samson are immersed in a world of dirty tricks and routine betrayals by their morally loathsome superiors, all of whom might have been, like Deighton's Dicky Cruyer, "short-listed for the Stalin Prize in office politics" (*SH*, 45). Still Greene, in suggesting that distinctions between good and evil do not exist on the political level at all— that is, that the problem is much deeper than the tendency of secret services to use Gestapo tactics to preserve the liberal democracies—has gone a step further. "Each side," thinks Castle, "shares the same clichés," or, as Halliday would put it, for every Afghanistan there is a Vietnam. In this political context, surely anyone could understand Castle's willingness to make personal gratitude the grounds for what others would regard as a political decision.

[22] The book in question is Zdenek Cervenka and Barbara Rogers, *The Nuclear Axis: The Secret Collaboration between West Germany and South Africa* (New York: Times Books, 1978).

[23] Leopold Duran, "El factor humano de Greene," *Arbor* 413 (May 1980): 80.

It is this paradox that surrounds the private life of the spy, the man or woman sworn to secrecy, a part of whose life is radically private, unknown to closest friends, yet whose vocation and fate are radically determined by public history. The "Philby" of the autobiography avoids the conflict, as indeed many popular fictional spies do, by excising the personal life. Le Carré's Bill Haydon is of one piece; like the historical Philby le Carré evokes in his introduction to *The Philby Conspiracy* and the fictionalized Kim Philby of Alan Williams' *Gentleman Traitor*, Haydon is as willing to betray a friend or lover as a country. But Greene's spy lives with both terms of the paradox; since intense personal loyalties motivate his disloyalty to England, his wife can forgive it: " 'We have our own country. You and I and Sam. You've never betrayed that country, Maurice' " (*HF*, 246). He is drawn to both Communism and Catholicism when in the presence of good men who espouse them, but finds himself essentially "born to be a half-believer" (*HF*, 140), with as little "trust in Marx or Lenin" as in "St. Paul," and can only cling to the personal decency that gratitude to Carson represents. One of the deep questions his situation poses is if it is indeed possible to live outside all group loyalties.

Conor Cruise O'Brien, who is not given to saying such things lightly, stresses the echoes of Kafka in Castle's name and calls him a Christ figure: "There seems indeed to be a kind of inversion or diversion of Kafka, perhaps a Christianization: not just people in quest of the inaccessible Castle, but the Castle itself engaged in a quest: man seeking Christ, and Christ seeking man."[24] Castle's faithfulness to his own conception of right, his suffering, loneliness, humility and obscurity (a "dullish man, first-class . . . with files" [*HF*, 44]) are consonant with a certain romantic idea of Christ, also a "man outside state sympathy." Castle is at home with other Greene protagonists whose unattractive exteriors conceal their genuine virtue even from themselves. Castle's search for a confes-

[24] "Greene's Castle," review of *The Human Factor*, *New York Review of Books*, 1 June 1978, 4.

sor needs, however, to be seen in more specific terms; it is above all a need to talk, to ease the terrible isolation that drives him, having failed to find his Moscow control, into the confessional of a modern Catholic church whose priest tells him that he needs a doctor (*HF*, 242). In spite of the great dependence of the plot on Castle's love for Sarah and her son he is never free of the loneliness his double life imposes on him. Telling Sarah the truth is only a prelude to their separation. Not only does Castle's espionage lead to the death of Davis, who comes closer than any other man in England to being his friend, but it leaves his wife immured with his censorious mother in a country in which she can never feel at home. The necessity of shooting Sam's repulsive but much loved dog, Buller, in order to prevent his barking from alerting the neighbors becomes even more horrible when the reader learns that it is finally the wounded dog's moaning—the shot does not kill him—that summons them. That Castle must leave England disguised as a blind man is surely no accident.

Castle's decision to live out a personal commitment without ties to country, party, or church leads him inexorably to the two-room flat in Moscow. It is interesting that in the last chapter Greene comes closer to evoking the historical Philby than at any other point in the novel. For, although it is almost possible to imagine Philby committing himself to Communism in the early thirties out of a feeling for his young Jewish wife, which matches Castle's love for Sarah (also a victim of racial laws), so many of the other details of Greene's novel move away from Philby's life that we might be inclined to forget the parallel. Philby in Moscow, both as an object of historical record and of novelistic speculation, is an important part of the legend. The image of a bored, vaguely discontented spy wearing out his old school ties and following cricket scores through the air mail edition of the *Times* is the focus of Williams's novel and Bennett's play. Until Philby's death in 1988, and the publication in 1989 of Knightley's *The Master Spy*, this part of the legend drew some of its impetus from occasional sightings of him and from the odd photograph of the old spy in a fur hat posing in Red Square, but the main text is Eleanor

Philby's *Kim Philby: The Spy I Loved*, a not particularly in-sightful view of the expatriate spy's life. The third Mrs. Philby provides a wonderfully superficial perspective on defection to Moscow, which at its best conveys to the reader a Flaubertian dizziness before the depths of stupidity: "We ordered marvel-ous cuts of meat, red caviar, special tinned fruits and vegeta-bles, the best brands of Russian champagnes, wines, beer and soda water. All these . . . would be delivered to the flat by a cheery man in a smart white coat. . . . One pays cash on de-livery."[25] This perspective does, however, make Eleanor Philby an excellent source for the novelist. Greene borrows her flat in "an enormous gray building" (*HF*, 70) and moves the Philby's large television set into it; he turns their blue wicker settee into a green wicker chair, and follows Eleanor Philby in informing the reader that, although an unfurnished flat in Moscow includes a kitchen stove, everything else, in-cluding the toilet, has to be bought. Like Eleanor Philby, Castle makes a stab at learning Russian from a housekeeper named Anna. "Cruikshank and Bates," British defectors who preceded Castle, dine like the Philbys and Macleans at the Aragvi Restaurant. By evoking the wraith of Philby in Mos-cow, Greene reminds the reader that a real story resonates behind his fiction even as his hero remains a readier object of sympathy than his real-life counterpart. Castle soon learns that the KGB has deceived him and that his real value to it had not been in liberating Africans but in providing credible cover for a Russian triple agent; the leak that ended Castle's career had been engineered by the KGB. The dead telephone in his wife's hand at the end of the novel signals the beginning of an isolation that is worse than any he has known. For Greene, as for other British novelists and essayists, the endless Moscow winter is a ready-made symbol. "This was not the snow he remembered from childhood," thinks Castle. "This was a mer-ciless, interminable, annihilating snow, a snow in which one could expect the world to end" (*HF*, 330). The comparison

[25] *Kim Philby: The Spy I Loved* (London: Hamish Hamilton, 1968), 102.

with the icy circle in which Dante placed his traitors is inevitable.

Greene succeeds in showing the possibility of sympathizing with the spy in the terrible punishment of his isolation. One may respect Castle's sense of loyalty even as he betrays his country and brings deep unhappiness to those for whom he undertook the betrayal. This complicated sympathy is gained at the price, as we have seen, of effacing most of the public context in which Castle operates and displacing its significance to the plane of the private life and conscience. Yet precisely because in the end Castle's private choice has left him alone in the snows of Moscow, the novel cannot be read as an apology for political betrayals. Forster's famous opposition—"if I had to choose between betraying my friend and betraying my country I hope I should have the guts to betray my country"—proves impossible to sustain, even in this novel, which is remarkable for its lack of interest in public events (*TCD*, 76).[26] Castle embodies the bourgeois, liberal individualism his last name suggests (every man's home is . . .) every bit as much as the Bloomsbury cult of personal relations that his first name evokes. A half-believer without ideological commitments, we can expect him to die in Moscow the strange death of liberal England. And since neither Catholicism nor Communism is presented in the novel as a wholly satisfying faith—only rarely does the "human face" of either shine forth in a saint like Carson—the book ends as bleakly as *Tinker, Tailor, Soldier, Spy*.

. . .

[26] Boyle points out that Guy Burgess was given to quoting this remark "to anyone within earshot" (*The Fourth Man* [New York: Dial-James Wade, 1979], 181) and quotes Goronwy Rees as saying that Anthony Blunt used it as text when trying to persuade him not to make a voluntary statement to M15 identifying Burgess as a Soviet spy: " 'I said Forster's antithesis was a false one. One's country . . . was itself made up of a dense network of individual and social relationships in which loyalty to one particular person formed only a single strand' " (Ibid., 384).

Both private and public issues are central to Joseph Hone's *The Private Sector*, where the search for the spy's identity takes place in exotic Cairo. The setting is informative. It was in the Middle East that Philby spent his last years before fleeing to Moscow; more importantly, he was very much the product of the colonial world this novel analyzes. Although there are many questions about the direction it takes, all of Philby's biographers concede the importance of St. John Philby's influence on his son. A second-rate Lawrence of Arabia, creature of Ibn Saud and convert to Islam, St. John Philby was imprisoned by the British for his profascist sympathies at the outbreak of World War II. In his last years, he took up with a former slave girl, Umferhat, a gift of King Saud I (*PC*, 53); in his grotesquely overweight presence the already middle-aged spy was photographed with the little Arab boy who was his half-brother. In a general way Hone's setting evokes Philby's father; the book also specifically refers to the spy himself. Williams, the fictional chief of sis's Middle East Intelligence Section in 1967, is identified as the elusive Fourth Man who had recruited Philby "and his two friends" in the early thirties (*PS*, 151). Through Williams, history and fiction converge, as in the warning to his Moscow contact: "don't swamp the air waves on the Moscow circuit up at the Embassy—that's how they first got onto Philby" (*PS*, 160). However, although Williams is the author of the elaborate plot that takes the narrator to Cairo, gets him jailed for treason, and even provokes the Six Days' War, he remains a shadowy background figure.

The double agent around whom most of the novel turns is Henry Edwards, a British colonial who begins his triple career in Soviet, British, and Egyptian intelligence in his native Cairo. Most of the novel is narrated by Peter Marlow, an obscure deskman in Middle East Intelligence whom Williams sends after Edwards when the latter is suspected of defecting. In the process of finding Edwards, Marlow discovers a whole system of betrayals: Henry, although once his best friend, has had an affair with his wife, Bridget; and he himself is being used, like his colleague Marcus, as the unwitting carrier of a microdot forgery that will encourage the Egyptians to go to war with Israel. Moreover, in Cairo, Marlow is reminded of his own betrayal; there he had briefly doubled for Colonel Hamdy, now the head of Egyptian Intelligence and, as Marlow finally discovers, an Israeli agent. Thus the novel evaluates not one betrayal but several of varying political and personal consequence.

Hone is definitely among those writers who are fascinated with the psychological motives of the double agent and he seeks these motives, like any good analyst, in childhood. Even Williams, treated so briefly, seems to link his espionage for the Russians to a Russian doll his mother had given him when he was still an only child and that he came to associate with the unexpected birth of a brother: "he remembered the feeling of despair that had come over him . . . real children, too, went on forever, one inside the other in the body of their mother . . . the knowledge of the endless ramifications of deceit" (PS, 129). More than a convention, his clandestine life as a homosexual seems seriously connected with his career in espionage. Faithful, rather unimaginative Marlow knows that his own spying on his wife and his brief career as an insignificant double for the Egyptians had once given him "a taste for . . . deceit," a "loyalty towards betrayal" (PS, 124). In such oxymorons the accents of Greene can be heard; in a similar passage, where Marlow finds the word *turn*, as spies use it, misleading, a stylistic and philosophical dependence on Greene becomes unmistakable: "one is 'turned' in this way from the very beginning, through some reverse or imagined slight, or some long-nurtured sense of injustice; it can start in childhood, or later through a childish response . . . one is 'turned' only from the business of sensible life" (PS, 124).

Hone's Marlow, like his predecessor in Conrad, seems drawn to the protagonist of the story by half-acknowledged affinities with him. Henry, like Philby, is always charming, and although he had manipulated and betrayed Marlow on several levels Marlow never loses his residual affection for him. Henry himself professes no deep belief in Communism, and dreads the idea of going to Moscow. When Marlow asks him about Stalin and the invasion of Hungary, he says " 'I believed in the belief, not the facts. I've never been to Russia' " (PS, 293). Like Greene's Castle Henry compares Communism to Christianity, which has its own historical atrocities: " 'The English martyrs, the Thirty Years' War, the Huguenots" (PS, 293). Believers, in his view, always disregard facts: " 'No one believes in the loaves and fishes. He was a fraudulent caterer and quack doctor. But that doesn't seem to have mattered' " (PS, 293). Henry claims to have evolved a public argument for his spying; recalling Philby's distaste for the English "political outcast . . . railing at . . . the God that had failed me" (MSW, xx), he says "I wasn't interested in being a professional left winger writing for the Telegraph colour mag" (PS, 293). But the real reason has nothing to do with such arguments. His decision to be a Communist spy, he says, had been born in a terrible moment in childhood when his father had forced an old Nubian waiter to give up three months of his salary to pay for a broken crystal decanter. Marlow suspects that something else is involved: "Though of course the child wouldn't know . . . it was the denial by the father which had driven him underground in anger . . . where he had remained all his life. Children are the most undetectable double agents; Henry had become a professional child. . . . Hungary, five million peasants—the greatest repression—can mean nothing to such people whose political faith is formed in childhood, a creed inextricably related to the pain and happiness of a seven-year-old" (PS, 293–94). It is perhaps because he lacks such motives that Colonel Hamdy, who has spent his whole career in Egyptian Intelligence as an Israeli agent, is able to understand that he has come to love Egypt far more than the country for which he has betrayed her; ideologies must necessarily prove more flexible than childhood scars.

This deeply Freudian view of espionage can also be seen at other levels in the novel. The sis as Marlow describes it is certainly unglamorous and, like Greene's Davis, Marlow complains of the insignificance of his desk job in London. Recruited while teaching in an upper-class Egyptian school that apes Eton in every possible way, Marlow persistently imagines the world of espionage as an extension of the public school. "Williams," he says, "looked at me . . . as if I'd kicked him in the crotch during a house match" (PS, 15); Bahaddin congratulates him on his recruitment by SIS "like an old cricket coach from the boundary, determined to offer some acknowledgement of my honour, albeit clandestinely" (PS, 100). His discovery that both East and West want the Egyptian government to fall is a realization "that the powers had identical interests in this airing cupboard, in seeing matron topple" (PS, 305). Along with the imputation of childish motives goes a strong sense that British history, like a man's life, is much more of a piece than most people admit. The key scene in which Henry confesses to Marlow takes place in an old colonial church, Cairo's Cathedral of All Saints, and is punctuated, like Leon's seduction of Emma Bovary, by the comments of a persistent guide. Filled with plaques commemorating the forgotten battles of forgotten wars, the church strikes Marlow as having "nothing remotely Christian" about it; "the building was simply a memory of violent life" (PS, 288). That violent life still goes on, colonial wars are still fought: "The brave and foolish went to the wall, just as they had always done, but at midnight now, not high noon. . . . It was a foolish story about history" (PS, 289).

That Hone is able to evoke so much of the psychological resonance of espionage, and at the same time remind us that his is a story about history, is a genuine accomplishment. Imbedding the narrative within the story of the outbreak of the Six Days' War, he is able to develop suspense (will the central characters, all implicated in the outbreak, get out of Egypt before it is too late? Will Marlow avoid being framed by Williams?) that the early identification of Edwards and Williams would otherwise dissipate. The consequence of the spy's actions, just as importantly, are made to seem real both in public and in private. Hone's Durrellian evocation of Cairo—scorching, gritty, ragged, corrupt—is sometimes overblown ("its electric vacancy which begins by making every plan possible and ends by making them all unnecessary" [PS, 260]), to be sure, but in the end the effect is to give a real face to at least the Egyptian victims of the war. Marlow, returning to England, finds that he is unable to convince his superiors of Williams's guilt and ends up with a twenty-eight-year jail sentence for espionage. British Intelligence, having learned the wrong lessons from Philby's case, justifies its severity and perseverance in the face of weak evidence by evoking his name: "Such was the case with Philby; he was trusted in high places to the bitter end" (*PS*, 312).

The fiction that Kim Philby inspired, like his autobiography, has many fascinations and limitations. A vehicle for exploring the decline of England, the morality of betrayal, or the relationship between private life and public responsibility, the Philby myth threatens to leave the man safe behind his mask. Perhaps a future novelist will take up the implications of a comment by Alan Bennett's Philby figure, Hilary, who remarks that his essence is irony, "the English specialty." "We're conceived in irony. We float in it from the womb"; the "best disguise," he says, "is to be exactly what you say you are."[27] Each of the novels, Greene's by no means excepted, betrays certain stylistic difficulties as well. For, although the conventions of the spy novel certainly lend themselves to an exploration of this famous "double," the straining to transcend a popular genre seems in each case to lead to a troubling portentousness. The immersion of each author in Conrad has not always had beneficial results;[28] as we have noted, there are

[27] From *The Old Country* (London: Faber, 1978), 62.

[28] Greene's affinities with Conrad, who provides the epigraph for *The Human Factor*, are too well known to require commentary; Hone's use of a narrator named Marlow is only the most obvious sign of Conrad's influence. John Halperin discusses several indications of Conrad's influence on le Carré (including the repetition of the phrase "one of us" in *The Looking-Glass War* and Jerry Westerby's re-reading of Conrad in *The Honourable Schoolboy*. Halperin points out that Smiley, in *Tinker, Tailor, Soldier, Spy* says "I tell you . . . no one has any business to apologize for what I did" (*TTSS*, 206; "Between Two Worlds: The Novels of John le Carré," *South Atlantic Quarterly* 79 [Winter 1980]: 17). The Israeli spymaster of *The Little Drummer Girl* is named Kurtz. The anxieties of this influence are noted by Harold Bloom in his introduction to the Chelsea House casebook: "Le Carré's overtly allusive counterpointing of Conrad and Greene against popular spy fiction formulae

passages in Hone that seem to imitate Greene slavishly, as there are passages in Greene that read like self-parody. One is occasionally sympathetic with Kingsley Amis's protest against the "cultural Puritanism that does not encourage the writers of thrillers or . . . any of the genres unless it can be maintained that the genre in question is being used as no more than a vehicle, a metaphor, and that the author is really going on about modern society and the human heart with the rest of them" (*WBJA*, 68–69). Greene seems to have sacrificed too much of the spy novel's suspense in the interest of psychological complexity that one misses in le Carré's portrait of Haydon. Hone, the least well-known of the three novelists, seems in this respect to have been the most successful, retaining the strengths of the genre while expanding its significance. Yet its derivative style, along with the problems created by a two-dimensional love story that runs through the novel, keeps it from assuming the originality and stature of the best of Greene, let alone Conrad. A story as deeply enmeshed in public history and popular consciousness and as resonant with fundamental moral and psychological questions as Philby's is not easily exhausted. Although Greene, le Carré, and Hone have added depth to Philby's ironizing self-portrait, the spy's life still remains a story in search of an author.

. . . seems to me a defense against the enormous influence upon him of Conrad's *The Secret Agent* and Greene's spy novels" (from *John le Carré* [New York: Chelsea House, 1987], 1).

CHAPTER FIVE

Iris Murdoch's *Nuns and Soldiers*

THAT LOSS of confidence in England's ruling classes that we saw in the story of Kim Philby is also a loss of confidence in a shared vision of history and public life. In Iris Murdoch's *Nuns and Soldiers*, we see an England in which such a shared vision is a missing center; the very absence of English history in this novel is an ominous indication of present perils. The story is apolitical: Guy Openshaw, middle-aged patriarch to a family of assimilated English Jews, dies of cancer. The novel traces his wife Gertrude's subsequent courtship by an emigrant Pole and a young artist whom she eventually marries, and takes time along the way to explore the spiritual crises of, among others, Anne Cavidge, a college friend of Gertrude's who has just emerged from fifteen years in a convent. Moreover, the novel is stripped of those elements of full social and political documentation that allowed Michael Holquist to say of nineteenth-century novels that "there is a sense in which they are all historical."[1] Set in 1977–1978, the novel records only one public event of those years, the election of a nameless "Polish pope" (*NS*, 461). No one talks about North Sea Oil, striking labor unions, or James Callaghan and Margaret Thatcher. People gossip continually, but not about Louise Brown, the world's first test-tube baby, or Princess Margaret's divorce, or the indictment of the Liberal party leader, Jeremy Thorpe, on charges of conspiracy to murder his lover, Norman Scott. The social context is blurred: characters go on National Assistance, have trouble finding teaching jobs, do volunteer work among native speakers of Urdu, or regard Northern Ireland as a place where being killed by a

[1] "Whodunit and Other Questions: Metaphysical Detective Stories in Post-War Fiction," *New Literary History* 3 (Autumn 1971): 145.

terrorist bomb is a distinct possibility, but these isolated details are never linked to a historical process that might include, for example, Idi Amin, the promotion of unemployment as a check to inflation, or the Irish Treaty of 1921.

Yet, as in Bowen and Farrell, history in *Nuns and Soldiers*
is a signifying absence, a missing center that makes the novel
an eloquent commentary on the failure to see one's life historically; more pessimistic than either *The Last September* or
Troubles, Murdoch's *Nuns and Soldiers* seems to suggest that
her largely upper-middle-class English characters feel estranged from the past and unable to influence the present.
Yet, despite the absence of a conventional historical subject,
the word "history" recurs frequently in *Nuns and Soldiers* as
a signal of the book's concern with how people remember,
tell, and respond to their own past. One is reminded of Carlyle, whose *Frederic the Great* fascinates Murdoch's insom-
niac Pole. For Carlyle the difficulties we experience in telling
the truth about our past are deeply connected to the problems
of writing public history: "All men are historians . . . our very
speech is curiously historical," for we usually "speak only to
narrate . . . what we have undergone or seen." In our memory, he continues, we find our own history, "the whole fortunes of one little inward kingdom, and all its policies, foreign
and domestic."[2] Murdoch's characters are such historians,
each seeking a relationship to a past denied easy continuity
with the future. The novel criticizes each character as an in-
terpreter. *Nuns and Soldiers* is deeply pessimistic about the
possibilities that a true past is recorded, told and understood:
it is a novel in which what Murdoch has called the "essential
elements of trickery and magic" in aesthetic form seem more
apparent than its ability, at least where the past is concerned,
"to communicate and reveal" (*FS*, 78).

We have already seen some of the implications of the past
tense in fictional discourse. Whether one stresses the notion
that the past tense is used ordinarily to convey a sense of pres-

[2] "On History" (1830), in *A Carlyle Reader*, ed. G. B. Tennyson (New York: Random House, 1969), 56.

ence, or agrees with Hamburger that "it creates no time at all, no past, it obliterates time,"[3] we can certainly agree with Roy Pascal's conclusion that "the meanings of the tenses cannot be equated with the temporal functions they have in normal discourse."[4] This insight, when coupled with the Jamesian tradition of telling, not showing, may explain the discomfort we feel when an author seems as determined as Murdoch, in the first one hundred or so pages of *Nuns and Soldiers*, to use the past tense to create a past that we experience as just that, a world of previous experience that has already ended. Guy's death and Anne's departure from the convent are deeply connected, "endings," "eternal partings" that must be accepted as such from the beginning (*NS*, 356). Murdoch indulges in long selective expositions of the characters' pasts: Anne's theological crises, the Count's childhood, education, and career; Tim's childhood, and Daisy's; the history of Gertrude and Guy's marriage. The past is thematized in other ways: Anne has a degree in history, a subject that preoccupies the Count, whose reading is limited to historians like Gibbon, Thucydides, and Carlyle and to novelists with a strong sense of the past, such as Trollope, Tolstoy, and Proust. We become aware from the beginning that even minor characters will be defined in terms of their relationship to history. Thus "les cousines et les tantes," Guy's extended family that functions as a chorus throughout the book, are introduced in terms of their complicated relationship to Openshaw family history. Ethnically Jewish, or half-Jewish, where religion is concerned, they are a confusing mixture of pious converts to Roman or Anglo-Catholicism, converts in name only, highly assimilated agnostics, and devoutly Orthodox Jews. Their return to Orthodoxy suggests that some Openshaws feel the intractability of Jewish identity, but on the surface they all appear comfortably adapted to British upper-middle-class life. The historical dangers of being Jewish are articulated

---

[3] *The Logic of Literature*, trans. Marilynn J. Rose, 2d ed. (Bloomington: Indiana University Press, 1973), 64.

[4] "Tense and Novel," *Modern Language Review* 57 (1962): 11.

only in the Count's vivid nightmare in which he becomes a Polish Jew on his way from the Warsaw Ghetto to Treblinka (*NS*, 252–54).

Defined in large measure by their characteristic ways of responding to the past, the Count, Tim, and Gertrude become vehicles for an exploration of the ways in which human beings generally respond to their history. Each of these responses needs careful analysis, but let us begin with the most obviously "historical" figure, Wojciech Sczepanski, the Count. The child of emigrants, he had once wished to evade the implications of history. To some extent his identity is still suppressed, his "dog's breakfast of a name" having long since fallen victim to the Anglo-Saxon disdain for foreign sounds (*NS*, 11). Instead, he is known by more allegorical titles, Tolstoyan and Biblical: "Count" or "Pierre" or "Peter": "I love not Christ but Peter," Anne thinks (*NS*, 304). In both English and Polish, he speaks with a foreign accent and lives alone in "featureless" rooms (*NS*, 20). The Count's life seems to be conducted almost exclusively in the past tense, its direction ruthlessly determined by historical accidents: his father's failure to die for Poland, his brother's death in the bombing of a London church at Christmas, the crushing of the uprisings first of the Warsaw ghetto and then of the Polish Underground Army. As a child he was "determined not to be damaged by" such "horrors," but of course he is (*NS*, 9). As a child, too, he had personified history as a force that destroys Poland: "obviously history intended . . . Poland to be subservient to Russia" (*NS*, 9). As an adult the Count has "interiorized Poland, he was his own Poland, suffering alone" (*NS*, 13): "I am like Poland, my history is and ought to be a disaster" (*NS*, 42).

Poland, in fact, comes to stand for public history in the novel, its generals and politicians and dates enumerated as their counterparts in English history are not—Kosciusko, 1226, Mickiewicz, the Poznan riots. The English characters are so oblivious to history that the Count wonders if Poland is invisible (*NS*, 13). Even Guy has no books about Poland, although the Count believes that "every intelligent person must be interested in Poland" (*NS*, 390). For him and for the novel, Poland becomes a "symbol" of "the sufferings of oppressed people everywhere" (*NS*, 39). Closer to home, the Joycean overtones of "nightmare" suggest that Poland is a good deal like Ireland; as Gertrude observes, the Poles "always discuss their history . . . they are like Ireland" (*NS*, 227).

In *Nuns and Soldiers*, then, to be ignorant of Poland is to refuse one's affinities with either the victims or the oppressors in the history of small nations. Yet, the haunting of the Count by Polish history cannot be seen as ideal. For the Count, Polish history is a version of Quentin Compson's South; his body is like Quentin's, "an empty hall echoing with sonorous defeated names."[5] The Count is paralyzed by his tragic sense of Polish history; as unable to die for Poland as his father was, he becomes passive in every human relationship, compulsively reading this myth of Poland back into his personal story: "The image of Gertrude shone in sad Warsaw like the image of Christ in Limbo" (*NS*, 228). Quite appropriately the woman he loves is inaccessible throughout most of the novel; losing her for good only confirms his personal myth: "Maybe it's all to do with being Polish. My country has had nothing but persecution and misery and the destruction of every hope" (*NS*, 445). On the evening that the Cardinal from Crakow becomes Pope—the other Peter, the embodiment of a more positive reading of Polish history—the Count, reduced in the reader's eyes, settles for mediocre happiness as an adjunct to Gertrude's marriage to Tim.

Obsession with history, as the Count suspected as a child and demonstrated as an adult, is dangerous. The extreme alternative is to be like Tim, who is always "prepared to settle for the contentment of 'the man who has no history' " (*NS*, 77). In a novel in which each of the major characters first appears to be neatly opposed to another, Tim seems to be the counterpart of the defeated Polish exile. His "history . . . is unsatisfactory" (*NS*, 74), the story of a deserted consumptive

---

[5] William Faulkner, *Absalom, Absalom!* (New York: Random House, 1936), 12.

mother, an anorectic sister, and a feckless father, all dead by the time he is fourteen. His Irish father, who might have nurtured an identification with oppression like the Count's, has bequeathed instead an instinct for avoiding a settled adult life. Like the Count he is imaged as one of the novel's soldiers, but instead of seeing himself committed to a "soldier's dullness and circumscribed lot and extremely small chance of glory" (*NS*, 14), he sees "himself sometimes as a soldier of fortune, a raffish footloose fellow, a drinker, a wandering cadger, a happy-go-lucky figure in a shabby uniform (not of course an officer) who lived from day to day avoiding unpleasantness" (*NS*, 77). And, of course, Tim, after a brief courtship, wins the woman whom the Count has loved futilely for years.

Most significantly Tim's aesthetic sensibility is divorced from history. He haunts the British Museum, enraptured by "Greek vases and Etruscan tombs and Roman paintings and Assyrian reliefs," but knows "nothing of their history" (*NS*, 81). He has "no identity, no 'personal style' "; he paints "pseudo-Klees, pseudo-Picassos, pseudo-Magrittes, pseudo-Soutines" (*NS*, 80), going from purely formal works that resemble elaborate diagrams or networks to sentimentalized pictures of cats, which, by the novel's end, have already appeared on ceramic mugs and may soon appear on matchbooks.

This artist without a history illustrates the sorts of reservations about art that Murdoch analyzes in *The Fire and the Sun*. Tim is a copyist whose copies always remain inferior to the originals; a "destiny as a great faker" evades him only because he lacks patience, talent, and knowledge of chemistry (*NS*, 80). Murdoch has analyzed this practical incompetence, which Tim repeatedly illustrates, as one of Plato's fundamental objections to artists—the painter of beds who cannot make a bed (*FS*, 6). Even more important, he is what Plato thought artists were always likely to be: a liar. For Tim wishes to escape notice ("his motto was *Lanthano*") and to think of himself as a child: London's pubs are "innocent places" where he and Daisy are "innocent children" (*NS*, 83). These impulses connect to his lack of respect for history and motivate lies about his past: "He had . . . to rewrite history so as to obliterate

Daisy from it. But without Daisy it was a false history" (*NS*, 341).

"That pure clean blessed beginning-again feeling" (*NS*, 154–55) is perhaps Tim's happiest emotion, setting him outside of time, free of consequences and responsibility. A certain kind of art collaborates in this fantasy: "Gertrude would save him, as good women always saved sinful men in stories. He thought again about . . . the 'new innocence and the fresh start' " (*NS*, 214). Traditionally, Christianity has also fostered this notion of being purged of the past, purified and born again as a little child. Tim in fact is "baptized" twice in the novel in near-drownings described in language both religious ("he prayed," [*NS*, 423]; "he blessed," [*NS*, 424]) and Wordsworthian ("there was a presence in the glade," [*NS*, 417]). Yet, the encounter with the "Great Face" does not permanently change Tim, who cannot integrate these moments into the history of his life. At the end of the novel he is still hedging about if he will ever lie to Gertrude, still painting cats.

That such secular baptisms are ever efficacious is an idea more seriously explored in the case of Anne Cavidge, nun to Tim's soldier. Having lost faith "in a personal God" (*NS*, 65) and "the anti-religious idea of life after death" (*NS*, 66), she comes back into the world and nearly drowns there. As is the case of Tim's near-drownings, Gertrude is the first person Anne sees after she comes ashore. Anne's life does not seem to change after her brush with death. A convert, like so many of the Openshaws, she seeks in Catholicism what Tim had always sought in the world, a "quiet conscience": "she would regain her innocence and keep it under lock and key" (*NS*, 56). Always a Protestant's idea of a nun (impossibly unaffected by Vatican II, apparently knowing only the King James version of the Bible), Anne has lived as much outside of time as possible for fifteen years. Life in the convent meant wearing medieval garb, marking the hours in patterns prescribed by the order and by the "holy repetition" of the liturgical year (*NS*, 236). Life with Gertrude, on the other hand, means acquiring a few fashionable clothes and falling in love with the Count. When the convent ethic of self-sacrifice meets the world of sexual love, both are distorted. Anne, ceasing to be "God's spy" (*NS*, 303), begins spying on Daisy and on the Count. She lies to Gertrude about Mrs. Mount's letter, withholds from her the information that Tim has gone back to Daisy, and then that he has returned to Les Grandes Saules. At the time, she thinks she is behaving selflessly but has no regard for the harm to others that might come from her behavior, which she finally realizes; absorbed in defeating her own hopes, she had no "thought to spare for catastrophes which her selfless masochistic morality might be bringing about in Daisy's life" (*NS*, 495).

A new secular beginning proves as impossible for Anne as for Tim; yet, throughout the novel, unlike him, she attempts to make historical sense of her life. The slower, less dramatic change is at the heart of her vision of Christ and allows her at the end to preserve an intention to go into the world to help the poor, to understand her mistakes, and to make a serious effort to prevent their recurrence. The Christ Anne sees does not wholly correspond to the myth that had originally drawn her into the convent; he particularly does not correspond to his depiction in paintings. He criticizes her desire for innocence as "sentimental," repeatedly saying that salvation, goodness, and miracles depend on her. The scene echoes Julian of Norwich's *Revelation of Divine Love*, which Murdoch admires for the "evident combination of purity and realism" that it shares with "the Gospels, St. Augustine, and parts of Plato," and that also characterizes "good art" (*FS*, 83).

Elizabeth Dipple discusses this scene at some length, perceptively analyzing the "ironic connection" between Anne's vision and that of Julian. Julian's Christ "encourages a human resting on his divine power to perform what looks impossible to the human mind," whereas Anne's Christ teaches that "she alone is responsible . . . for whatever shall be well in the world."[6] The two Christs agree on only one issue, "the size of the universe," but the dissimilarity of the inferences they draw is seen in the differences between the objects they use

[6] *Iris Murdoch: Work for the Spirit* (London: Methuen, 1982), 329.

to illustrate the point. Anne guesses that her Christ is holding a hazelnut because she has read Julian; actually he hands her a small gray stone. Her Christ is also, Dipple points out, "wrenched . . . from his traditional identification with life to an equivalence with death" (*NS*, 326). Like Guy and like Murdoch's *The Sovereignty of Good*, Anne's Christ emphasizes the value of contemplating death: " 'Indeed it is one of my names' " (*NS*, 291).

Anne's ambiguous vision—we are probably meant to take it as real but the psychoanalytical escape hatch is left open—not only "domesticates"[7] Christ but also historicizes him. The vision does not restore Anne's faith in the Christ of the church but continues a change that had begun in her in the convent. When she thinks of the Passion it is "now like something she had read about in the newspapers": "Now there were no angels, no Father, only a man hanging up in an unspeakable bleeding anguish, of which for the first time she was able to grasp the details" (*NS*, 354–55). The goal of her personal religion is to follow a "nomadic cosmic Christ" who is, nonetheless, conceived historically, "a pathetic deluded disappointed man who had come to an exceptionally sticky end" (*NS*, 500). The question becomes, can she "relive his journey and his passion while knowing that he was after all not God?" (*NS*, 500). This movement from a conception of time figured in transcendent moments to a conception of the ordinary time of a slow historical process is also reflected in Anne's changed evaluation of her relationship with the Count. She realizes that she had been wrong to live on "perfect moments," "the pure honey of love": "I was afraid to move on with him into the horrors of history" (*NS*, 496). In this movement of mind, Anne reverses the procedure by which the Count had made Polish history into a tragic personal myth and makes herself an actor rather than a victim.

Anne thus chooses a relationship to the past while the Count sees himself historically determined to have no choice. Tim, desiring to live without history, is committed to making

---

[7] Ibid., 309.

himself safe from the past: "He must be able to speak of Daisy as something belonging to the past, and so he had better wait until she *was* past, or rather more past then she was now. But when was this pastness going to begin?" (*NS*, 223). The old question of when it is decent for a widow to remarry becomes such a question in the novel. Gertrude wonders if she has only "fallen in love with the first man with whom, after Guy's death, she has been really alone? How quickly can the past lose its authority; what *is* its authority?" (*NS*, 195). For Gertrude herself the answer to the second question is "*very quickly.*" When Guy dies she loses any connection with philosophy, with the systematic examination of moral issues in which he had always engaged. "Model," "king," "judge" (*NS*, 1), this patriarch seems to embody what he says he despises, the idea of God the Father (*NS*, 65). His death issues in a time of moral uncertainty in which his widow's major task appears to be making herself happy, as he had wanted her to be.

According to conventional wisdom, Gertrude's marriage to a shiftless young man who used to steal from her refrigerator should make her unhappy, but it does not. Art, religion, history and philosophy variously mediate the responses of the other major characters, but Gertrude lives entirely for personal relationships. Among the damaged and the dying she is a natural survivor, an emblem of the healthy self-seeking ego. She learns the double-think of survival: "There are terrible things which cannot be different, and which the mind stores and deals with in the process of surviving" (*NS*, 466). She does not ask too many questions about why Guy would have disapproved of her love pact with the Count; she does not notice that Ann is in love with him, nor does she see any harm in her desire to have everything, "like a sheepfold with the sheep gathered in" (*NS*, 467).

Through each of its four major characters, then, *Nuns and Soldiers* presents a way of looking, or failing to look, at the past. Forgetting and rewriting are presented as fundamental, perhaps even necessary, impulses. Still there is the question of the content of the past, the difficulty of knowing the truth not only about Hannibal or the Soviet Army, but about one's own history. Looking back, characters in the novel are always "re-interpreting" (*NS*, 296), afraid that a present act may violate or "spoil" the past (*NS*, 35). But Murdoch does not allow the reader to remain an innocent spectator; the novel becomes an interpretative trap in which we are continually caught in our own, too hasty judgments. At its simplest the technique consists of deferring vital information, forcing us to reinterpret what we have read. We must reach the end of the novel before we discover that Anne had taken charge of Sylvia Wicks during a period when it was assumed that she was given over exclusively to mystical visions, migraines, and the activities of unrequited love. Manfred has really been as much in love with Anne as she had been with the Count; Guy, on his deathbed, had spoken Yiddish.

Of course from one perspective such revelations are simply unfair, although they may be justified as a reminder of the limits of our knowledge of any fictional character, whom we will not permit to have a life between the pages. But Murdoch's traps are more sophisticated; if we look back we can see that what she has called "the instinctive completing activity of the client's mind" has been at work in us (*FS*, 85). Like Stanley Fish's students, who can turn a list of famous linguists into a seventeenth-century poem, we require only the smallest scraps of information to build an interpretive whole to defend against further information. Many readers, for example, will rush to judge Guy's significance in the novel. The family's instinctive reverence for him, his patriarchal role, the words "king" and "royal," even his name, encourage the equation, Guy = God. And, as we have already said, this interpretation has some validity and usefulness. Nonetheless, toward the end of the novel Murdoch undermines this interpretation by introducing a secondary meaning: the Count thinks of Tim as "a sort of guy or faked-up devil" (*NS*, 449). Of course Guy is much too charitable and scrupulous to turn into Satan, but we are forced to consider evidence that his views were not always as infallible as his wife and friends suppose them to be. In fact, he does tell Tim that "it did not matter, having no identity" (*NS*, 80), and he "often" says to Gertrude "that time was

unreal," a line she finds consoling when she contemplates remarriage (*NS*, 279). Tim and Gertrude's behavior suggests the
limits, even the dangers, of such views; when they are acted
on, they encourage a denial of consequences. The final revelation that Guy had spoken Yiddish on his deathbed is deeply
moving, not only because it suggests a previously unknown
dimension of this outwardly assimilated Jew, but because it
suggests a return to a historically grounded identity that his
family is still denying or at least deferring. "I shall be there
myself tomorrow," says Veronica Mount. "Chattering Yiddish
in Abraham's bosom" (*NS*, 492).

One of the novel's traps is imbedded in the binary opposition its title suggests. *Nuns and Soldiers* is a nineteenth-century title, a presumably deliberate echo of *The Red and the
Black* or *War and Peace*. Obviously, Anne is a nun and the
Count thinks of himself as a soldier; almost immediately, however, we must acknowledge that Tim and Daisy "soldier on"
(*NS*, 73) and Gertrude says a "widow is a kind of nun" (*NS*,
103) and she wears "her mourning like a nun's veil" (*NS*, 305).
The Shakespearean allusions also remind us of how Hamlet
used that word. Then, too, the Count's life, with its poverty
and isolation, is more monkish than military; Daisy and Tim's
favorite pub has an "ecclesiastical atmosphere" and "little cu-
bicles, like confessionals" (*NS*, 71). Daisy fears being "reduced to drinking the left-overs in the pubs, like bloody Frog
Catholics living on the Eucharist" (*NS*, 88).

The opposition of nun and soldier—peace versus war, contemplation versus action—begins to seem less important than
the similarities of the two: both take vows / oaths, wear uniforms / habits, submit to discipline / order, set themselves
apart from civilian / worldly life. As the reader proceeds the
apparent interpretive convenience of the terms dissolves; the
classification scheme they suggest breaks down. The difference between the words seems to be of the sort that Barbara
Johnson has called "critical difference." According to her,

difference . . . is not what distinguishes one identity from another.
It is not a difference between (or at least not between independent

units), but a difference within. Far from constituting the text's unique identity, it is that which subverts the very idea of identity, infinitely deferring the possibility of adding up the sum of a text's parts or meaning and reaching a totalized, integrated whole.[8]

What is at issue is not a nihilistic denial of any distinctive meaning whatsoever but a sense of the deep connection between the concepts of nun and soldier. Meaning seems to reside in the impossibility of effecting a perfect separation between the terms, for the most contemplative life can have consequences in the actions of other people. Anne seems to speak for the author when she tells the Count that his isolation does not make suicide acceptable: no one "can tell where his life ends"; there is an "infinite responsibility" that arises from our deep and largely unconscious connection to other people (NS, 446).

The novel repeatedly proposes such facile oppositions: the Day Nurse versus the Night Nurse, Guy ("the man who has everything") versus Tim ("the man who has nothing" [NS, 307]), God versus Mammon, Mary versus Martha, Christ versus Peter, liars versus truthtellers, the selfish versus the selfless. The opposed terms remain meaningful, but are not the shorthand for avoiding thought that is at first supposed. Anne, for example, is deeply connected to Daisy and Tim by her search for innocence, to the Count by the dream vision of a garden with a great copper beech, to Tim by baptism, to Manfred by the capacity for unrequited love. She is the opposite number to no one, requiring constant attention and remaining morally a little enigmatic even at the end.

Expectations that the reader brings to the novel as a form can be another kind of trap. Dipple correctly points out that "*Nuns and Soldiers* is in relatively small measure about the subject of its greatest area of expansion," the Gertrude-Tim plot. "This bourgeois surface" does indeed "skirt the domain" of what she unhappily calls "women's fiction."[9] "The reader's

[8] *The Critical Difference: Essays in the Contemporary Rhetoric of Reading* (Baltimore: Johns Hopkins University Press, 1980), 4.

[9] *Iris Murdoch: Work for the Spirit*, 307.

impatience with the pair," says Dipple, "is part of the strategy of the novel, which offers their marriage," ironically, to "satisfy the conventional hunger of readers for traditional material."[10] Murdoch's ironic intentions seem clear enough; the reader's desire for a happy ending, provided for the mediocre characters but denied the more admirable ones, points to the insufficiency of his or her own reflexes about happiness, domesticity, what Dipple refers to several times as "at-homeness in the world." As much as this view fits into my own sense of Murdoch's strategies, I would add that she has not avoided all of the dangers of provoking the reader's impatience, that the longueurs of the love story must inevitably strike many readers as crying out for editing.

Most successful are the allusions. Murdoch's belief in the ethical value of great literature is complicated, as has already been noted, by her sensitivity to the seductions of form and the capacity of art to gratify the desire for a simplified view of the world. Allusions can supply such a convenient pattern for the reader, who is thereby trapped into substituting a literary past for the present. We observe how the Jamesian formula, "we shall never be as we were" (*NS*, 367)[11] seems to suggest that the characters are willing to believe that Tim and Daisy had plotted to live on the proceeds of a rich marriage because they unconsciously tie that "plot" to James's *The Wings of the Dove*. Similarly, if Murdoch names a character Manfred and tells us that he is handsome and writes an "affected Italianate script" we are likely to use these scraps to build a character for him that excludes the charity and restraint that are finally revealed in his behavior.

The most obvious of the novel's allusions are to *Hamlet*, as we could see even from the plot synopsis: an attractive widow named Gertrude marries hastily an indecisive younger man who spends his spare time at a pub called The Prince of Denmark. He calls her his "queen" (*NS*, 230), behaves with her

[10] Ibid., 312.

[11] The phrase echoes the last line of James's *The Wings of the Dove*, "We shall never be again as we were" (Harmondsworth: Penguin Classics, 1986), 507.

like "a hereditary prince in a peaceful happy feudal state" (NS, 256), and worries as little as possible about the feeling that her dead husband was "like a father to me" (NS, 478). The tragedy we may expect the allusion to supply never occurs. Murdoch takes the latent Freudian content of the tragedy, which a twentieth-century reader cannot help seeing, and plays it out. Let Hamlet marry his mother; they will not do so badly, after all. In a world of uninhibited gratification, there is no tragedy, only a mediocre settling for a nursery atmosphere of games and orality, "incompetent chess" and "another bottle of Beaujolais" (NS, 473, 474).

The end of the novel refuses its implied reader's desire for order, pattern, and certainty. We are back with Anne, the character who seems, after Guy, to be the only one to choose her actions in ethical terms, and we find that even she is flirting with the idea of giving up on goodness as "too hard to seek and too hard to understand" (NS, 504). Even as Anne looks forward to her future in America, the text's literary allusions draw the reader back into the past. In the last scene, the silence, the falling snow, the "hissing" of the street lamps, the color brown, the subdued puns (Anne thinks of heaven as "countless"), all take the reader back into that model of literary ambiguity, the final epiphany of *Dubliners.* Joyce's journey westward associates itself with death, but for Gabriel Conroy "the west" is also rich with the history of Ireland, which he had long ignored. Anne's westward journey ("tomorrow she would be in America") is a shade darker, heavy with the irony of another new beginning at the end of a novel that begins with death and connects new beginnings to illusions. In the "hypnotic silence" the scene reminds her of a "picture or a dream," looks "*like* the heavens spread out in glory, proclaiming the presence and goodness of its Creator" (NS, 504, emphasis added). Anne is left "*feeling* lightened of her burdens" (NS, 505, emphasis added). The language reinforces the sense that she looks to a world of appearances and wishful thinking, of automatic consolatory responses conditioned by art.

Readers of *Nuns and Soldiers*, then, must to some extent

share with the characters the problem of understanding the past, if only as it is figured in their reading of earlier sections of the novel; they must particularly acknowledge the inadequacy of a response based on the finding of forms and the completing of patterns. All too successfully, Murdoch frustrates the reader's desire for a character who will serve as a model, for the illusion of having once and for all understood (gained mastery over) a character, but especially for the consolation of form. In a negative way, the novel seems to offer conclusions—that the human task is to examine one's past and to live faithfully within it without becoming its victim. Change is painfully slow and transcendent moments are illusory unless slowly contemplated and understood. A philosophy, aesthetics, or theology that presents the possibility of transcending this sort of historical process is not conducive to good behavior, a point Murdoch makes in *The Sovereignty of Good*, where she connects the concept of "individual history" to moral perfectability (*SG*, 26). The question that remains is if the novel allows for the possibility of communicating more than the problem, as Murdoch characteristically argues that art ought to: "The great artist, while showing us what is not saved, implicitly shows us what salvation means" (*FS*, 80). This novel, exemplifying a relationship between the telling of stories about the past and lying, seems to insist on the intractability of the barriers between human beings. Anne's quiet charities commend to our attention a persistent obscure goodness in her, but the last two images of her—drinking alone in a bar while overhearing lies about her past, walking alone in the snow—seem more than accidentally linked to this goodness. It is easy to see why Dipple argues that the "main point" of the novel "is that although the characters of the good . . . may yearn for a place in the comfortable middle space of the world, their essential state is one of alienation and separation."[12] "The Son of Man hath not where to lay his head" (*NS*, 105).

The novel's fragmentary and negative association of public

[12] *Iris Murdoch: Work for the Spirit*, 322.

and private histories hedges this vision of alienated goodness. Murdoch goes to some length to show the intersection of Polish history with the Count's life and to suggest how unsatisfactory the lot of the assimilated British Jew is. A reasonably attentive view of one's link to the history of a people that yet preserves a sense of a separate personal identity is suggested as psychologically and morally desirable. Yet a similar sense that her characters might benefit from closer attention to the public history of the time and place in which they are living is altogether missing. And this absence, at the heart of a novel filled with so many references to "history," is perhaps its most chilling statement about the possibilities of constructing, telling, and responding to a truthful version of the past. Enmeshed in the permanent crisis of a largely uncommunicable personal past, they "do not even know they do not know" a shared world of public history. Perhaps in a world where an unspecified "cosmic disaster" (NS, 309) seems scientifically credible—the novel's famous astrophysicist has seriously considered suicide—public history is simply either too remote or too difficult for most people to face. Abetting the characters' ignorance, the narrator suggests that we must fear not only our tendencies to apply to public history the whole deceptive apparatus we erect for our own lives, but our desire to avoid looking altogether.

PART THREE

Apocalypse

CHAPTER SIX

Paul Scott's *The Raj Quartet*

NOT THE LEAST of the paradoxes of Paul Scott's *The Raj Quartet* is that its two thousand pages of impeccably researched historical fiction end with a lyric poem. Patrick Swinden shows us some of the sources of the poem's power. Its themes—the "inevitability of loss and the heartbreaking illusoriness of dreams"—echo those of the novel; more important, the poem links several characters, makes their "circles" coincide; and "coincidence of this kind is what Paul Scott's fiction is all about" (*PS*, 101–2). The point, as we shall see, is essential; still, to end a vast historical novel with a lyric poem is to do more than unify diverse stories; it constitutes a shift from a genre that demands commitment to social reality and political events to one that offers freedom from them. This movement from objective event to subjective regret, from panorama to image, from history to timelessness, is the novel's fundamental impulse. Scott's fiction explores the history of Anglo-India and betrays a deep skepticism about the ways in which human beings understand, remember, and act on their history. This skepticism extends to the genre in which *The Raj Quartet* is written, making its apparent conformity to the conventions of the historical novel a mask for its persistent subversion of them.

To be sure, the conventional elements are the most visible: pages of straightforward historical narration ("Hitler was dead"), characters who go off to fight in Burma or North Africa or write letters to Gandhi, the brutal boredom of a wedding reception at the Mess, the cruelties of the bridge table, the heat and dust of a journey by train to Calcutta appear in striking period pieces. What distinguishes this novel from much historical fiction, however, is the constant tension between its realistic texture and its tendency to turn history into stories and stories into myths that seek to explain history. The process begins on the first page of *The Jewel in the Crown*, when the narrator announces that his novel is "the story of a rape" (*JC*, 1). This fictional story has a precise historical setting, "1942, the year the Japanese defeated the British army in Burma and Mr. Gandhi began preaching sedition," yet it is also a metaphor for a process that "ended with the spectacle of the two nations in violent opposition . . . still locked in an imperial embrace of such longstanding and subtlety that it was no longer possible for them to know whether they loved or hated one another" (*JC*, 1). Although Scott indicates the centrality of the rape story on the first page, it is characteristic of his method that he delays telling it until he establishes a broader mythological context with another story, that of a murder. Since both stories figure heavily in the novel's private mythology, a brief summary may be useful. The murder story focuses on Edwina Crane, a schoolteacher who drives from Dibrapur to Mayapore with an Indian colleague, Mr. Chaudhuri. They are stopped by a mob, which kills him; she blames herself for his death and is found sitting beside his body in the road, holding his hand. Weeks later she dresses herself in a white *sari* and sets herself on fire, an act of *suttee*. In the "story of a rape" the theme of interracial love and violence is brought to a higher pitch. Hari Kumar, an Indian boy, grows up in England and attends Chillingborough, a prestigious public school. His father goes bankrupt and commits suicide, forcing his son to return to India, where he is an outcast, experiencing English racism in, among others, Ronald Merrick, an English police superintendent with homosexual inclinations. Hari falls in love with an English girl, Daphne Manners, and makes love to her in the Bibighar Gardens. They are interrupted by a gang that rapes her; to protect him, Daphne urges Hari to keep silent about his presence at the scene. In spite of the silence of both lovers, Ronald Merrick arrests Hari and tortures him on suspicion of rape; Hari Kumar is subsequently jailed without a trial for imagined political activities. Daphne dies giving birth to a daughter, Parvati, whom we see in the first volume as an accomplished raga singer.

The "story of a rape" and the story of Edwina Crane's journey from Dibrapur are repeated, reevaluated, and expanded through the four volumes. The narrator in the first volume describes himself as possessing a "lepidopteristic" intention to understand the story of Hari Kumar (*JC*, 91). He sets out like a journalist or historian, visiting scenes, interviewing survivors, reading newspaper articles, letters, unpublished memoirs. From the beginning, even this modest exercise in butterfly-pinning proves problematic. Hari Kumar has disappeared; Daphne Manners and Ronald Merrick are dead; most of the British have returned to England and the Indians who remain do not remember: "these things are forgotten and we are living different lives" (*JC* 359). Pictures and photographs are as lifeless as letters, which "do not resurrect the dead. They are merely themselves" (*JC*, 87, 88). The biases of history-writing quickly become apparent: Laxminarayan, a Hindu publisher, "is writing a history of the origins of Indian nationalism that will probably never be finished, let alone published: his apologia for many years of personal compromise" (*JC*, 255). To examine Brigadier Reid's unpublished memoirs, to listen to the mystical Sister Ludmila and the incessant monologues of Lili Chatterjee is to experience all of the distortions imposed by temperament and rhetoric. Some element is always missing: "History doesn't record the answer or even pose the question" (*JC*, 74).

Yet if the rape story fails as scientific history—at least so far as the narrator fails to pin down its "historical" details, it does begin to function as a myth with historical significance, explaining at least some of the history of Anglo-Indian relationships. Important themes are drawn into it: for example, the relationship between the English class system at home and colonial racism. In India, a man of lower-class origins like Merrick has the freedom, because he is white, to assimilate himself to the upper classes, but this freedom, depending as it does on color, makes him an ardent racist (*JC*, 193).[1] We are

[1] For a full discussion of this phenomenon as seen in late-nineteenth-cen-

meant to feel the power of Merrick's unacknowledged sexual feelings, but we also are meant to see his persecution of Kumar as exacerbated by his resentment of the Indian's public school accent (DS, 314). Educated by the English and then rejected by them in his own country, Kumar is like Nehru, whose "revolutionary" ideas are really only liberal British ideas made unacceptable because they are advocated on behalf of Indians (JC, 63, 266; S, 444). Experiencing the shock of Kumar's return to India, we glimpse something of what Gandhi felt when he came back after spending almost twenty-five years abroad. Perhaps the distinctive contribution of Gandhi to politics, "to introduce the element of doubt into public life," is owed to that sense of estrangement from his own culture (JC, 332). The violent end of the love affair is a symbol too obvious to require comment; if there is any hope, it lies with Parvati, the next generation, "but she is another story" (JC, 469). Quite similarly, Edwina Crane's story represents the failure of liberal progressive ideas unaccompanied by transcendent love (JC, 60, 70).

The novel's first response to public history, then, is to distill it into its own stories, to which it attributes a core of stable meaning. Yet, perhaps more crucially, the novel also demonstrates a distrust of stories and the kind of history they yield. The inaccuracies in stories and their seductiveness once they become myths can compel disaster. The most striking extended example is the story from which *The Day of the Scorpion* derives its title. The Laytons' Indian servants observe that a scorpion placed in a circle of fire will die before the flames reach it. Failing to understand that the scorpion is scorched because of its extreme sensitivity to heat, they make up a story that transforms him into a romantic suicide who kills himself, like a soldier falling on his sword in battle, because the odds are hopeless. Even at twelve, Sarah Layton

---

tury colonial literature, see Hugh Ridley, "The Unexpected Elite," in *Images of Imperial Rule* (New York: St. Martins, 1983), 124–45: "Violence . . . came from the whites' view of themselves just as much as from their view of the blacks. . . . people wanted to show they were masters—though in their hearts they knew how close they were to being slaves" (143).

seeks out the truth about scorpions and rejects the implications of the story: it is "more practical" and "braver" of the scorpion to try to sting the fire than to sting itself (*S*, 84). Susan Layton, however, remains at the mercy of the story. Pregnant with her first child, she believes that "people like us were finished years ago" and have nothing to offer the next generation (*S*, 358). When her son is born she calls him Edward, a name with resonances suggested by another character's description of an Anglo-Indian family "preserved by some sort of perpetual Edwardian sunlight that got trapped between the Indian Ocean and the Arabian Sea" (*S*, 444). In the depths of depression following the deaths of her husband and her aunt, she places Edward on her parents' lawn and builds a fire around him, perhaps believing that this child who symbolizes the hopeless future of the raj will also commit suicide. Some of the members of the club offer another interpretation, which is based on a more accurate view of scorpions: "Susan had made a statement about her life or that somehow managed to be a statement about your own . . . which reduced you . . . to the size of an insect; an insect entirely surrounded by the destructive element . . . doomed . . . not by the forces ranged against you but by the terrible inadequacy of your own armour" (*TS*, 286). We see the terrible price of such myths again in the career of Susan's second husband. Ronald Merrick, the "hollow man," was shaped by "all that Kiplingesque doubletalk that transformed India from a place where plain ordinary greedy Englishmen carved something out for themselves . . . into one where they appeared to go voluntarily into exile for the good of their souls and the uplift of the native" (*DS*, 217). As sustaining fiction, the white man's burden gives a long-range historical purpose to present acts of cruelty and discourages introspection.

Moreover, the raw materials of history are endlessly vulnerable to interpretation. "The history of their relationship," says Guy Perron of Daphne and Hari, "could be made to fit almost any theory one could have of Kumar's character and intentions" (*DS*, 317). Liberal progressive narratives of the sort Herbert Butterfield disposed of in *The Whig Interpreta-*

tion of History are a particular target. Ronald Merrick is defined by his invisibility to such histories: "a man . . . who
lacked entirely that liberal instinct which is so dear to historians that they lay it out like a guideline through the un-
mapped forests of prejudice and self-interest as though this
line, and not the forest, is our history. . . . There he is, the
unrecorded man, one of the kind of men we really are" (*DS*,
314). When Lady Manners has her vision of the disaster in
which British India will end, she realizes that what history is
likely to record will be the "actual deed," the granting of independence, but such a record will be false: "We must remember the worst because the worst is the lives we lead, the
best is only our history and between our history and our lives
there is this vast dark plain where the rapt and patient shepherds drive their invisible flocks in expectation of God's for-
giveness" (*S*, 318). Elsewhere, Robin White, former Deputy
Commissioner of Mayapore, writes to the narrator of their
shared fascination with the "beat" and "pulse," the "unrecorded moments of history" (*JC*, 348). He wishes to relate this
theory to his own life, but in doing so finds himself falsifying:
"even in attempting to relate it, I'm back in the world of de-
scribable events" (*JC*, 348). As if to compensate for this tendency of written history to drift away from actual lives, the
novel constantly seeks to establish an identity between public
events and the private experiences of its characters.

Just as the novel draws historical panorama into the narrow
circle of its own myths, it continually assimilates public events
to the lives of the characters. For all their psychological veri-
similitude, the major characters are in one way or another
representative of political movements or social strata: Mohammed Ali Kasim, the enlightened Muslim; Edwina Crane
and Barbie Batchelor, earnest lower-middle-class missionaries, women of liberal goodwill; Colonel John Layton, the flag-
ging idealism of the officer caste; Aunt Charlotte, the English
public's ignorance of Indian conditions; little Edward Bingham, the future of the raj. Place names move out of history
into fiction: Chillianwallah Bagh, the section of Mayapore in
which Hari Kumar lives with Aunt Shalini, recalls Jallianwal-

lah Bagh, the scene of General Dyer's massacre, which, as K. Bhaskara Rao observes, becomes the Gillian Waller of Mabel Layton's uneasy sleep.[2]

The same dates have public and private significance. Edwina Crane's journey from Dibrapur takes place on the afternoon of 8 August 1942; Daphne Manners is raped that night. The eighth of August was the day the All-India Congress Party voted in favor of Gandhi's Quit India resolution. T. Walter Wallbank summarizes: "Before the Congress could carry out its campaign of mass civil disobedience, the government of India acted and all Congress leaders—including Nehru, Gandhi, and Azad—were arrested on August 9. Immediately serious and widespread disorders broke out."[3] Thus, major actions of the fictional story tend to constellate around the landmarks of the historical one. Sometimes, of course, the process is inevitable, as when M. A. Kasim, fictional Congress Party leader, is jailed on the same day as his historical counterparts. But Scott carries the process of assimilating history to fiction to the point where history seems almost subsumed. Barbie Batchelor resigns as superintendent of a mission school in September, 1939. On D-Day, Mabel Layton dies, Sarah Layton loses her virginity, and Susan Layton goes into labor. Captain Purvis, who thinks of the Second World War as a "criminal waste" he will "never be able to forgive" (*DS*, 27), commits suicide just in time to escape hearing about the bombing of Hiroshima on August 6, 1945, the day Barbie Batchelor dies.

These mechanisms not only allow Scott to draw diverse historical elements into a novelistic story, but they allow him to explore an alternative idea of history. Such a view locates the meaning of public events in the lives and consciousness of single people.[4] Emerson, in his famous essay, "History," as-

[2] *Paul Scott* (Boston: Twayne, 1980), 103.

[3] *A Short History of India and Pakistan* (1951; New York: Mentor, 1958), 207.

[4] Suzanne Kim touches on this point briefly but suggestively. "On peut certes parler d'un traitement autobiographique de l'Histoire chez lui [Scott], encore que l'Histoire dépende autant, sinon plus, d'une vue mythique de

sumes that historical facts are impossible to come by or are inherently unstable: "No anchor, no cable, no fences avail to keep a fact a fact. Babylon, Troy, Tyre, Palestine, and even early Rome, have passed or are passing into fiction."[5] He is undismayed by this prospect: "Who cares what the fact was, when we have made a constellation of it to hang in heaven an immortal sign?"[6] The facts as external events do not matter because "there is one mind common to all individual men"; we can all experience history in our own lives, through our own self-knowledge: "We are always coming up with the emphatic facts of history in our private experience, and verifying them here."[7] Emerson's view of history as biography is consoling to the historical novel's traditional claims, since it affirms the validity of imaginatively experienced history and its accessibility to the well-intentioned and reasonable reader.

The novel's examination of Emerson's theory centers around Barbie Batchelor, perhaps the most complicated and sympathetic of Scott's characters. Barbie becomes obsessed with Emerson when she comes across these lines in "History": "If the whole of history is one man . . . it is all to be explained from individual experience. There is a relation between the hours of our life and the centuries of time" (*TS*, 68). Barbie "began to feel what she believed Emerson wanted her to feel: that in her own experience lay an explanation not only of history but of the lives of other living people" (*TS*, 68). We might ask what sort of history she finds there and how finding it changes her.

Like other major characters in *The Raj Quartet*, Barbie can be read as representative of a group—in her case the ear-

l'Inde et de propositions métaphysiques pessimistes sur la vie humaine." ("One can certainly speak of an autobiographical treatment of history in him [Scott], yet the history depends as much, if not more, on a mythic view of India and on pessimistic metaphysical propositions about human life.") ("Histoire et roman," *Études anglaises* 38 nos. 2–3 [1983]: 170.)

[5] From *The Collected Works of Ralph Waldo Emerson*, vol. 5 (Cambridge: Harvard University Press, 1979), 6.

[6] Ibid.

[7] Ibid.

nestly Protestant lower middle class. She comes to India as a missionary strongly motivated to convert Indian children and is disappointed when she discovers that official attitudes, even in the missions, are moderate and secular: "Moreover, the authorities, both civil and military, seemed to take considerable trouble to enable Hindus to go on being Hindus and Muslims to be Muslims . . . by giving official recognition to the communal differences between them" (*TS*, 3). A story told about one of Barbie's experiences as a young teacher attributes to her the sort of cultural insensitivity one expects of zealous missionaries. A little girl in her class had colored the face of Jesus blue because that was the color of Krishna in the picture her parents had at home. To prevent a repetition Barbie took away all the blue crayons, "and then the children had no way of coloring the sky" (*TS*, 8). As she is introduced to us in September 1939, she remains "a believer in the good will and good sense of established authority" (*TS*, 1). Yet, inside, Barbie is not the same: she has begun to feel that her life has been wasted doing something of which God disapproves (*TS*, 4).

Outward incidents in the remaining six years of her life are few. Barbie moves to Pankot, where she is a paying guest of Mabel Layton at Rose Cottage, and grows to love her; when Mabel dies Barbie is grief-stricken because the family refuses to honor Mabel's wish to be buried in Ranpur. That grief worsens as Mabel's daughter-in-law Mildred immediately evicts Barbie. She attempts to give Susan Layton a set of apostle spoons as a wedding gift, but Mildred humiliates her by returning them; she walks miles in the rain to present them to the Mess, but her attempt fails when she discovers Mildred in bed with the officer in charge. The pneumonia that follows this walk leaves Barbie's voice weakened but she decides to accept a teaching post anyway. She returns to Rose Cottage for a last visit, meets Ronald Merrick there, and gives him her copy of the "Jewel in the Crown" picture. On the way home, her heavy trunk causes her tonga to overturn; the driver is killed and Barbie herself is pushed over the edge toward madness.

We can read Barbie's life and private experiences as history. Her recognition that the civil authorities encourage the divisions between Hindu and Islamic communities, for example, is a crucial perception for the last volume, which ends with the religious massacres of 1947. Her Protestant zeal, however misguided, represents the idealistic hope that Britain can leave behind a unified India, and perhaps the more basic hope that the best of its civilization is a positive legacy for India. The symbolic value of Rose Cottage has already been suggested by Patrick Swinden, who sees the loss of Paradise as the subject of Scott's novels (*II*, 1). The cottage is the Eden of Anglo-India; as Mabel says, "It often strikes me as something the gods once loved but forgot should die young and that there's only me left to love it" (*TS*, 22). Mabel herself represents much of the best of Anglo-India. The widow first of a British officer and then of a Deputy Commissioner, Mabel had rebelled against her class by contributing one hundred pounds to a fund for the victims of Jallianwallah Bagh when her friends were collecting for General Dyer, and, insofar as possible, she dissociates herself from the Club. With her death the reader must sense that Anglo-India has lost her conscience, and that the English will soon be dispossessed forever. Mildred Layton's long antagonism for Barbie also has symbolic overtones. Mildred, who drinks heavily and sleeps with an ambitious junior officer while her husband is a prisoner of the Nazis, is always unattractive, but with Barbie she is ruthless. She despises her immediately for being Mabel's guest, and therefore for keeping the Laytons out of Rose Cottage. Her first act upon inheriting it is to have the fabled roses ripped out and replaced by a tennis court; her renovations strip the house of its "secluded, tentative" air, and restore "its functional solidity, an architectural integrity which belonged to a time when the British built . . . with their version of India aggressively in mind and with a view to permanence" (*DS*, 139). Yet, ironically her restoration fails because "she had robbed the place of . . . the quality of survival and the idea behind it—that survival meant change." Twelve Upper Club Road, as Mildred calls the cottage, begins to look, even when the family is home, "like a place of historic interest, visited but not inhabited" (*DS*, 140). The parallel with English attempts to return during the war to an earlier phase of colonialism and the consequences of doing so is readily drawn. Her success in keeping Barbie from giving her apostle spoons either to Susan or to the army is a desperate rejection of Christian values and of the lower middle classes whose tastes the spoons reflect. The picture of Queen Victoria accepting India, the jewel in the crown, is first given to Edwina Crane as a reward for facing down a rebellious Indian mob; both she and Barbie use it to teach the language and values of the English and jettison it when they have become disillusioned. For Barbie to give it to Ronald Merrick means conceding the colonial project to its most ruthless advocate. Her perception of Ronald Merrick as the devil goes little further than the novel does in seeing his racism and ruthlessness as "the dark side," the worst elements in British colonialism (*S*, 362).

Yet, although Barbie's life provides a good example of Scott's tendency to correlate private experience and public history, what happens to her as she embarks on the Emersonian search for history marks a separation between Emerson's optimism and Scott's deep pessimism, and in this respect the encounter between her consciousness and history is paradigmatic of the novel's. Under Emerson's spell, other people come alive for Barbie as they never have, and as they do, her perception of them changes. Daphne Manners, for example, is transformed from the rape victim the Club imagines into her more essential identity: "the girl's hand was no longer pressed inverted against her forehead but held by another which was brown like the dead teacher's" (*TS*, 68). Such moments in which the lives of other people are experienced truthfully in the imagination are not limited to Barbie: Sarah Layton has a similar revelation when she goes riding with Ahmed Kasim: "this morning as I rode home . . . she was alive for me completely. She flared up out of my darkness as a white girl in love with an Indian. And then went out because—in that disguise—she is not part of what I comprehend" (*S*, 158). Sarah, who finds Emerson "tiresome" (*DS*,

398), is a survivor whose moments of intense sympathetic identification will always—mercifully—end in incomprehension. But Barbie's imagination is greater. Not only does she absorb the lives of other people into her own life but she begins to confuse them:

> She was no longer sure of what she saw: Edwina guarding the body, Mabel kneeling to grub out weeds or inclining to gather roses; or herself, Barbie, surrounded by children she had presumed to bring to God; or Miss Manners in some kind of unacceptable relationship with a man of another race whom she was intent on saving. From these there emerged a figure, the figure of an unknown Indian: dead in one aspect, alive in another. And after a while it occurred to her that the unknown Indian was what her life in India had been about. (*TS*, 69)

As Barbie watches him, the unknown Indian begins to howl. But after reading about Edwina Crane's suicide she understands who he is: "the dead body was the one Edwina guarded—her life in India come to nothing" (*TS*, 89). For Barbie, who equates despair with the devil, this is an image of damnation, and the "revelation of Edwina's despair uncovered her own, showed its depth, its immensity" (*TS*, 89). In her consciousness every British life lived in India has "come to nothing."

Barbie's conflation of the lives of Daphne Manners and Hari Kumar, of Edwina and Mr. Chaudhuri, of Mabel and herself, replicates the process by which Scott draws history into his fictional stories. These are the "coincidences of circles" of which Patrick Swinden speaks, the tendency of Scott's characters to "borrow . . . identities and in some cases their destinies" from each other to which David Rubin alludes.[8] Not only does the love story of Daphne Manners and Hari Kumar parallel the story of Miss Crane on the road from Dibrapur, but it looks back to the story of old Mr. MacGregor and the Indian girl he loved and forward to the never-realized

---

[8] *After the Raj: British Novels of India since 1947* (Hanover, N.H.: University Press of New England, 1986), 136.

story of Sarah Layton and Ahmed Kim. This process of collapsing stories blurs the identities of characters who never meet, or makes apparently random actions seem related. Similarly, Ronald Merrick believes that Edwina Crane has committed suttee because she "felt that the India she knew had died"; Teddie Bingham's death in a burning jeep is a result of a foolishly outdated mixture of idealism and paternalism. "Sitting there with Teddie made it all seem to connect . . . what she had done all that time ago . . . and what he had just done . . . there was the other similarity—death by fire" (S, 413). Sarah, who as we have seen thinks of Ronald Merrick as "one of us," "our dark side," extends the perception to Susan in her madness: "We sense from the darkness in you the darkness in ourselves, a darkness and a death wish" (S, 501). Doing so, she prepares us for their marriage and for Ronald's murder, which, like Teddie Bingham's death in combat, is little more than a suicide. Such links are continually forged: Sister Ludmilla and Guy Perron might seem to have nothing in common, yet both see that Ronald Merrick "chooses" his victims (JC, 150; DS, 214). In Guy Perron's dream, "Purvis was Kumar, seated, looking up at me through the eyes of this other man who kept saying, I don't think I'll ever forgive it" (DS, 337). Occasionally such links are bizarre, as when the narrator, bathing at MacGregor House, "closing the eyes against the contrary evidence of sex, attempts a re-enactment of Miss Manners refreshing herself after a hard day" (JC, 93).

Emerson believed that such links to the "common mind" liberate the understanding and free an ordinary person to possess the history of kings: "He must sit solidly at home, and not suffer himself to be bullied by kings or empires, but know that he is greater than all the geography and all the government of the world, he must transfer the point of view from which history is commonly read, from Rome and Athens and London to himself."[9] But in Scott's novel the history of Anglo-India is too terrible to liberate the reader into his or her own life. As the stories collapse into each other, they become one

[9] *Collected Works of Emerson*, 6.

story, from which no escape is possible. Lady Manners watches Hari Kumar's interrogation and projects into the Indian future Barbie's vision of Edwina Crane's well-intentioned life "come to nothing": "It will end . . . in total and unforgivable disaster. . . . The reality of the actual deed would be a monument to all that had been thought for the best" (S, 318). Confusion of identity finally becomes a symptom of madness; in the asylum, the nurse greets Barbie, "Good morning, Edwina . . . or are we Barbie today?" (TS, 382).

It is not surprising, then, that the novel comes to depict history as a burden, a maze, a prison. To the list of actual prisons in which M. A. Kasim, his son Sayed, Hari Kumar, and Colonel John Layton are locked are added the nursing homes and hospitals in which Poppy Browning's daughter, Barbie Batchelor, and Susan Layton experience their madness. Guy Perron and Sarah Layton wander through the old summer residence of the British government in Pankot as through a "maze of imperial history" (DS, 348). To Guy, Sarah seems to possess nothing but the "unreality" of Anglo-Indian history and "to belong to it like a prisoner would belong . . . to a cell his imagination had escaped but whose door he was not permitted to open" (DS, 349). They move on to the Moghul Suite, which at first seems to offer release "from the stupefying weight of nearly a century of disconnexion from the source. But the Moghul suite was no less burdened by that weight; it was the inner box of a nest of boxes" (DS, 349). Susan's christening dress is made of lace in which butterflies appear to shimmer, but the lacemaker, a blind woman who lives in a tower, calls them "prisoners" and regrets that they will never fly out of the lace (S, 371). Susan dresses little Edward in the lace before trying to burn him; "Little Prisoner," she murmurs, "Shall I free you?" (S, 502). Barbie wears a piece of it like a bridal veil when she sets out on the tonga ride that ends in death and madness. The too-heavy trunk that causes the accident is always identified as Barbie's life in India. It is "her history and without it according to Emerson

she wasn't explained" (*DS*, 358); "without it she did not seem
to have a shadow" (*TS*, 7).[10]

Experienced both as myth and biography, history is a
shadow, a prison, a treacherous burden, a story with only one
ending. Through Barbie the novel explores the possibility of
escaping history by escaping language. All her life Barbie has
been a compulsive talker, a teacher with a carrying voice. She
dislikes her own chatter and admires Mabel's "gift for still-
ness" (*TS*, 247). Shortly before Mabel's death, Barbie begins
to experience "imaginary silences" in which she cannot even
hear herself speaking. These silences leave her with a "vivid
sense of herself as new and unused . . . no longer in arrears
. . . because the account had not been opened yet" (*TS*, 176,
177). This sensation is so attractive that she thinks "Emerson
was wrong, we're not explained by our history at all . . . it's
our history that gets in the way of a lucid explanation of us"
(*TS*, 176). Barbie begins "to enjoy the sensation of her history
and other people's history blowing away like dead leaves; but
then it occurred to her that among the leaves were her religious principles and beliefs" (*TS*, 177). She tries to reshape
her silence so that it will not "destroy contact but create it"
(*TS*, 177). Her silence is a mystical state of waiting for God to
speak: "I want to create around myself a condition of silence
so that it may be broken, but not by me. But I am surrounded
by a condition of Babel" (*TS*, 187). In death Mabel is depicted
as a "fallen tower" (*TS*, 247); losing her and rejecting Babel,
Barbie has no alternative but to drift toward the towers of silence that give the third volume of *The Raj Quartet* its name.

When she is ill with pneumonia, Barbie tells Sarah that in
her hospital bed "she has no history, just the hours of the day"

[10] James Longenbach provides an excellent discussion of "Nietzchean an-
tihistoricism" as a modernist theme. In "Ibsen's *Hedda Gabler* (1890), Mor-
ris's *News from Nowhere* (1890), Mann's *Buddenbrooks* (1901), Gide's *The
Immoralist* (1902), and Joyce's 'The Dead' (1907) . . . history is felt to be a
burden, something to be avoided or destroyed. Yet, at the same time, the
persistent effect of the past is finally unavoidable" (*Modernist Poetics of History* [Princeton: Princeton University Press, 1987], 7, 8). In this respect and
others Scott is closer to modernism than most of his contemporaries.

(*TS*, 326). Sarah argues that she does: the trunk still carefully stored at Rose Cottage; but after the tonga accident, Barbie finally succeeds in living outside history. Claiming to be under a "vow of silence," Barbie communicates only in brief notes (*TS*, 383). Given a calendar turned to the first anniversary of D-Day (and of Mabel's death), Barbie rips it up; by 6 August 1945, the date of her own death, she has passed into a state where all dates are meaningless: "The calendar was a mathematical progression with arbitrary surprises" (*TS*, 386). Sarah, coming to visit in late June, is distressed because Barbie seems to have lost her memory, but more precisely what Barbie has lost is meaningful language: "She remembered a great deal. But was unable to say what it was. The birds had picked the words clean" (*TS*, 385).

This image of language stripped clean is an image of death. The towers of silence are literal as well as metaphorical, a place visible from Barbie's barred window where vultures pick clean the bodies of the Ranpur Parsees. Perhaps Barbie associates these birds with her reading of the essay, "History": "She was not cut out for the philosophical life but through Emerson it impinged on her own like the shadow of a hunched bird of prey patiently observing below it the ritual of survival." The bird in turn associates itself with Barbie's devil, "not a demon but a fallen angel" who "was despair as surely as God was love" (*TS*, 89). Sick and weeping over Edwina's suicide, Barbie orders him to leave, "then caught her breath at the sound of a slow ungainly winged departure as of a heavy carrion bird that had difficulty in overcoming the pull of gravity" (*TS*, 90).

It is possible to see a mystical value in Barbie's patient waiting for God's voice; Barbie herself enters madness believing that she falls "like Lucifer but without Lucifer's pride and not . . . to his . . . destination" (*TS*, 382). But her destination must be outside history and time, and almost outside language. Within historical time she dies on the same day as the victims of Hiroshima, virtually as one of them: "They found her thus, eternally alert, in sudden sunshine, her shadow burnt into the wall behind her as if by some distant but terrible fire" (*TS*, 386). Remembering that shadow was one of the novel's words for history, the reader knows how complete that immolation is. It consumes Barbie's belief, secure in September 1939, in the good sense of established authority; it consumes Emerson, who believed we could understand ourselves and our history without going mad; it consumes all missionary fervor, all belief that the West brings progress and humane values to the East.

As we have seen, the novel's metaphors for history suggest the futility of action: history is a shadow (*TS*, 326), a too-heavy trunk, a burden (*TS*, 269), a dead hand (*S*, 139), a carapace (*S*, 415). Edwina Crane imagines "the moral drift of history," a naive conception of a river flowing into a sea, losing as it runs on all the "debris" of prejudice and disharmony (*JC*, 25). Robin White tells the narrator that the impetus for this drift comes from "our consciences," which work in the "dangerous area" of personal risk, "with or without us, usually without" (*JC*, 348). Thus, changes occur almost without our knowledge or consent: "It was . . . a question of the greater morality outlasting and outweighing the lesser. Which was why . . . the Indians won" (*JC*, 348). Ronald Merrick, however, explores the possibility of making one's participation in history more conscious. "History," he tells Hari Kumar, is "a sum of situations whose significance was never seen until long afterwards because people had been afraid to act them out. . . . They preferred to think of the situations they found themselves in as part of a general drift of events they had no control over" (*S*, 309). Binding Kumar to a trestle, beating him, then offering him a drink of water: for Merrick these are all elements of a "situation of enactment" (*S*, 309) that makes both men "for the moment . . . mere symbols" (*S*, 310). Merrick does not think one can necessarily "change the course of events by acting out situations" but believes that doing so "you'd understand better what that situation was and take what steps you could to stop things drifting in the wrong direction, or an unreal direction" (*S*, 309). In Merrick's view, he and Kumar are acting out not only the subjugation of colonial people, but its basis, "contempt," which is the "prime human emotion" (S, 312). English liberals and intellectuals are as contemptuous of Indians as he is; "no human being was ever going to believe all human beings were created equal" (S, 312). From the course of his career, it is easy to see how unproductive Merrick's enactment is for himself: he "takes steps" as a policeman, an army officer, and a special agent of the princely state, Mirat, but is brutally murdered on the eve of Indian independence.

But just as Sarah thinks of Merrick as the "dark side of [our] history" (S, 362), so his conception of the intractability of racial hatred is one of the novel's nightmares. If the luminous examples of interracial love that the novel offers can ever be realized on the plane of its public history, whose most characteristic landmark is the genocidal massacre, is a question Scott leaves unanswered. For Hari Kumar the only response to Merrick is detachment: "the situation only existed in Merrick's terms if we both took part in it. The situation would cease to exist if I detached myself from it" (S, 315). In his detachment, Kumar joins his grandfather, who went *sannyasi*, that is, renounced family and property to wander India as a religious beggar; and he seems linked to the many characters in the novel who detach themselves from history through exile, madness, and suicide.

The alternative to such detachment is positive action, and of this *The Raj Quartet* offers less than more traditional historical novels. Great battles and decisive meetings take place off-stage; Merrick's description of Teddie Bingham's bungled attempt to encourage a former Muzzafirabad guide to desert from the Japanese-sponsored Indian National Army is as close as we come to combat in the Second World War. For action Scott substitutes the idea of action, which he embodies especially in M. A. Kasim and John Layton. These men devote their lives, respectively, to politics and the army, yet each— the bare fact already indicating Scott's bias—is a prisoner for most of the novel. Kasim is Scott's most admirable politician, an immensely attractive man who serves in Ranpur as provincial chief minister until 1939, when he resigns as part of the

Congress Party's boycott of the English war effort. It becomes increasingly difficult for him to remain loyal to the Congress Party, which most of his fellow Muslims perceive as seeking to substitute a Hindu *raj* for a British *raj* (*DS*, 409). Kasim, however, foresees the violence that must accompany partition and resists all appeals to desert to Jinnah's pro-Pakistan Muslim League, even though he disagrees with all of the major decisions Congress has made since 1939, and regards its cap, which he wears, as a "crown of thorns" (*S*, 495; *DS*, 415). The British first try to suborn, and then imprison him. Partly because of Kasim's imprisonment, his son Sayed, a British officer, deserts to the Indian National Army. Kasim is repelled by this breach of contract and by the INA in general; if allowed into the army of a free India, such men will represent a constant threat of military dictatorship. In Kasim's eyes Sayed has thrown away his future. Moreover, since he himself cannot expect to be elected to public office if he withholds support for the INA, he must move, at least temporarily, "hors de combat." Freed by the British, he must "cultivate his own garden," a skill he learned in prison (*DS*, 461). Kasim's apolitical son, Ahmed, brings his father a moment of happiness by supporting his decision to remain loyal to Congress. But in the novel's last major episode, Ahmed is killed by Hindus in one of the massacres that preceded partition. Thus, in the moment of victory—the achievement of independence—Kasim appears defeated, deprived of a future and of the ability to act.

In John Layton, a less well-realized character, Scott similarly translates victory into defeat. Layton is *The Raj Quartet's* Ashley Wilkes, or, to be more charitable, its Mr. Compson— a gentleman whose code has become outdated, a man who cannot quite live up to his own conception of himself. Layton is taken prisoner in North Africa; he is imprisoned in Italy and then Germany and returns to India with a decimated regiment. He has acquired prison habits, such as pocketing bits of food and cleaning his own bathroom, that are out of place in a country where an English gentleman never puts on his own shoes unaided. Scrupulously honorable, he refuses to return to Pankot before the last of his men is released from hospital in Bombay. Yet once in Pankot, Layton cannot bring himself to visit the family of Havildar Karim Muzzafirkhan, the only member of his regiment to go over to the German equivalent of the INA, the Frei Hind, who has committed suicide in British captivity. Every day for weeks he rides to the dead man's village but can go no farther, "the intention collapsing under the weight of his notion of its futility," for the old relationship with his men has failed to survive the war (DS, 358). His daughter Sarah sees that he "believes himself dishonoured—not by anything he had done but by his talent, which turning out limited had narrowed the whole area of his self-regard" (DS, 359). He can no more prevent Susan's marriage to Ronald Merrick than he can prevent his wife from ripping out the roses in his garden; both are defeats that would have been unthinkable before the war. The last recipient of Captain Purvis's much-traveled Scotch, he studies "the pale liquid in his glass, perhaps seeing in the whisky of one dead man the face of another" (DS, 288). Observing this exhausted patrician, the reader scarcely remembers that England won the war.

In John Layton and Mohammed Ali Kasim Scott transforms the man of action into an honorable prisoner. Seen through the eyes of his Indian nationalist, the independence of 1947 is a defeat of Indian unity; through the eyes of his English colonel the allied victory signals the end of the British Empire and the beginning of the nuclear age. In India, "the British came to the end of themselves as they were" (S, 4); in "India: A Post-Forsterian View," Scott adds: "the Fieldings as well as the Turtons."[11] To have lost world power and colonial possessions is not as important to Scott as the loss of one's belief in liberal humanism. Scott is convinced that England's rapid demission of power in India after the war was an abandonment of that nation to warfare between religious factions that England itself had fostered. Well-meaning people like Guy Perron's Aunt Charlotte bear a responsibility for the massacres of 1947: her belief that only the Indians actually killing each

[11] In *Essays by Divers Hands* n.s. 36 (1970): 125.

other are to blame confirms his "impression of the overwhelming importance of the part that had been played in Brit-
ish-Indian affairs by the indifference and the ignorance of the
English at home" (*DS*, 230, 231). Those terrible massacres in
turn exemplify the fate of England's colonies in the immediate
postwar period. In his essay Scott comments on how, in the
former colonies, "in most cases the opposite of what had been
worked for had been achieved; and in other cases, where a
hope had been fulfilled" one was led to suspect "that the ful-
fillment revealed flaws in the arguments in favour of it."[12] In
the novel's myth-making, Anglo-Indian history becomes a
myth of its own, a story of the end of colonialism as a surrender of the Third World to the violence and racism that are the
real legacy of the colonizers. Mr. Gopal's nephew, Ashok,
"wishes to be the first Indian to make an atomic bomb" (*DS*,
199).

For all its sympathies with India and Indians, then, *The Raj
Quartet* is a radically conservative novel that resonates with
the conviction that human beings can do little to change their
oppressive history. The genre in which Scott writes demands
that he record their struggles and acknowledge their politics,
ambitions, and wars. But when it is all over, when the immediate price of India's freedom is at least a quarter of a million lives and a future of religious massacre, then Scott moves
gracefully, almost with relief, to another genre. Time in the
lyric is at last released, as Barbie was in her madness, from
the constraints of the calendar.[13] The Indian poet offers time-

---

[12] Ibid., 121.

[13] For an extended analogy between Scott and Proust, see David Rubin.
Rubin, accurately observing that Scott has more in common with Proust than
with Tolstoy, finds history "secondary" in *The Raj Quartet* (*After the Raj*,
120–21). Drawing a parallel between Parvati Manners and Mlle de Saint-
Loup, he finds some "consolation" in the vision of this young woman who
"reconciles in herself Britain and India" and "will one day bring to England
her performances of a traditional Indian art, successfully bridging 'the dark
currents of a human conflict' " (151). Scott's fiction presents "a striking justi-
fication of the novel genre . . . as opposed to what is generally called history"
because "it explores universal human potentialities and destinies for which
history can provide only a deplorably inadequate record" (156). Even in

less images of mutability—the dying flower, the running deer, the flying hawk. So much history ends in so few images, "fleeting moments: these are held a long time in the eye / the blind eye of the aging poet" (*DS*, 623). The last, most characteristic gesture of this historical novel is to empty itself of history, to turn to the beauty we "can imagine in this darkening landscape" (*DS*, 623). The lyric asserts that human beings make an art that is better than their history, yet all that long history lies like a shadow over it.

Proust, however, the consolation of timeless art is hedged. Subsumed in his novel into a symbol of the public history art must transcend, the historical Dreyfus Affair, demonstrating the power of the Right in French politics and the capacity of Western Europeans for hysterical anti-Semitism, has resonances for us that the novelist could not have known. Half-Jewish, homosexual, a chronic invalid, Proust—had he survived into his early seventies—might well have been a victim to forces his novel dismisses. Scott's numerous references to nuclear war in the *Raj Quartet* suggest that he is well aware of the sort of irony that historical hindsight lends to *A la recherche du temps perdu*. While the Proustian project clearly appeals to Scott, I think the text acknowledges its impossibility much more bleakly.

CHAPTER SEVEN

Doris Lessing's *Children of Violence*

FOR PAUL SCOTT, history is a prison from which human beings long to escape; in Doris Lessing, it is a fortress excluding women and colonialized peoples; to be free is to be able to act in public history. In the fourth volume of her *Children of Violence* series, *Landlocked*, the narrative, usually anchored in Martha Quest's consciousness, slips for a few pages into her mother's mind. Her daughter's oldest antagonist, Mrs. Quest has steadily opposed Martha's politics, her divorce, every symptom of what she regards as her self-indulgence and reckless freedom. But as she sits quietly in her drawing room, the momentarily bitter disappointment that her husband's sickness will prevent her from attending the colony's Victory Parade triggers more profound unhappiness: "It seemed to her that for years, for all her life, she had sat, forced to be quiet, listening to history being made. She, whose every instinct was for warm participation, was never allowed to be present" (*L*, 71). That absence of women from history of which Jane Austen and Virginia Woolf complained is seldom overtly recognized in the novel; throughout her lifetime, Martha is deeply involved in politics: not only during her Communist period, with its interminable meetings and rounds of tract-distributing, but also during the long years in Bloomsbury, where the Coldridge house, as Catharine Stimpson says, "entertains all of postwar English politics and culture."[1] Yet, throughout the novel Martha, like her mother, remains a spectator and victim of a public history that excludes her. In this exclusion lies her ominous typicality; this fundamental absence from history

---

[1] "Doris Lessing and the Parables of Growth," in *The Voyage In*, ed. Elizabeth Abel, Marianne Hirsch, and Elizabeth Langland (Hanover, N.H.: University Press of New England, 1983), 188.

makes her not only a representative woman, but a representative citizen of the twentieth century.

With its author's goal of describing the "individual conscience in its relation to the collective" (*SPV*, 14), *Children of Violence* belongs to a genre—the multivolume autobiographical novel sequence—that enjoyed great popularity in England after the war. Works such as Anthony Powell's *Dance to the Music of Time*, C. P. Snow's *Strangers and Brothers*, Evelyn Waugh's *Sword of Honour*, and Olivia Manning's *Fortunes of War* similarly explore the evolution of a single character against a background of war and massive social change. All of these books, to the extent that they are committed to analyzing the exchange between a single consciousness and public events, are historical novels. This genre, Nicole Ward Jouve argues quite convincingly, relies on an assumption true "in Balzac's time," that "the world of an individual could be put into correspondence with—*represent*—the world. The vision an individual had of the world, the fate of an individual, could act as a *valid model* for what was happening at a universal level." Given the "monumental and divisive complexities" of contemporary life, Jouve wonders how Lessing and others "can go on writing like this."[2] For Waugh and Powell, at least, the answer might well be that their own world views are not radically different from those of Balzac, or at least those "of Balzac's time." The central personae of most series novels are either apolitical or politically conservative; indeed that genre, congenial to nostalgia, is also congenial to political reaction. As I have argued extensively elsewhere,[3] the major unifying device of the series novel is the representation of memory, which allows the central character to hold fast to his or her past even as the world changes and to discern those patterns of recurrence that are the source of so much irony and con-

[2] "Of Mud and Other Matter—*The Children of Violence*," in *Notebooks / Memoirs / Archives: Reading and Rereading Doris Lessing*, ed. Jenny Taylor (Boston: Routledge and Kegan Paul, 1982), 126, 128.

[3] Margaret Scanlan, "Memory and Continuity in the Series Novel: The Example of *Children of Violence*," *Modern Fiction Studies* 26, no. 1 (1980): 75–86.

solation in Proust and his descendants. For Lessing the answer is more complicated. Since she distrusts irony almost as
much as she distrusts nostalgia, since her Martha Quest finds
repetition a nightmare (*PM*, 77, 95) and is unusually successful at blocking out her past, *Children of Violence* was doomed
from the start to seem less well-unified than, say, *The Dance
to the Music of Time*. Moreover, as Jouve and Frederic Stern
have noted, the Martha Quest of the final volume is a less
well-realized character than the earlier Martha, a transpar-
ency through whom the author speaks "almost directly."[4] If
unity, the careful conservation of an engaging and credible
personality, is what we expect, then *Children of Violence* dis-
appoints. Yet that disappointment does not necessarily signal
the failure of the series. In the process of writing the series,
Lessing seems to have discovered the problematic of the individual's relation to the collective of which Jouve speaks. Its
succeeding volumes show the stages of the protagonist's struggle to understand and act in a world to which she is often
invisible. The tension between the radical (whether Marxist,
feminist, Laingian or Sufi) writer and her reactionary genre
produces an insightful if ultimately pessimistic vision of the
relation between women and the public historical life that excludes them.

As an adolescent, Martha reaches out to that life through
books; among the first we see her reading are *The Decay of
the British Empire* and H. G. Wells's *Concise History of the
World*. She reads such books slowly, puzzled, aware that "the
memoirs of Lloyd George, or histories of the Great War"
seem to have no "reference to the farm, to the gangs of native
labour, to what was described in the newspapers, or even to
Mein Kampf (*MQ*, 27). Such books lack the emotional power
of her father's stories about the First World War, the fearful
glamour of words like "Gallipoli" and "Boche" "which affected
her so strongly, who had nothing to do with what they stood
for" (*MQ*, 25). Throughout her life Martha remains conscious

---

[4] Frederic Stern, "The Changing 'Voice' of Lessing's Characters: From Politics to Sci Fi," *World Literature Written in English* 21, no. 3 (1982): 463.

of the distance of official written history from her own experience. She and her friends in London, for example, are firmly convinced that anything learned in school "under the heading of history, or art, or literature, was particularly dangerous, since by definition it couldn't be true—was necessarily the product of derivative minds representing temporary academic attitudes congealed into temporarily rigid formulas" (*FGC*, 376, 377). History, written by victors, necessarily excludes the victim; the "history" of Zambesia is that of its "white occupation" (*L*, 245). Even Johnny Lindsay, who has given his life to leftist causes, refers to labor history as the struggle of white miners against "their government," and has no answer to the black man who asks when his people "enter the picture" (*L*, 126). In the colony "desperate Mashona had fought the raiding Matabele" only to die nameless: "a few of the corpses had been white, with names that appeared in history books and on monuments" (*L*, 134).

If official histories are exclusive, popular history is mythic, legendary. With no distant past of their own, the colonists transform recent history into "the fabulous past of kaffir wars, and pioneers, and violence. How exciting life must have been then, sighed the people in the district, remembering their distant origins—and yet the district had not been settled much more than thirty years" (*MQ*, 45). Even the present is susceptible of being mythicized, for such is the power of words to transform its relation to the past. Martha, arriving in London, is struck by the poverty of the working classes and the persistence of the class system, although the radio and newspapers suggest that she is "in the middle of the Russian revolution." She concludes that "this was a country absorbed in myth . . . nothing was as it was described—as if a spirit of rhetoric . . . had infected everything, made it impossible for any fact to be seen straight" (*FGC*, 16). The origins of Nicky's Committee of a Hundred "were already swallowed in myth" within a few months, and Lessing asks rhetorically, "what event does not get swallowed in lies and half-truths within weeks?" (*FGC*, 378).

Lessing's rejection of all available versions of the past goes further than that of any of the other writers we have seen because it is connected to her heroine's rejection of the versions of female life provided by literature and society. Especially in *A Proper Marriage*, Lessing figures the education of her heroine as a radical rejection of everything she has been taught. Her disillusionment with Douglas and the crystallization of her previously vague sense of racial injustice are linked together in this process. Long before her actual separation from him, "that image of a lover that a woman is offered by society . . . had divorced itself from Douglas, like the painted picture of a stencil floating off paper in water" (*PM*, 27). Literature does not describe the concerns about which she and Alice and Stella speak: "women in literature were still what men, or the men-women," wished they were (*PM*, 62). Her labor does not progress as "the book" (*PM*, 206) says it should, and the dominant emotion produced by caring for a small child, "boredom like an illness" (*PM*, 206), is suppressed by everyone Martha knows. The novels and diaries Martha reads seem to imply that women do not mind being trapped in small rooms with small children: "Do you suppose they didn't tell the truth, the novelists?" (*PM*, 205).

Gradually Martha comes to associate the lies that shape women's roles with wartime propaganda and the rhetoric of officially sponsored racism, and comes to discern that they serve the same faceless masters. Young men go off to die in bombers; they become "Knights of the Air"; "certain poets were partly responsible for this charming figure—the newspapers are not to blame for everything" (*PM*, 162). Since the voice of authority in Lessing is always "anonymous" (*PM*, 92) it is difficult to say who is behind it all—presumably a conglomerate of white male business interests—but on the eve of her separation from Douglas, Martha realizes that newspapers and husbands speak the same way:

> She was considering such questions as, What did the state of self-displaying hysteria Douglas was in have in common with the shrill, maudlin self-pity of a leader in the *Zambesia News* when it was complaining that the outside world did not understand the sacri-

fices the white population made in developing the blacks? For
there was a connection, she felt. Not in her own experience, nor
in any book, had she found the state Douglas was now in. Yet precisely that same note was struck in every issue of the local newspapers—goodness betrayed, self-righteousness on exhibition,
heartless enemies discovered everywhere. (*PM*, 334)

This "*Zambesia News*," run in the interests of white mine
owners, continues in the remaining African volumes to represent the ability of the press to manipulate public opinion. A
meeting between whites and Africans in which Labour Party
members urge blacks to form trade unions engenders the
headline "Agitators Inciting Africans to Revolt" (*RS*, 225).[5]
Throughout the General Strike of 1948, the "violent and ex-
clamatory newspapers" carry exhortations "to keep calm and
use moderation, under enormous headlines of Strike, Total
Strike, National Strike, Threat, Danger, Alarm" (*L*, 253, 254).
In *The Four-Gated City* Lessing pillories the English newspapers that inflame the Cold War; Miles Tangin, the reporter
who hounds the Coldridges after Colin's defection and Sarah's
suicide, is easily the most repellant character in the whole series. But newspapers can only manipulate people because
they have too little memory to see the inconsistencies that
Martha discerns when she goes through the issues of the *Zambesia News* for 1940–1942 and sees that the Russians have
been transformed from "dastardly and vicious criminals" into
"a race of battling giants" (*PM*, 278). By 1956 people at dinner
parties are making remarks that had been treasonable as recently as a year ago, for "people had forgotten" (*FGC*, 295);
in America Graham Patten owes his great popularity to his
Marxism, "which had the charm of novelty, for no one could
remember hearing anything like it . . . so far behind them

[5] Murray Steele, in his "*Children of Violence* and Rhodesia: A Study of
Doris Lessing as Historical Observer" (Local Series Pamphlet no. 29, Salisbury: Central Africa Historical Association, 1974), points out that, although
Lessing's description of the African Branch controversy in *RS* is generally
"close to fact," the actual headline in the *Rhodesia Herald* for 18 February
1944 was the much blander "Native Labour Congress" (18–19).

was the age of Joe McCarthy, enormous numbers of people could not remember it, and were saying it never had happened" (*FGC*, 341). Lacking memory, the masses have always been at the mercy of history books, a "substitute" or "false" memory, "the dirty smoke left in the air after the fire of events" and are vulnerable to "the deliberate creation of false history" by totalitarian ideologies (*FGC*, 598).

If one cannot accept another's version of history, if one cannot read oneself into history, then it seems logical to try to make history oneself, to commit oneself to public action. For Martha, like her creator, who wrote the first two volumes of *Children of Violence* before she officially left the Communist Party, Marxism *is* public action. She debates radical politics with Joss and Sol Cohen in Part One of *Martha Quest*; leaves her husband for a Marxist group at the end of *A Proper Marriage*; is actively engaged in the Communist movement throughout *A Ripple from the Storm*, in which novel she marries a bona fide German Communist refugee; withdraws herself slowly from both marriage and movement in *Landlocked* and, in *The Four-Gated City*, although no longer politically active, lives out the repercussions of the defection of her employer's brother to the Soviet Union in the middle of the Cold War and remains generally more sympathetic to the Left than to the Right. Marxism, in short, is pervasive as subject matter, but *Children of Violence* itself never reads very much like a Marxist novel. Not only does its genre encourage all sorts of bourgeois individualist preoccupations—with the symptoms of Martha's pregnancy and the dissatisfactions of her sex life, her green linen dresses and the fluctuations in her weight— but its vision, necessarily limited to her experience, largely excludes blacks. That "the Africans are the proletariat of this country" but "the political structure is such that no white person can easily make contact" (*RS*, 90) is a major theme of *Ripple from the Storm*; the novel embodies the same contradiction that keeps the Communist cell segregated, and therefore ephemeral to black African experience. The cruelties, hypocrisies, and interests of the ruling class are analyzed at length, but the proletariat as a class is represented in absentia, by a handful of cooks, "boys," "nursies," by Elias the informer, and by the admirable but necessarily atypical Mr. Matushi. On her arrival in England, Martha eagerly immerses herself in working-class life, remaining long enough to realize that everything the newspapers say about it is a lie, but then immures herself in Bloomsbury for the rest of her dramatized life, where she has if possible less contact with the proletariat than she had in Africa.

The difficulty of making contact, the barriers, both literal and figurative, that thwart the attempts of Lessing's more dedicated Communists, such as Jimmy Jones, to join the African masses seem to arise whenever her characters attempt to move to the center of political or historical activity. In the early novels, many of her characters are displaced persons, exiles and refugees; in *The Four-Gated City* madwomen and psychics replace them. In Zambesia, everyone knows that he or she is at several removes from European history; even the perfect Zambesian civil servant, Douglas Knowell, longs to go north to fight in the war and is desolated when an ulcer sends him home. Thomas Stern briefly achieves his dream of joining history when he goes to fight for Israel, but comes back to die of blackwater fever on the Zambesi river. If even the men largely experience history as ripples from a storm, certainly a young provincial woman has little chance of sailing into its eye.

For Martha, Zambesia's tiny Communist party at first represents not only freedom from traditional female roles but participation in history. When the party finally dwindles into herself and three other members, Martha feels "cut off from everything that had fed her imagination: until this moment she had been part of the grandeur of the struggle in Europe, part of the Red Army, the guerrillas in China, the French underground, and the partisans in Italy, Yugoslavia and Greece" (*RS*, 278). The reader, more modestly, senses that she has been temporarily cut off from committee meetings, bicycle trips to the Coloured Quarter, and occasions for peddling *The Watchdog*. For politics never inscribe themselves in the novel as anything larger than the tedious power-jockeying that goes on between Anton and the RAF members. The language of political meetings is a language cut off from ordinary discourse; as Piet du Preez says, "when I go to one of the union meetings from one of our meetings, I'm scared stiff I might use some of the bloody jargon by accident—they'd think I'd gone off my rocker" (*RS*, 278). It is a language divorced not only from ordinary people but from its speaker's intentions: "Martha did not listen to what was being said: the shortest acquaintance with politics should be enough to teach anyone that listening to the words people use is the longest way around to an understanding of what is going on" (*RS*, 13). Given the alienation inherent in their own use of language, the Zambesian communists inevitably live in a fantasy world, refusing, for example, to look into Solly's charges (*RS*, 82) that Stalin is responsible for the murder of several hundred Soviet Army officers. Martha can only see Stalinist atrocities after the virtual demise of the group, when she has begun to adopt a new standard of truth. Reading a Russian prison memoir "was her first experience . . . of using a capacity she had not known existed. She thought: I *feel* the book is true" (*L*, 222).

Disillusioned with the masculine abstraction and hermetic logic of Communism, Martha has begun a long journey into the intuitive and irrational. Her comrade Marie had been ridiculed for making a similar statement in a debate about the impropriety of a Communist's involvement with the coloured population: "her husband, Piet, who had been grinning throughout this exchange, now let out a great laugh, and said: 'Women. She *feels* it is wrong, and so that's enough' " (*RS*, 91). The Zambesian Communist party, indeed, has proven to have relatively little sympathy for women, as the female comrades frequently observe (*PM*, 316; *RS*, 57, 99, 100, 134, 135). Marriage with Anton Hesse means finding again in a remarriage with a radical all the platitudes of marriage to a civil servant, dealing "with all the practical details of life" (*RS*, 205). The conceptions of the family she draws from Communism reinforce in her what she comes later to regard as the "mad" (*FGC*, 69) decision to leave her daughter, Caroline: "we abolished the family. In our minds. And when the war was over and there was Communism everywhere, the family would be abolished" (*FGC*, 70).

Marxism thus critically fails to bring Martha into the center of historical activity and misleads her about her personal life. Its ideology does not fit her experience, but neither does it seem to fit the experience of other, male characters. Real choices do not seem to be made in terms that Communists use, as we see in the case of Anton Hesse. His relentlessly analytical mind, his narrow devotion to the line from Moscow, his eagerness to see that every step of a procedure is followed correctly make him, for a time, an excellent Communist. Yet, when the war ends, the petit-bourgeois in him, visible earlier only in the ugliness of his furniture, makes him the ideal employee and future son-in-law of a businessman. Wherever any character is explored in depth, his or her choices prove to have little relation to their overt ideological content: when Thomas Stern goes off to fight for Israel, he has really gone "to get his own back on Sergeant Tressell" (*L*, 194).

For Doris Lessing, the failure of Communism to lead Martha Quest into the center of meaningful activity is emblematic of the failure of all well-intentioned political ideologies and not of any particular inadequacy of Marxism. Although she sees the repressions of the Right as being real enough, and is able to describe quite vividly the English Red-baiting during the early 1950s, the Left, as she depicts it, has no real impact. The dedication of Johnny Lindsay and the heroism of Mrs. Van leave southern Africa as racist as ever; *The Four-Gated City* makes much, as we have seen, of the persistence of class division in England and minimizes or ignores such mitigations in the lot of working people as National Insurance or free university education. It is generally heartening, Lessing seems to say, but finally useless that in 1956 the Hungarians said no to the Soviet Union and the British said no to Anthony Eden. It is charming that a young mother holds up a sign that reads "Caroline Says No," but "Mark, Lynda, Martha . . . sat quietly together, three middle-aged people with nothing in their experiences of the world to help them to faith in the utility of Caroline's saying no" (*FGC*, 413). By ending her novel with

an unspecified nuclear accident that makes England uninhabitable, Lessing guarantees that antinuclear protest will seem
as futile, in her novel, as peaceful protest against the racial
policies of Rhodesia and South Africa in the 1940s.

For, in spite of Lenin's cry that "men make their history"
(*RS*, 62), in *Children of Violence* history never seems to be
made by identifiable people. One notices that even in the
early volumes many of the commanding personalities of the
war years—Hitler, for example, or De Gaulle, or Churchill—
are scarcely mentioned, while Stalin's name, more frequently
mentioned, is a mere barometer of the times: Anton refuses
to speak to Martha for days after she calls that glorious leader
"Uncle Joe." In the last volume Lessing seems close to accepting the reactionary Mr. Maynard's view: " 'What is history? A record of misery, brutality and stupidity. That's all.
That's all it will ever be. What does it matter who runs a country? It's always a bunch of knaves administering a pack of
fools' " (*RS*, 54). For no matter how strongly Martha continues to protest against Mr. Maynard's disbelief, irony, and rid-
icule (*FGC*, 558), the narrator tells us straight out that "the
history of the twentieth century as far as we've got with it is
of sudden eruptions of violent mass feeling, like red-hot lava,
that destroy everything in its path—First World War, Fas-
cism, Communism, Second World War" (*FGC*, 480). As Mr.
Maynard might ask, does it matter which mass eruption? It is
clear, as Jean Bethke Elshtain argues, that by 1969 for Lessing
"there are no transformative possibilities within history; thus
no set of partial solutions or less-than-total responses can meet
the dimensions of the apocalyptic reality she sees."[6]

If attempts to engage and act in historical reality are always
doomed to failure, if one is seemingly as far from the centers
of power, as "landlocked," in Bloomsbury as in Zambesia /
Rhodesia, then perhaps it is the frantic struggle for engagement that is wrong. Perhaps our historicity and our relation
to our own time are already in us. This view, which Lessing

[6] "A Controversy on Language and Politics I: The Post-*Golden Notebook*
Fiction of Doris Lessing," *Salmagundi* 47–48 (Winter–Spring 1980): 97.

adopts on a mystical, apocalyptic level at the end of *The Four-Gated City*, is one the series examines in more traditional ways in its earlier volumes. The first glimpses of Martha in adolescence suggest that Lessing had intended her to be fully grounded in history, with attitudes determined by and representative of a particular time and place: "She was adolescent, and therefore bound to be unhappy; British, and therefore uneasy and defensive; in the fourth decade of the twentieth century, and therefore inescapably beset with problems of race and class; female, and obliged to repudiate the shackled women of the past" (*MQ*, 8). Now this sentence has its ironies: in the first place, it is attributed to authors Martha has been reading and whom she accepts uncritically, and in the second, it represents a level of consciousness that she has not yet earned. The "shackled women of the past" will be meaningless until she too has been tied to a small child and a boorish husband. But still Martha does act as a kind of world-historical female, and at times with a rueful consciousness of doing so; for example, to Mr. Maynard she explains her first marriage by saying "the international situation positively demands it of us" (*PM*, 58).

In *Landlocked*, the relationship between a person and his or her time is more complicated. Characters are not so much doomed to act out, in miniature, the crises of their time, as to be its victims. When Thomas and Martha discuss Maisie, whose first two husbands were both killed in the war and whose third, a Scotsman, went home without her at the war's end, they know that this young woman's life has been wrenched out of shape by distant events: "She saw Maisie, if there had not been a war: married to her first husband. . . . Soon she would have been a fat middle-aged woman with reserves of lazy good nature, and spoiled children. . . . Instead . . . she was sleeping with men from the bar, and probably for money" (*L*, 158). The author *says* much the same about Anton Hesse, "linked with the fate of his country so deeply and by so many fibres that the cataclysm which had engulfed Germany had also engulfed him who had fled from it and had been living so many thousands of miles away" (*L*, 216). Perhaps going into business and marrying the boss's daughter is for him as grave a transformation as Maisie's drift toward prostitution, but his character is seen so much from the outside that it is difficult to know. More deeply disturbing as history's victims are the Jewish refugees, Thomas Stern and Sarah Coldridge. Both have escaped the crematoriums and typhus of the European camps but die abroad the deaths the Nazis had planned for them. Sarah gasses herself in the oven of her flat in Cambridge and Thomas dies of blackwater in an African village where he had gone into a self-imposed exile: "what else had he been wanting," Martha thinks, "but to die, futilely, away from his own people, and among strangers?" (*L*, 248).

More problematic is the kind of historical determination suggested by a key passage in *Landlocked* that glosses the title of the series:

> Every fibre of Martha's body, everything she thought, every movement she made, everything she was, was because she had been born at the end of one world war, and had spent all her adolescence in the atmosphere of preparations for another which had lasted five years and had inflicted such wounds on the human race that no one had any idea of what the results would be.
>
> Martha did not believe in violence. Martha was the essence of violence, she had been conceived, bred, fed and reared on violence. (*L*, 195)

The passage suggests a radical historical determinism that is not so easily documented in the text as Sarah's suicide or Maisie's promiscuity. In what sense is Martha the "essence of violence?" We never see her advocating it; she never strikes out physically at anyone, not even when Douglas takes to pummeling her; her behavior—except in relation to her mother—is impeccably civilized; she's even too polite to stop having sex with Anton. Neither her outward behavior nor her usual emotions seem to *be* violent, nor in any obvious sense caused by violence; it is quite possible in short that the passage is an instance of narrative anachronism, of the author adverting to views of her character set forth in the first volume and subsequently dropped. The power of this conception of Martha as a historically determined character can be seen rather in the force with which Lessing battles against it in the last volume of her series.

The Four-Gated City is a passionate attack on history that, as the first four volumes demonstrate, ignores, lies about, and victimizes most of the human race, but is felt to do so with particular force by women. In *The Four-Gated City*, the difficulties of understanding and affecting public life extend even to men born at the center of the British Empire. In Mark Coldridge, Lessing at last introduces a sympathetic member of the British ruling classes; in his brother Colin, an Alan Nunn May figure, she introduces the only character in her series who corresponds closely to a well-known public figure. Colin, a Cambridge physicist working on the bomb, defects to the Soviet Union at the height of the Cold War; his wife immediately commits suicide, leaving their son for Mark to raise. Everyone in the Coldridge family comes under intense suspicion in an England that is starting to behave like a client of the United States. Badgered by journalists, hard-pressed financially, Mark nearly goes mad: "The gap between what a Coldridge believed was possible and what was happening had widened to the point that he was in a kind of collapse" (*FGC*, 167). Mark repeats some of Martha's struggles to make sense of the world; he goes through a Marxist phase, "using language identical with hers of ten years ago" (*FGC*, 183); Martha "watche[s] Mark as if she were watching her own young self" (*FGC*, 186). Yet Communism "had never gone deep" (*FGC*, 214); and with Stalin's death, Mark becomes disillusioned and emerges essentially unchanged. Years later, he goes to Moscow, where he confronts the brother whose dramatic defection has caused him so much grief, and meets only a self-satisfied, thoroughly apolitical scientist and family man "in whose life there appeared to be a gulf which made irrelevant anything that happened before" (*FGC*, 330). Evidently those born to rule, and those who actually act on the world's history, understand it no better than the powerless.

Mark's study becomes the physical symbol of his most dramatic attempt to understand the world. On its walls and ceiling he copies random pieces of information from newspapers; these are marked with colored stars and triangles that connect them to each other and to observations made by Lynda, his schizophrenic wife; a "fifth wall" consists of entries from a diary kept by Lynda's equally mad roommate that detail the domestic frustrations of modern life: rude and inefficient workmen, appliances that break the first time they are used. Clearly Lessing believes that Mark, striving for a whole picture that makes concealed connections and acknowledges the force of the irrational, is constructing the only valid history of the recent past. Such a history suggests no clear line of present action. Martha, Mark, Francis, and Paul go into the study to think, waiting to learn what to do. To a young man who argues that stating the problem is not enough, Lynda suggests that the answer lies in developing paranormal powers: going beyond acknowledging that one's thoughts influence other people to learn to control the nature of the influence, "so that ripples go out exactly as one foresaw" (*FGC*, 443). Mark, however, is a rational creature committed to action and ill-suited for parapsychology; appropriately he spends the years after England's collapse running a refugee camp in Africa, that is, applying traditional humane solutions to problems that largely defy them.

In a panel discussion following *The Day After*, the 1983 television movie about survivors of a nuclear war, Elie Wiesel commented that the straggling lines of hollow-cheeked fugitives looked strangely familiar, as if the whole world had become Jewish. When Mark Coldridge reenacts Martha's frustrations at being unable to understand or influence history, we see how far the men who traditionally ruled England have been brought to the condition of women. The history of their own time is alien; its outcome is determined by men in other countries armed to the teeth with an incomprehensible technology; the truth is never told in public. This deep pessimism—who'd be a woman?, as Maisie McGrew used to say— is offset for Lessing and her characters by a growing sense of the possibilities of the irrational. In isolation, passivity, and madness are answers that public life never provides; the mad-woman in the basement is the real seer: "if society is so organized, or rather has so grown, that it will not admit what one knows to be true, will not admit it, that is, except as it comes out perverted, through madness, then it is through madness and its variants it must be sought after" (*FGC*, 375). Defeated at every attempt to connect meaningfully with the world of public events, the heroine explores her unconscious mind and discovers that history is already there.

Early in *The Four-Gated City* Martha resists Mark's argument that at some time in the future the moral terms in which we regard the Second World War will come to seem irrelevant: people will simply say, "War expressed itself thus and thus in the years between 1939 and 1945" (*FGC*, 132). Martha at that stage still believes that it matters whether or not one fought Hitler. But later it is not so easy to be sure, so convinced has she become that everyone has a Whitmanian capacity for containing worlds and that emotions are external forces, wavelengths, into which we tune. When she deliberately drives herself mad, she finds herself "sounding like Goebbels": "I am what the human race is. I am 'the Germans are the mirror and catalyst of Europe' and also: 'Dirty Hun, Filthy Nazi' " (*FGC*, 539). The real Goebbels perhaps only did not know that one "can choose to be them ['the subhuman creatures"] or not" (*FGC*, 551).

At the end of the novel proper, Martha sets out for a walk and finds herself asking "Where? But *where*. . . . Here, where else, you fool, you poor fool, where else has it been, ever" (*FGC*, 591). "It" has no clear referent, but a wide scope—truth, perhaps. The earnest young girl on the veld, reading for life; the tired young wife in the stifling meeting room; the efficient matron charged with all the functions of a house in Bloomsbury and the happiness of its tenants: these Marthas have learned too well that history makes no account of them. Very well, then, they will abolish history, they will internalize the world, they will tell its story as their own story, foretell its future under their own signs of passivity and anguish.

The Appendix is that foretelling, an undramatized essay in the form of news reports, memos, and letters, the old science fiction device of the history of the future. Its burden is that a "Catastrophe," a nuclear accident of some unspecified kind, has left England uninhabitable. The Catastrophe had been predicted by Lynda Coldridge, who had a vision of England looking "like a poisoned mouse lying dead in a corner" (*FGC*, 566) but of course such schizoid premonitions are not the basis of public policy. Millions died; the survivors are scattered around the world, which has been divided into large Orwellian zones. The picture of huge populations dying of bubonic plague in camps, surrounded by their monstrously deformed children, has its terrors, as does the image of sinister world governments already engaged in acquiring dossiers on their citizens and writing lying histories of the Catastrophe.

Yet, for all these terrors the underlying fantasy of nuclear survival is a consoling one, especially as described in Martha's letters from a small Scottish (*FGC*, 634) or Irish (*FGC*, 639) island where a group of seventy-three leads an arcadian life, growing crops and wearing "good sheepskin clothes" (*FGC*, 640). Their own mutants are superior beings, more highly evolved "Guardians" whose kind will one day inherit the earth. Part of their superiority lies in their instinctive understanding of the horrors of the past, which makes them invulnerable to the propaganda already being written on the mainland: "they are beings who include . . . history in themselves and who have transcended it" (*FGC*, 647). One is doubtless intended to rejoice that just before her death Martha manages to send one of these little prodigies to Francis Coldridge in Africa.

On those of us who have little faith in the evolution of the race through radiological mutation, the optimism of Lessing's ending is lost. We reject her telepaths and Memories, diagnose them as the schizophrenics their psychiatrists always told them they were, go on speaking in our small personal voices and believing that our emotions and moral decisions are meaningful. But Lessing's apocalypse continues to haunt and anger. For women, whose history in this century is a long struggle to move to the center of politics, to speak and be heard, to act and see the public consequences of one's acts, it is galling to be told that Mrs. Quest, resentfully lighting another cigarette while the radio crackles on about distant catastrophes, is a true image of our relation to history. For men, it must be unthinkable. A dozen liberal reasonable arguments against that image leap to mind and we can scarcely forgive ourselves if, huddled around our television sets, tuned to the news from Chernobyl, we momentarily think that there might, after all, be something to it.

CHAPTER EIGHT

Anthony Burgess's *The End of the World News*

MOST contemporary British historical fiction seems to be about the end of a world, whether of Anglo-Ireland or Anglo-India or even, in Doris Lessing, contemporary England. As its title indicates, Anthony Burgess's *The End of the World News* goes a step further, envisioning the destruction of the earth and the death of human culture; more centrally, it envisions the obliteration of virtually every aspect of the historical past and the reduction, in some imagined future, of the few remaining shreds of collective memory into kitsch. To imagine a time when all of human history has been reduced to two video cassettes—one a television docudrama about the life of Sigmund Freud, the other a musical comedy about Leon Trotsky's visit to New York in 1917—is to evoke farce. Yet, Burgess's novel is also metaphor, a vehicle for exploring the anxiety he shares with many of his contemporaries who believe that interplanetary catastrophe is not a necessary prelude to wholesale disregard for the contingent, linear, unrepeatable contents of the past. Were we to lose our archives— the Liberty Bell, the text of Louis XIV's will, the bed in which Van Gogh slept—our history would not, says Claude Lévi-Strauss, cease to exist, but it "would be exhibited in synchrony" (*SM*, 242). In *The End of the World News* Burgess arranges that exhibit, displays the cold inadequacies of a view of the world in which the present is seen spatially, as a set of self-contained relationships, and not in any significant sense as a product of the past.

Generically, we are inclined to regard the end of the world as belonging to visionary literature or science fiction; Burgess asks us, however, to see it as a subject for historical fiction.

The elusive "present" of the narrative is actually a "future perfect"; in the epilogue we discover that one of the three stories we have just read—the one about the destruction of the earth by the runaway planet Lynx in 2,000 A.D.—has been told in a spaceship to a group of schoolchildren whose ancestors were its central characters. We also discover at the end that the work's other two stories—a "novelization" of the life of Freud and the musical comedy about Trotsky—are transcriptions of the only other remaining narratives of human history, remembered because the spaceship's first captain was a friend to the actor who starred in them and had preserved tapes recording the television performances of those stories. Naturally such tapes have no literary merit and only limited claims to historical accuracy; naturally, too, the children of the future can scarcely understand them at all. Like *The Red and the Green* or *The Big Chapel*, *The End of the World News* is not so much "about" the past as it is about the need to recognize how limited our knowledge of it really is and to become more conscious and critical of the habits of perception that influence our understanding of both past and present. To these general concerns of the "other" historical novel Burgess adds a more specific concern with the relationship between high and low culture, with the tendency to spatialize history that may well be a common bond between television programming and, say, the works of Lévi-Strauss.

As is appropriate for a novel concerned with spatialized history, *The End of the World News* is from beginning to end an assault on historical chronology. The three stories spliced together to make the novel interrupt each other almost randomly; Freud's story is not presented sequentially, but in flashbacks; besides, the foreword and epilogue offer two different levels of "present" narrative time. The foreword is in fact a serious introduction to many of the novel's themes. Writing with stolid pedantry, "John B. Wilson, B.A." claims to have found the manuscript in the bathroom of its author's home. Geppert has noted how in Wilhelm Raabe's *Das Odfeld* a discussion of antiquated documents, ostensibly intended to authenticate the novel's historical claims, has the opposite effect, calling attention to its fictiveness, and to the time gap that separates novel and event, by means of elaborate descriptions of the physical characteristics of the documents.[1] Quite in keeping with this technique, "Wilson" (Burgess's real name) makes free with otherwise irrelevant detail: "There seemed . . . a double unity—that of the typeface (Olivetti STUDIO 45) and that of the typing paper (Gevafax 70)" (*EWN*, viii). Like Vladimir Nabokov's Charles Kinbote, Wilson views his subject through the distorting lenses of temperamental incompatibility, with a mixture of reverence and contempt; and, as in *Pale Fire*, commentary threatens to overwhelm text. The dreadful style with which Wilson characterizes the novel as "sub-literary" introduces the theme of language as a barrier to understanding. People who write the way he does are incapable of understanding vulgar jokes; solemnly, he reports having discovered the manuscript "packed in a shopping bag marked boldly UPIM, this being the name of a celebrated Italian chain store" (*EWN*, viii). Anachronism—in the age of plastic bags one does not discover manuscripts—and incomprehension, but these may be the point. Regrettably, it is from Wilson's clumsy hands that we must snatch whatever straws of interpretation the foreword can provide. From him we learn that the novel's technique was inspired by a photograph of Jimmy Carter watching three television sets simultaneously, and that the late novelist was much interested in the musicalization of fiction. Wilson reproduces a letter in which the author says that the "greatest events of the past century" were "the discovery of the unconscious by Sigmund Freud, the Trotskian doctrine of world socialism, and the invention of the space rocket" (*EWN*, x). Finally, we are informed of the author's belief that: "You can take your choice of time and space. In matters of history, you can't have both, especially if you're German. Young K, a German, thinks me more capable of Nazi sentiments than himself, because I was brought up in the Nazi period" (*EWN*, ix).

[1] *Der "andere" historische Roman*, 46.

Given these alternatives, the novel will, in effect, choose space over time, subsuming the unique and unrepeatable to the elements of a timeless pattern or—as Wilson's younger brother might say—replacing diachrony with synchrony.

This assault on chronology is carried on all three narrative channels, but in each case the technique is different. We can begin where the novel proper begins, with the Sigmund Freud story. Anachronisms in this story are fairly subtle and the genre ("novelization," as of a reasonably upscale television serial) is only partly at odds with the subject matter. Even if Irving Stone had not schooled us to accept the elements of romantic, soft-core sensational fiction in the great man's life, the novelistic qualities of Freud's *Interpretation of Dreams* and the therapeutic significance of narrative would have broken down our resistance to the form. To the extent that novelizing Freud's life means putting the ideas back into the context of ordinary life, it is an imitation of his own technique. The humor in Freud's mother urging him to eat more chicken (" 'Let me cut you a nice piece of the breast' " [*EWN*, 84]), or of his wife pointing out the fantastic element in the early sexual traumas of his patients (" 'If she only imagines she killed her mother, why can't she imagine that horrible disgusting business with her father?' " [*EWN*, 80]) is only vaguely demystifying. Blatant anachronism is rare enough, a matter perhaps of Freud's ignoring the "Freudianism" of his wife's criticism of his smoking (*EWN*, 81). More often the author relies on the reader's extratextual knowledge to underscore the difference between Freud's perspective and ours. "Never, never, never, Jung is a good Freudian" (*EWN*, 258), like the observation that "Nuremberg is a city of . . . tolerance" (*EWN*, 221), gains irony only from hindsight. Perhaps because novelization risks being almost too congenial to his subject, Burgess keeps the language barrier high, virtually insisting on the anomaly of an English-speaking Vienna. The Freud story begins with long passages of dialogue between Ernest Jones and various Nazi officials that take place in German with English summaries labeled "subtitles" (*EWN*, 4). German phrases and frequent references to translation underscore this sense of the inadequacy of English to this story.

This sense of inadequacy to historical truth is developed in other ways. Most of the story is presented in a series of flashbacks, the memories of a dying old man whose life's work testifies to the disguises the past takes in the service of the needs. "How can we trust memory? Was it really like that?" he asks, and the reader shares his concern (*EWN*, 143). The narrator is willing to agree with his character that the story is to some extent provisional. Anna Freud, leaving her Gestapo interrogators, sees a "*Stürmer* nose . . . thrust into a dish of *Schlagobers*. No, no, but it could have happened" (*EWN*, 17). At the beginning at least one obvious literary influence reminds the reader of a cultural as well as linguistic barrier between author and subject. Ernest Jones acquires more than a touch of Lucky Jim and of John Lewis, the hero of *That Uncertain Feeling*: he smiles "something filthy in Welsh" (*EWN*, 4) at an uncomprehending Nazi, tells an "SA swine what he was in tuneful Welsh and what his Fuhrer was too" (*EWN*, 5). To his mind, a Nazi band plays "very four-square music . . . like a speeded-up Bread from Evans's" (*EWN*, 12). Even Freud appears to have read about the Welch's house party: as Jung laughs disdainfully at his suggestion that they have supper, he wonders "if the word had perhaps a special obscene meaning in the German of Zürich" (*EWN*, 170).

As Burgess tells the Freud story, there is much that will strike the reader as bizarre or improbable. One's usual responses to terminal cancer and Nazis are constantly diverted by jokes: German compounds, for example, keep getting longer, until Freud on the verge of leaving Vienna is informed that he must pay an exit tax called the "*Unbedenklichkeitserklärung*" (*EWN*, 10). Recuperating from cancer surgery, he begins to hemorrhage and owes his life to his roommate, a "cretinous dwarf" (*EWN*, 303). Asked to sign a statement that the Nazis have treated him fairly, Freud has the improbable no-blindfold-please courage and wit to append, "I can heartily recommend the Gestapo to anyone" (*EWN*, 19). In transit to London, he opens a letter from Samuel Goldwyn offering him one hundred thousand dollars to take charge of a series of films about the great lovers of the past (*EWN*, 203).

But what strikes the reader as improbable is in fact historically true. Although everything in the novel's tone suggests that the four details noted above are comic inventions, a reading of Jones's biography of Freud will confirm them all, even to the spelling of *Unbedenklichkeitserklärung*.[2] Jones's Freud, like Burgess's, complains of the inaccessibility of U.S. toilets,[3] and the obsession with meeting trains early, which Burgess makes much of, has its roots in real life, although Jones's Freud wishes only to be one hour, rather than two hours, early. So given were the early psychoanalysts to enacting their own theories that Freud twice fainted in Jung's presence while Otto Rank, shortly after learning about Freud's cancer, burst into a "fit of hysterical laughter" at the mention of his name.[4] Seen in this context, even the cheapest of Burgess's inventions, "You're a freud, Dr. Fraud," acquires an unexpected plausibility (*EWN*, 102).

Burgess has, in short, been willing to exaggerate a little, but not much. The comic texture of the Freud story owes much more to careful selection of the bizarre or unflattering (one would scarcely wish one's biographer to immortalize one's views on public toilets, whatever their correctness) than to outright invention. This selectivity keeps Freud from seeming awesome, and the quarrels with heretics who refuse to accept the sexual etiology of the neuroses are as tiresome in the novel as they are in the biography. Nonetheless, Burgess's Freud remains sympathetic, while his Jung, on the other hand, is a caricature from the beginning. Transposed in the novel into a speech before jack-booted Nazis, Jung's 1934 essay, "The Present State of Psychoanalysis" is more chilling

[2] Ernest Jones, *The Life and Work of Sigmund Freud*, ed. Lionel Trilling and Steven Marcus (London: Hogarth, 1961). "Unbedenklichkeitserklärung" (516); "cretinous dwarf" (439); "I can heartily recommend" (518); Sam Goldwyn (453). The Goldwyn incident, however, occurred in 1925.

[3] Ibid., 269.

[4] Ibid., 11; 266; 441.

than ever, and explains Freud's sense of betrayal: " 'In my opinion, it has been a grave error in medical psychology up to now to apply Jewish categories indiscriminately to German . . . Christians' " (*EWN*, 322).[5] "Novelized," Freud's theories seem even more intimately connected to his own psyche; in a dream he ends a ringing denunciation of women, who " 'have made few contributions to the discoveries and inventions of civilization,' " with a plaintive " 'Is that all right, momma?' " (*EWN*, 344) The long struggle with cancer is faithfully transposed, prosthetic "Monster" and all; one has only to bring oneself to compare Burgess's treatment with Stone's sentimentalization to see how much more moving is a death accompanied by indignity ("a boiled egg for dinner and you dribble most of it through your nose," his personified cancer tells him, [*EWN*, 307]) than is the ecstatic agony of a genius. Overdosed with morphine, Burgess's Freud goes to his death dreaming of his mother: "A small naked child crawled out of the light and into the comforting darkness" (*EWN*, 368). It would be a hard-hearted person indeed who would wish to refute the death wish.

Burgess has in effect defamiliarized Freud; selectivity and exaggeration have produced such an *irréalisation* of the biography that most readers are likely to confuse fact with invention. At the same time, much of the larger historical context of Freud's life—the medical theories of his day, for example,

[5] "Meines Erachtens ist es ein schwerer Fehler der bisherigen medizinischen Psychologie gewesen, dass sie jüdische Kategorien, die nicht einmal für alle Juden verbindlich sind, unbesehen auf den christlichen Germanen . . . verwandte." "Zur gegenwärtigen Lage der Psychotherapie," in *Zivilisation im Ubergang* (Olten: Walter, 1974), 191. Note that Burgess omits the qualifying phrase, "die nicht einmal für alle Juden verbindlich sind" (which are not even applicable to all Jews). Similarly, Burgess quotes the phrase, "the Aryan unconscious has a higher potential than the Jewish," without noting that this higher potential results in Jung's view from the Aryan's closeness to barbarism: "Das arische Unbewusste hat ein höheres Potential als das jüdische; das ist der Vorteil und der Nachteil einer dem Barbarischen noch nicht völlig entfremdeten Jugendlichkeit" (The Aryan unconscious has a higher potential than the Jewish; that is the advantage and the disadvantage of a youthfulness that is still not fully estranged from barbarism) (191).

or the Jewish culture of Central Europe as more than family life à la Dan Greenberg—is effaced. It is consistent with this displacement of context that Burgess's Freud is frequently seen on trains, or as a visitor or refugee in English-speaking countries. Burgess's emphasis on Freud's identification with Oedipus, Moses, and Hannibal similarly takes him out of his historical context. But the full consequences of this treatment of Freud cannot be assessed until we examine the other two stories with which his story intersects.

To "novelize" Freud's life is no very radical distortion, as we have seen. Yet, as a vehicle for the life of Trotsky, the musical comedy can only compete in a demolition derby. The genre itself is frivolous, antirealistic, in a word, bourgeois— and besides, Burgess travesties it so well. There are *Fiddler on the Roof* evocations of Trotsky's childhood, for example: "Yanovka, Yanovka, where the hunter wound his horn / And the undulant gold corn / Was house high" (*EWN*, 105). One doesn't need a score to sing along with the following duet: "Trotsky: Caviar with blinis / Means slaughtering a fish. Olga: I'd rather feed on wienies . . . Trotsky (fiercely): *Chilled* caviar. *Hot* wienies" (*EWN*, 93). The chorus of "We're having a socialist party" rings in the ears (*EWN*, 151). As if the genre itself were not enough to trivialize any topic, the setting also detracts from Trotsky's stature: as Tom Stoppard was not the first to realize, there is something comic as well as pathetic in the image of Lenin at the Zürich Public Library, Marx at the British Museum, or Trotsky in New York. As in the Freud section, Burgess calls attention to the fact that the central figures in the story were not native speakers of English, although with an even broader appeal to the English speaker's instinctive feeling that foreign languages are inherently funny: no wonder Olga Lunacharskaya prefers to be called plain Olga Mooney.

Whereas the Freud story adheres relatively closely to known fact, although always self-conscious enough about its distortions, the Trotsky comedy has little regard for historical fact. It is true that Trotsky visited New York before the revolution, living in an apartment on 164th Street for which he paid eighteen dollars a month, including his first telephone. Like Burgess's Trotsky he tried to organize American workers and dissuade them from fighting in the First World War; Robert Payne's book on Trotsky also tells the charming story of how Trotsky's son got lost trying to satisfy a curiosity natural enough in a resident of 164th Street: he wanted to find out if "there was a 1st Street."[6] The rest, however, is pure invention, replete with a love story; characteristically, the narrator remarks of Natalia Trotsky: "She is not at all like the historical wife of Leon Trotsky."[7] But for all its conscious travesty, trivialization, and *irréalisation*, the Trotsky story is more than farce. The very incompatibility of the genre to Trotsky's ideas is the point.

Revolution, as every early Marxist knew, was supposed to start in developed countries like the United States. As every Trotskyite knows, revolution can only be sustained in an undeveloped country like Russia, by support from more developed societies: hence, the necessity of "world socialism" (*EWN*, x) or permanent revolution. The isolation of the Soviet Union from the developed world in the 1920s and 30s thus explains the failure of the revolution and the devolution into Stalinism. In Burgess's version, failure to revolutionize comfortable American workers (never mind what sweatshops were like in 1917; this is musical comedy) and therefore the incompatibility of his ideas with U.S. "reality," is a serious failing. Trotsky himself is partially seduced by U.S. materialism and political apathy ("I like these folks / Who like being slaves, / I like their jokes / And Gillette shaves" [*EWN*, 238]); he even betrays a human side: "The women are striking / But the workers are not / I am liking the women a lot" (*EWN*, 240). Falling in love with Olga Mooney, he is almost persuaded that lofty theories about inevitable class struggles have little to do with real musical comedy life. As Olga says " 'to some people the working class is only a kind of abstraction' " (*EWN*, 124); "you don't give a damn about people' " (*EWN*, 125).

---

[6] *The Life and Death of Trotsky* (New York: McGraw-Hill, 1977), 175.
[7] Ibid., 263.

Promotion of respect for reality in a musical comedy is a tricky matter. Trotsky himself keeps coming back to the verse, "All through history / Mind limps after reality. / What is reality?" The answers change as Trotsky's affair with Olga evolves. "What's damn well there" (*EWN*, 127), an appropriate Marxist response, is replaced with something more Freudian: "I don't think I know . . . The truth may well be that the root of all human miseries and joys is / Something any good Marxist is shocked even to find himself minimally even vestigially thinking of" (*EWN*, 184). This song is still on Trotsky's lips as he sails off for revolutionary Russia (*EWN*, 381). Only the girl he leaves behind knows that there's "no such thing" as a new world: it can only come, this radical future, "The day after / the day after / the day after" (*EWN*, 381). We do not need our history books to tell us that it will all be a terrible failure. Trotsky's fate lies before him, evoked by a Mexican who comes out of nowhere to strum mournfully on his guitar: "Mexico, Mexico, / A good place to die" (*EWN*, 153, 379).

In Freud and Trotsky's stories, in varying degrees assimilated to popular literature, we have seen two of the three greatest events of the twentieth century. The third, the invention of the space rocket, has not of course had as much time to influence our culture. Burgess's author explains its significance: "physical, as opposed to merely psychological or ideational, transcendence of our dungy origins" (*EWN*, x). For the first time, one might add, it has become possible to believe that human life could survive the destruction of the planet. The third narrative channel is tuned to the depiction of that possibility as credible historical fact and, consequently, the mode of its narration is noticeably more realistic than the other two sections of the novel. Although the narrator warns his audience of unidentified children that "all this happened a long time ago . . . I am vague on detail" (*EWN*, 20), the details are nonetheless abundant—place names, brand names, lists of people, and minute descriptions of places; the narrative in this third of the novel loses its provisional tone and is more easily accepted than, for example, Sam Goldwyn's offer to Freud.

By the same token, although the anachronisms of the other two sections tend to modernize, the language of the year 2,000 is closer to that of the nineteenth century, ornate and even stuffy. The president goes on television to announce that the government of the Commonwealth of the Democratic Americas is moving to Texas: "In very crude and blotchy colour the Stars and Stripes fluttered to the blurred brass of the old song that honoured them" (*EWN*, 254). Although numerous futuristic details are evoked—blepophones, nuclear hanglines, portable artificial lungs for cancer victims, the transformation of the map of Europe into "Teutophone" and "Francophone" states—Burgess is at pains to keep the world recognizable. The name of Sixth Avenue has been changed— to Sixth Avenue (*EWN*, 161). Although the Fourth Vatican Council has abolished Roman Catholicism, essential structures remain—from the hangline over New York City one can see such sights as the Newman Tower, Patmore Center, the Scotus Complex, Paternoster Convention City, and the Tractarian Folly (*EWN*, 26). Muriel is a professor, but Fidels and Solzhenitsyns are cigars. The names of Nat Goya, Dashiell and Calvin Gropius, Zwingli Gilroy, and Wyclif Wilock testify to a certain conservatism in the late twentieth century. Assuming that the author of *A Clockwork Orange* and the script of *Quest for Fire* is acutely sensitive to such details, one notes that late-twentieth-century American English is a curious mixture of 1930s American, 1980s American, and modern British. Phrases such as "thirty dollars a day and all found" (*EWN*, 256), "to have rather a fancy to" (*EWN*, 290), "high-gloss aubergine" (*EWN*, 291), "cold roast joint" (*EWN*, 348), "air hostesses" (*EWN*, 355), and words such as "layby" (*EWN*, 308) and "arse" (*EWN*, 311) mingle indiscriminately with elevators, windshields, gasoline, johns, and more dated usages, such as "C-notes" (*EWN*, 277), "palookeroney" (*EWN*, 313), and "blubbing" (*EWN*, 329).

What results is a curious displacement of the future into the past that parallels the temporal dislocations of the historical sections of the novel. Whereas Burgess emphasizes the bizarre elements in the Freud biography and trivializes Trotsky, he establishes a more matter-of-fact tone toward the apocalyptic events of the future. It is easy to identify with the hero of this story, Val Brodie. An English professor and writer of science fiction, he nonetheless deplores the trend to replace courses in high culture—" 'Shakespeare, Milton, Harrison and Abramovitz . . . Blake and Gerard Manley Hopkins' " with science fiction, " 'a university course in, let's face it, trash' " (*EWN*, 30). The story line revolves around a government plan to build a spaceship called the *America* that will take fifty people out of the earth's atmosphere before the planet Lynx strikes; at issue is the question of who will be on the ship and how it will go about saving human culture.

Thus conceived, the plot quickly discloses an old-fashioned moral debate. According to the original plans, drawn up by Vanessa Brodie and her father, Hubert Frame, the ship is intended to carry off the best physical and mental specimens, mostly scientists capable of contributing to the ship's technology. When these people assemble at the Center for Advanced Technology (CAT) under the leadership of Maxwell Bartlett (Boss Cat), certain troubling tendencies develop. Bartlett insists that the group wear black uniforms; a cat emblem ("the symbol of a sitting cat, back view, with a single thunderbolt" [*EWN*, 359]) looms over the center, increasingly referred to as a camp. Bartlett rapidly becomes a dictator, ruthlessly crushing dissent; Nat Goya attempts to escape and, within hours, his "battered body" is "incinerated in the camp crematorium" (*EWN*, 231). Others are kept in line with drugs that abolish the literary memory along with the capacity for dissent: "*Henry V? Tom Sawyer? Portrait of a Lady?* Never heard of them" (*EWN*, 273). Thus, while Bartlett gives speeches about "our duty to salvage human knowledge" (*EWN*, 190), he is systematically destroying the conditions of humane civilization: "Justice, compassion, fairness, humour— even a modicum of decent human inefficiency" (*EWN*, 230). No doubt can remain about why the National Science group that had advised Frame in the early days was called Natsci.

Fortunately the survival of the human race is not left in the hands of Boss Cat for long—an outcome guaranteed by the condition of narrative itself, since, in a perfect Natsci state, this subversive story could never be told to children. Excluded from the survivor's list, Val Brodie meets the Rabelaisian actor Courtland Willett and endures a series of disaster-movie episodes in a flooded New York City before the two of them realize that he had predicted the location of CAT in one of his novels. Their arduous travels across a disintegrating America—in Wilcock, Missouri, the population has turned to ritual cannibalism—are matched by the efforts of Edwina Duffy Goya. Pregnant by CAT's first dissident, she is wildly in love with the electronic evangelist Calvin Gropius, whom she imagines to be her child's real father. She searches out Gropius in a frantic effort to get his help in reaching the *America*; not long after finding him, however, she realizes that her true passion is for his son Dashiell, who operates a gambling casino and has, as they say, close ties to the Mafia. In the story's climax, which evokes the penultimate scene of a James Bond movie, Val, Willett, Edwina, and company breach the barbed-wire barriers of CAT and board the spaceship. Because a revolt is already underway inside, their attempt is successful. Boss Cat's last speech, calling on his crew to fall into pre-arranged pairs for mating, has provoked hysterical laughter, and: "Laughing, it seemed, was a solvent of even the most potent chemical conditioner" (*EWN*, 333). Val Brodie replaces Bartlett as the spaceship's captain, Edwina gives birth to her miraculous son (Joshua, of course), and humanity goes off to outer space with whatever leavening a religious extremist, a gambler, and a writer of science fiction can offer a team of technical experts.

The meaning of this third story, and, in particular, the answer to the question of why the sympathetic Val Brodie insists on destroying the last Mozart tape, depends on its relationship to the other stories. The reader's experience, after all, is that of a television viewer watching three screens at once. The selection of the stories is arbitrary, whether we view them as the great events of the twentieth century or as constituting all of human history but, as Burgess has said, the discontinuity of much modern art is an illusion. Artists who claim to select elements at random are unaware that "the unconscious may well be imposing a coherence, which they're not consciously aware of." Even a newspaper, according to Burgess, is "unified by being diurnal, by saying this is what's happening today."[8] The assault on chronology and the temporal displacement that we have noted in the stories encourages the reader to impose this coherence. It is, in fact, fairly easy to identify common motifs that point to larger thematic unities.

One immediately notices, for example, the paradoxically timeless yet topical gloss that brand names contribute to all three stories: Trotsky celebrates Gillette razors; one Nazi cleans his teeth with Odol while another smokes Wahnfreud cigarettes, a joke that introduces a long series of plays with brand names of the apocalypse noted earlier. Like Freud, Hubert Frame is dying of cancer induced by compulsive smoking; his favorite brand of cough drops (Rasps Extra Strong) "bears a picture of an ancient genius coughing his heart up" (*EWN*, 23). Like Trotsky, Freud visits New York City, where Val Brodie finds himself at the beginning of his last year on earth. Freud, Trotsky, and the survivors of the human race all end up as refugees and exiles. The emphasis on foreign languages, accents, and translations—in a gross improbability Burgess depicts an American president who is actually multilingual—furthers the theme of displacement. Freud's preoccupation with Oedipus and Moses is matched by the science fiction section's concern with the Christmas story: the planet Lynx is first sighted during a Sunday School Christmas pageant, and there are several allusions to Noah and the Book of Revelations. Ernest Jones talks about his essay on Hamlet, Courtland Willett about his performance as a fat Hamlet. Bokharin "has a strong look of a younger Courtland Willett" (*EWN*, 73); as does Alfred Adler (*EWN*, 142), who also has "a most musical, Willettian voice" (*EWN*, 243).

There are explicit references to the end of the world in both

---

[8] Samuel Coale, "An Interview with Anthony Burgess," *Modern Fiction Studies* 27 (1981): 443.

the Trotsky and Freud stories. A journalist tells Trotsky that a report from Valparaiso says that " 'a planet has swum in from another galaxy. . . . It's going to collide with the earth' " (*EWN*, 338). Trotsky dismisses the report as a distraction from the "real issues": " 'There's only one world coming to an end, and we know which it is' " (*EWN*, 338). On the next page, in 1938, Freud has the same reaction to a Paris newspaper's headline about the "fin du monde": "Catchpenny nonsense. Anything to divert public attention from the real issues" (*EWN*, 339). Burgess's Freud has concentrated on the individual psyche at the expense of social reality, while Trotsky is dedicated to sublimating his private life to the needs of the working class; what unites them is a common concern with creating a *novy mir*. Like Trotsky, Freud believes that " 'if I'm right . . . the world will come to an end and then start all over again—a new world' " (*EWN*, 94). Such notions obviously link the two historical stories to the events of the year 2,000. Freud's story also provides another link; as Burgess has noted elsewhere, writers may be drawn to apocalyptic fiction because "we are all solipsists, and all die, the world dies with us. . . . Perhaps it is rage at the prospect of our end that makes us want to extrapolate them on to the swirl of phenomena outside."[9] The juxtaposition in the novel of Chamberlain's declaration of war and Freud's death to serve this function while of course remaining faithful to sober fact.

Each story is also about power, about totalitarianism and human beings who subvert it. Burgess's Trotsky may croon about the necessity of breaking eggs, but Olga explains his drive for power and fame and its necessary implications for dissenters: " 'Not just the whip to your body but the burning fire of rehabilitation. Only when a leader is dealing out punishment, comrade, does he know the real ecstasy of power' " (*EWN*, 126). Burgess's Freud, seen first as a victim of Nazi power, is later shown to have been too eager to protect his authority as the founder of psychoanalysis to listen to Adler's view that "behind sex lies power" (*EWN*, 146). Bartlett, the

---

[9] "The Apocalypse and After," *Times Literary Supplement*, 18 March 1983, 256.

dictator, would agree with Adler: "Power is the reality" (*EWN*, 271). As television viewer the reader looks from the psychoanalytic screen to the Marxist screen to the futuristic, Skinnerian screen and sees the same reality acted out in different costumes. Nazi brutishness, revolutionary violence, and the cold-blooded technological absolutism of the year 2,000 make equal claims on our attention. Since history has been so far spatialized, cause and effect seem casual matters; one might argue that Freud's insight into the mind, intended to liberate human beings, has contributed to the thought control techniques of the year 2,000, but the text does not insist on the point. Since specific historical causes of, say, Nazism or the Russian Revolution have been effaced or reduced to doggerel, what remains is a depiction of an innate craving for power that seems to characterize people in any period.

This bleak vision of transcendent evil, which Burgess's critics have learned to call Augustinian, is offset, in two of these stories, by the heroism of the central figure, and in all by the evocation of those timeless human qualities most at odds with totalitarianism. In this respect, we must note that each of the stories has some of the elements of an epic, or at least of an adventure story: trials and violence, wonders and monsters, the exhilaration of strange lands and alien people. In the year 2,000 people may fear a future "thin and mean and unloving" (*EWN*, 61), but these words describe neither their world, nor that of Freud and Trotsky. That heroes like Freud and Willett relish their meals, that Trotsky's temptation to fall in love is associated with his flirtation with "Ice cream and blueberry / Pie" (*EWN*, 240) is a reassuring indication that not all human appetites are evil. We know that Burgess's Trotsky is doomed when we see him rising above food and sex; one can tell that Jung is sinister when he cringes away from the offer of a good stiff drink. Humor, whether embodied in the text or in the hero's one-liners, undermines the seriousness totalitarian commitments require; as we have noted, hysterical laughter leads to revolt even among the half-brainwashed Ph.Ds of CAT. Burgess's Freud battles cancer with the courage of his historical counterpart, whom he quotes when he refuses a painkiller: " 'I prefer to think in torment than not to be able to think at all' " (*EWN*, 367).[10] Like the story of Val Brodie surviving fire and flood to do battle with Boss Cat, his is a success story along classical lines. The farce of the Trotsky story ends sadly for him but, to the exuberant New Yorkers he leaves behind, totalitarianism can have little appeal. Considered spatially, Burgess's stories confirm not only the idea that a timelessly recurring resistance to dictatorship is as natural to human beings as the drive to power, but the happy thought that in the end it wins out.

The spatialization of history, which makes such timeless stories possible, is not only a technique in the novel but a central idea. A tendency to view all times as if they were the present is a well-known characteristic of popular culture; Burgess's use of "sub-literate" genres—science fiction, musical comedy, "novelization"—suggests how close is the link between high and low culture. Among their other functions, brand names and advertising slogans remind us that even genius associates itself with the most vulgar manifestations of its period. Burgess's Anna Freud reads a "cheap, sensational novel in English" (*EWN*, 20); Jung tries out word association techniques on a cabin steward who "claims to have read something by Dr. Jones" (*EWN*, 206). Actually, the cabin steward had read *The Interpretation of Dreams*.[11] Burgess elaborates the point to show how quickly ideas pass into popular culture. Freud tells a patient to read the newspaper while masturbating (to suppress thoughts of his mother), then notes the headline, "Was Hitler Afraid of His Father?" (*EWN*, 366). In a pub, he hears an old woman chatting: " 'Proper mother's boy, scared of the outside world he was. Real Eedy puss complex I call it' " (*EWN*, 363). The process is reversible: the abolition of history implicit in the continuous topicality of television has its counterpart in serious culture.

In "The Democracy of Prejudice," a review of Brigid Brophy, Michael Levey, and Charles Osborne's *Fifty Works of*

[10] Ernest Jones, *The Life and Work of Sigmund Freud*, 529.
[11] Ibid., 266.

English Literature We Could Do Without, Burgess exposes the distortions of a relentlessly contemporary perspective. The book dismisses *Beowulf* as dull, disregarding the notion of the historical interest of learning "something about the aesthetic behavior of English before French and Latin got into it." The jettisoning of history," notes Burgess, "allows you to see the Middle Ages spatially" (*UC*, 178). Thus, Brophy, et al. go on to pan the York mysteries, pointing to frequent alliterations as proof that their authors were drunks since "alliteration is most frequently resorted to in intoxication" (*UC*, 178). Yet anachronism can readily be seen as a built-in danger of one of the most prestigious intellectual movements of our time. When Lévi-Strauss collates his manifestations of the Oedipus story, he is far more interested in its synchronic aspects—the repeated elements—than in particularistic explanations of changes in the stories. To watch three television screens simultaneously is a disturbingly similar process. The visual similarity between pages 266 and 267 of Burgess's novel, where Olga, Natalia, and Trotsky sing simultaneously in triple vertical columns, and a page of a critical text called, say, "The Morphology of the Musical Comedy," is striking. Throughout the novel, the desire to ignore or transcend ordinary public history is seen as dangerous. Freud's emphasis on universal patterns, as we have seen, blinds him to political realities; only Anna's interrogation by the Gestapo encourages him to stop talking about Moses and rebirth (*EWN*, 12) or the Destruction of the Temple (*EWN*, 7) long enough to realize the need to leave Vienna. Trotsky, who sees history as a force, nonetheless is much too ready to talk about its end. " 'History comes to a stop,' " he tells his son, when the " 'last thesis meets the last antithesis.' " A classless society emerges and " 'there's nothing more for history to do' " since the " 'two' " required for historical conflict no longer exist. His son disagrees. " 'All right. Where does the two come from when the Revolution comes?' " " " 'A split in the party,' " Serozha replies promptly (*EWN*, 337). " 'Mad to read history when history's at an end,' " says Hubert Frame, but we already know that even the death of the planet will not end human history (*EWN*, 269). In Val Brodie's view, history properly understood and remembered is the great glory of human beings: "the past has beaten the forces of destruction: possibility became fact, and fact cannot be willed away ever, not even by God" (*EWN*, 216).

Nonetheless, in the apocalypse it is the villain Bartlett who wants to "salvage human knowledge" (*EWN*, 190) and the hero, Val Brodie who, after permitting his crew to watch the earth's last minutes to the accompaniment of the last movement of the Jupiter symphony, gives the order that reduces human history before 2,000 A.D. to the contents of the novel. A necessary destruction? The novel insists that it is so, if human history is to avoid the ultimate spatialization. Without the old context—without the moon, or the sea, or four-legged animals—human culture will become meaningless. Willett returns to die with the earth out of a conviction that " 'We are earth. . . . We're not *mind* careering in outer space' " (*EWN*, 309). An American president who similarly refuses refuge in the spaceship predicts that " 'The games . . . will survive, but James and Toynbee will not. . . . What humanity will salvage from its long history is a few structures, a few rules in the void' " (*EWN*, 246). Val Brodie chooses life, but he also preaches " 'that all we can reasonably salvage from our past is the game of skill or chance' "; Dashiell Gropius, former gambling casino owner, will be " 'the most important man in . . . America' " (*EWN*, 385). If human culture is really to survive, human beings must create it out of the real materials of their own lives: the survivors have " 'no right to listen to instruments long dead' " (*EWN*, 386): " 'We must learn to make our own' " (*EWN*, 385).

Beginning with a pedant's radical misunderstanding, the novel ends with the even more radical misunderstanding of a group of schoolchildren. Divorced in time and space from the world the stories describe, they take its features as inventions, "lies": " 'It's not really history, is it? It's . . . myth' " (*EWN*, 387). We can understand the view that " 'It's a myth world, full of . . . clouds, trees, those things with four legs and things with four wheels' " (*EWN*, 387). They are not interested in creationist arguments for the existence of ancestors who built their ship: " 'Your generation talks about a journey. Our gen-

eration knows we're just here'" (*EWN*, 388). The baby Joshua
had indeed emulated his namesake in founding the first space
religion, but the children have lost belief in him. Freud and
Trotsky have also become myths: " 'Sike is making people go
to bed with their fathers and Pol is singing and dancing'"
(*EWN*, 389). "They had forgotten the story already," reads the
novel's last line. Yet, as the reader can see, these children are
as recognizably human as their ancestors; the structures of human behavior have persisted, beyond all misunderstanding,
and in this respect at least the forgotten Lévi-Strauss is vin-
dicated.

"The end of the world is, alas, a very trivial theme," Burgess remarks in his witty review of Warren Wagar's *Terminal
Visions*.[12] Surely everyone knows that serious "fiction is not
about what happens to the world, but about what happens to
a select group of human souls, with . . . catastrophe as the
mere pretext for an exquisitely painful probing, as in James,
of personal agonies and elation."[13] It is a salutary reminder of
what Burgess has rejected in purposely limiting the angst of
even Freud. A glittering pastiche of popular culture, the
book, all surfaces and structures, is something close to a si-
multaneous novelization of the theories of Lévi-Strauss and
Marshall McLuhan. *The End of the World News* illustrates a
spatial mode of perception that cannot help altering the way
we perceive our history. Impatient of depth and detail, the
contemporary viewer looks from channel to channel for the
big picture, the myth that transcends particular circumstance
and the old worn-out linearity of cause and effect. As we have
seen, the novel is very far from denying the notion that certain structures will survive any amount of tampering; but it
also urges respect for what does not survive, for the eccentric,
the temporal, and the contingent. The comedy grows blacker
as we realize how the novel begins and ends in misinterpre-
tation: nothing less than the end of the world and the death of
culture has, after all, taken place.

[12] "The Apocalypse and After," *Times Literary Supplement* 18 March 1983,
256.
[13] Ibid.

Afterword

IN THEIR apocalypses, Scott, Lessing, and Burgess all end a history, suggesting that whatever follows will carry only traces of the past. British writers of the late twentieth century are well aware that the phase of history into which they were born has already ended, and like le Carré's Bill Haydon, must occasionally feel the dismal contrast between the empire and contemporary Britain, "a poor island with scarcely a voice that would carry across the water" (*TTSS*, 345). Even the bitterest attacks on imperialism, such as Farrell's in the empire trilogy, occasionally evidence regret that the English, once so powerful, have no one left to oppress but a few hundred thousand Catholics in Northern Ireland and their own working class. The relationship between political and cultural hegemony is so self-evident that no one could expect novelists to welcome the reduction of their native country to a second-class status. Moreover, as relative outsiders—women, the sons of working- and middle-class families—even the Oxford graduates among these writers retain an ambivalence toward the traditional power structure whose standards they have met but with which they can scarcely identify completely.

As we have seen, the literary form of this ambivalence is an irony that risks paralysis. The direction this irony takes seems to grow progressively bleaker: *The Last September* indicts a small class, the Anglo-Irish Ascendancy; *The Red and the Green* indicts most of English literature, Shakespeare included; *The Raj Quartet* indicts all of European civilization, as it comes in contact with the Third World. Lessing and Burgess, in the shadow of nuclear war, describe its allotropes, nuclear accident and a collision of planets, the sort of "cosmic disaster" at which the astrophysicist in *Nuns and Soldiers* hinted, but which no one wanted to discuss. Although all of these novels depict characters of great charm, warmth, and intelligence, only Burgess's apocalypse is willing to show one of these people, rather than the sadists and boors, influencing the national destiny. The processes that allow human beings to ignore or distort their own historicity are so thoroughly displayed in all of these novels that their reader is tempted to conclude, with Paul Scott, that political action is futile. Today's empire builders, with their nuclear arsenals, are more dangerous than the British whom they succeeded in 1945, but no one would imagine that they are more thoughtful or tolerant. More often than one might wish, the novelists suggest that the liberal humane tradition to which they belong is an anachronistic survival of the days of England's glory, like Princess Diana or the invasion of the Falklands.

Much of what these novels tell us, then, is deflating, unwelcome: the natural response of human beings to their history is to ignore it, to mythicize it, even to end it, a real and not a metaphorical possibility. Fiction in the face of such apocalypse can neither subdue the world or promise to give it back to us whole. An imaginative construction like a daydream or a politican's speech, fiction—historical fiction more than most—always risks collaboration with our understandable but lethal habits of escape. Yet in their lucidity about the fictions by which we usually know it, these novels become a model of our experience of history. What gives them their special urgency is the sense that reader, characters, and author are bound together in the struggle to remember that we live in history and that, in this struggle, fiction may be an ally as well as an enemy. The critical spirit and vitality of these novels is evidence enough that the novel still responds to a living world of social experience, that the voice of British fiction still carries across the water.

Bibliography

Adler, Jerry, et al. "The Hard-Luck Christmas of '82." *Newsweek* 27 December 1982, 12–16.

Amis, Kingsley. *The James Bond Dossier*. New York: New American Library, 1965.

———. "A New James Bond." In *What Became of Jane Austen?* London: Jonathan Cape, 1970.

Barber, Michael. "John le Carré: An Interrogation." *New York Times Book Review*, 25 September 1977, 9, 44–45.

Barzun, Jacques. "Meditations on the Literature of Spying." *American Scholar* 34 (Spring 1965): 167–78.

Bennett, Alan. *The Old Country*. London: Faber, 1978.

Bergonzi, Bernard. "Fictions of History." In *The Contemporary English Novel*, edited by Malcolm Bradbury and David Palmer. Stratford-upon-Avon Studies 18, 43–66. London: Edward Arnold, 1979.

Binns, Ronald. *J. G. Farrell*. London: Methuen, 1986.

Bloom, Harold, ed. *John le Carré*. New York: Chelsea House, 1987.

Bowen, Elizabeth. *Bowen's Court*. New York: Knopf, 1942.

———. *The Last September*. 1929. New York: Avon, 1979.

Boyd, William. *An Ice Cream War*. New York: Morrow, 1983.

———. *The New Confessions*. London: Hamish Hamilton, 1987.

Boyle, Andrew. *The Fourth Man*. New York: Dial-James Wade, 1979. Published in England as *The Climate of Treason: Five Who Spied for Russia*. London: Hutchinson, 1979.

Bristow-Smith, Laurence. " 'Tomorrow is another day': The Essential J. G. Farrell." *Critical Quarterly* 25, no. 2 (1983): 45–52.

Brothers, Barbara. "Pattern and Void: Bowen's Irish Landscapes and *The Heat of the Day*." *Mosaic* 12, no. 3 (1978): 129–38.

Brown, Malcolm. *The Politics of Irish Literature*. Seattle: University of Washington Press, 1972.

Burgess, Anthony. "The Apocalypse and After." Review of *Terminal Visions*, by Warren Wagar. *Times Literary Supplement* 18 March 1983, 256.

———. "The Democracy of Prejudice." In *Urgent Copy*. London: Jonathan Cape, 1968.

Burgess, Anthony. *The End of the World News.* New York: McGraw-Hill, 1983.

———. *Tremor of Intent.* New York: Norton, 1966.

Carlyle, Thomas. "On History." 1830. In *A Carlyle Reader.* Edited by G. B. Tennyson. New York: Random House, 1969.

Cecil, Robert. "Legends Spies Tell: A Reappraisal of the Absconding Diplomats." *Encounter* 50 (April 1978): 9–17.

Certeau, Michel de. *L'écriture et l'histoire.* Paris: Gallimard, 1975.

Chesterton, G. K. *Charles Dickens: The Last of the Great Men.* 1906. New York: Readers Club, 1946.

Coale, Samuel. "An Interview with Anthony Burgess." *Modern Fiction Studies* 27 (1981): 429–52.

Colegate, Isabel. *The Shooting Party.* London: Hamish Hamilton, 1968.

Cookridge, E. H. *The Third Man.* London: Arthur Barker, 1968.

Cosgrove, Brian. "Ego Contra Mundum: Thomas Kilroy's *The Big Chapel.*" *Cahiers Irlandaises* 4–5 (1975): 297–309.

Cruise O'Brien, Conor. "Greene's Castle." Review of *The Human Factor*, by Graham Greene. *New York Review of Books* 1 June 1978, 4.

———. *Parnell and His Party.* Oxford: Clarendon, 1957.

Darnton, Robert. *The Great Cat Massacre and Other Episodes in French Cultural History.* 1984. New York: Vintage-Random House, 1985.

Daspré, André. "Le roman historique et l'histoire." *Revue d'Histoire Littéraire de la France* 75 (1975): 235–44.

Davis, Natalie Zemon. *The Return of Martin Guerre.* Cambridge: Harvard University Press, 1983.

Deighton, Len. *Spy Hook.* New York: Knopf, 1988.

Derrida, Jacques. *Of Grammatology.* Translated by Gaytari Chakravorty Spivak. Baltimore: Johns Hopkins University Press, 1976.

Dipple, Elizabeth. *Iris Murdoch: Work for the Spirit.* London: Methuen, 1982.

Donoghue, Denis. Review of *The Human Factor*, by Graham Greene. *New York Times Book Review* 26 February 1978, 1, 43.

Downey, James. *Them and Us: Britain-Ireland and the Northern Question, 1969–1982.* Dublin: Ward River Press, 1983.

Duran, Leopoldo. "El factor humano de Greene." *Arbor* 413 (May 1980): 71–84.

Elshtain, Jean Bethke. "A Controversy on Language and Politics I:

The Post-*Golden Notebook* Fiction of Doris Lessing." *Salmagundi* 47–48 (Winter-Spring 1980): 95–114.

Emerson, Ralph Waldo. "History." 1841. In *The Collected Works of Ralph Waldo Emerson*. 4 vols. Cambridge: Harvard University Press, 1979. Vol. 2.

Farrell, J. G. *The Hill Station: An Unfinished Novel, and an Indian Diary*. Edited by John Spurling. London: Weidenfeld and Nicolson, 1981.

———. *The Siege of Krishnapur*. London: Weidenfeld and Nicolson, 1973.

———. *Troubles*. New York: Knopf, 1971.

Faulkner, William. *Absalom, Absalom!* New York: Random House, 1936.

Feuchtwanger, Lion. *The House of Desdemona, or the Laurels and Limitations of Historical Fiction*. Translated by Harold A. Basilius. Detroit: Wayne State University Press, 1963.

Fleishman, Avrom. *The English Historical Novel*. Baltimore: Johns Hopkins University Press, 1971.

———. *Fictions and the Ways of Knowing: Essays on British Novels*. Austin: University of Texas Press, 1978.

Forster, E. M. *Two Cheers for Democracy*. London: Penguin, 1965.

Foucault, Michel. *The Archaeology of Knowledge*. Translated by A. M. Sheridan Smith. New York: Pantheon, 1972.

———. *The Order of Things: An Archaeology of the Human Sciences*. Translator not given. New York: Vintage-Random House, 1973.

Furet, François. *L'Atelier de l'histoire*. Paris: Flammarion, 1982.

Geppert, Hans Vilmar. *Der "andere" historische Roman: Theorie und Strukturen einer diskontinuierlichen Gattung*. Tübingen: Max Niemeyer, 1976.

German, Howard. "The Range of Allusions in the Novels of Iris Murdoch." *Journal of Modern Literature* 2 (1971): 57–81.

Gerstenberger, Donna. *Iris Murdoch*. Lewisburg: Bucknell University Press, 1975.

Ghiselin, Brewster. "The Unity of Joyce's *Dubliners*." 1956. Reprinted in *Dubliners: Text, Criticism, and Notes*. Edited by Robert Scholes and A. Walton Litz. New York: Viking, 1968.

Greene, Graham. *The Human Factor*. New York: Simon and Schuster, 1978.

———. "The Spy." In *Collected Essays*. London: Bodley Head, 1969.

Grella, George. "Murder and Loyalty." *New Republic* 31 July 1976, 23–25.

Halperin, John. "Between Two Worlds: The Novels of John le Carré." *South Atlantic Quarterly* 79 (Winter 1980): 17–37.

Hamburger, Käte. *The Logic of Literature.* Translated by Marilynn J. Rose. 2d ed. Bloomington: Indiana University Press, 1973.

Hardwick, Elizabeth. "Elizabeth Bowen's Fiction." *Partisan Review* 16 (1949): 1114–21.

Henderson, Harry. *Versions of the Past.* New York: Oxford, 1974.

Higdon, David Leon. *Shadows of the Past in Contemporary British Fiction.* Athens: University of Georgia Press, 1985.

Hill, Reginald. *The Spy's Wife.* New York: Pantheon, 1980.

Holland, Jack. *Too Long a Sacrifice: Life and Death in Northern Ireland since 1969.* Harmondsworth: Penguin, 1982.

Holquist, Michael. "Whodunit and Other Questions: Metaphysical Detective Stories in Post-War Fiction." *New Literary History* 3 (Autumn 1971): 135–56.

Hone, Joseph. *The Private Sector.* New York: Dutton, 1972.

———. *The Sixth Directorate.* London: Secker and Warburg, 1975.

Hutcheon, Linda. "Subject in/of/to History and His Story." *Diacritics* 16, no. 1 (Spring 1986): 78–91.

"In His Master's Service." Review of *My Secret War*, by Kim Philby. *Times Literary Supplement* 26 Sept. 1968; 1087.

James, Henry. *The Wings of the Dove.* New York Edition 1907. (Harmondsworth: Penguin Classics, 1986).

Jameson, Fredric. *The Political Unconscious: Narrative as a Socially Symbolic Act.* Ithaca, N.Y.: Cornell University Press, 1981.

Johnson, Barbara. *The Critical Difference: Essays in the Contemporary Rhetoric of Reading.* Baltimore: Johns Hopkins University Press, 1980.

Jones, Ernest. *The Life and Work of Sigmund Freud.* Edited and abridged by Lionel Trilling and Steven Marcus. London: Hogarth, 1961.

Jouve, Nicole Ward. "Of Mud and Other Matter—*The Children of Violence.*" In *Notebooks / Memoirs / Archives: Reading and Rereading Doris Lessing.* Edited by Jenny Taylor. Boston: Routledge and Kegan Paul, 1982.

Joyce, James. *A Portrait of the Artist as a Young Man.* 1916. Harmondsworth: Penguin, 1976.

Jung, C. G. *Zivilisation im übergang.* Olten: Walter, 1974.

Kemp, Peter. "The Fight against Fantasy: Iris Murdoch's *The Red and the Green*." *Modern Fictions Studies* 15 (1969): 403–15.

Kershner, R. B., Jr. "A French Connection: Iris Murdoch and Raymond Queneau." *Eire / Ireland* 18, no. 4 (1983): 144–51.

Kiely, Benedict. *Proxopera*. London: Victor Gollancz, 1977.

Kilroy, Thomas. *The Big Chapel*. London: Faber, 1971.

Kim, Suzanne. "Histoire et roman." *Études anglaises* 36, nos. 2–3 (1983): 168–80.

Knightley, Phillip. *The Master Spy: The Story of Kim Philby*. New York: Knopf, 1989.

Krause, David. *Sean O'Casey: The Man and His Work*. Enlarged edition. New York: Macmillan, 1975.

Krieger, Murray. *Theory of Criticism*. Baltimore: Johns Hopkins University Press, 1976.

La Capra, Dominick. *History, Politics, and the Novel*. Ithaca: Cornell University Press, 1987.

Laigle, Deirdre. "Images of the Big House in Elizabeth Bowen: *The Last September*." *Cahiers du Centre d'Études Irlandais* 9 (1984): 61–80.

Lascelles, Mary. *The Story-Teller Retrieves the Past*. New York: Oxford, 1980.

le Carré, John. "Introduction." *The Philby Conspiracy* by Bruce Page, David Leitch, and Phillip Knightley. New York: Signet-NAL, 1969.

——. *The Looking Glass War*. London: Heinemann, 1965.

——. *Tinker, Tailor, Soldier, Spy*. New York: Bantam, 1975.

Lee, Joseph. *The Modernization of Irish Society, 1848–1918*. Dublin: Gill and Macmillan, 1973.

Leitch, Maurice. *Silver's City*. London: Secker and Warburg, 1981.

Lentricchia, Frank. *After the New Criticism*. Chicago: Chicago University Press, 1980.

Lessing, Doris. *The Four-Gated City*. Vol. 5 of *Children of Violence*. 5 vols. 1969. New York: Bantam, 1970.

——. *Landlocked*. Vol. 3 of *Children of Violence*. 5 vols. 1958. New York: Plume-NAL, 1970.

——. *Martha Quest*. Vol. 1 of *Children of Violence*. 5 vols. 1952. New York: Plume-NAL, 1970.

——. *A Proper Marriage*. Vol. 2 of *Children of Violence*. 5 vols. 1954. New York: Plume-NAL, 1970.

——. *A Ripple from the Storm*. Vol. 4 of *Children of Violence*. 5 vols. 1965. St. Albans: Panther-Grenada, 1966.

Lessing, Doris. *A Small Personal Voice: Essays, Reviews, Interviews.* Edited by Paul Schlueter. New York: Knopf, 1974.

Lévi-Strauss, Claude. *The Savage Mind.* London: George Weidenfeld and Nicolson, 1966.

Locke, Richard. "The Spy Who Spied on Spies." Review of *Tinker, Tailor, Soldier, Spy,* by John le Carré. *New York Times Book Review* 30 June 1974, 1–2.

Longenbach, James. *Modernist Poetics of History: Pound, Eliot, and the Sense of the Past.* Princeton: Princeton University Press, 1987.

Lukács, George. *The Historical Novel.* Translated by Hannah and Stanley Mitchell. New York: Humanities Press, 1965.

McEwan, Neil. *Perspective in British Historical Fiction Today.* Wolfeboro, N.H.: Longwood Academic, 1987.

MacKenzie, Compton. *Water on the Brain.* London: Cassell, 1933.

MacLaverty, Bernard. *Cal.* New York: Braziller, 1983.

McMinn, Joseph. "Contemporary Novels on the 'Troubles'." *Études Irlandaises* n.s. 5 (1980): 113–21.

Mann, Wilfred Basil. *Was There a Fifth Man?* Oxford: Pergamon, 1982.

Martin, F. X. "Eoin MacNeill on the 1916 Rising." *Irish Historical Studies* 12 (1961): 226–71.

Merry, Bruce. *Anatomy of the Spy Thriller.* Dublin: Gill and Macmillan, 1977.

Murdoch, Iris. "Against Dryness: A Polemical Sketch." *Encounter* 16 January 1961: 16–20. Reprinted in *The Novel Today,* edited by Malcolm Bradbury. Manchester: Manchester University Press, 1977.

———. *The Fire and the Sun: Why Plato Banished the Poets.* London: Oxford University Press, 1977.

———. *Nuns and Soldiers.* New York: Viking, 1980.

———. *The Red and the Green.* New York: Bard-Avon, 1965.

———. *The Sovereignty of Good.* London: Routledge and Kegan Paul, 1970.

Murray, Dominic. "Schools and Conflict." In *Northern Ireland: The Background to the Conflict.* Syracuse: Syracuse University Press, 1983.

Newman, Judie. "Games in Greeneland: *The Human Factor.*" *Dutch Quarterly Review of Anglo-American Letters* 14, no. 4 (1984): 250–68.

Norman, E. R. *The Catholic Church and Ireland in the Age of Rebellion, 1859–1873.* Ithaca, N.Y.: Cornell University Press, 1965.

O'Casey, Sean. *Drums under the Windows*. New York: Macmillan, 1956.

O'Connor, Frank. *An Only Child*. New York: Knopf, 1961.

O'Connor, Ulick. *A Terrible Beauty is Born: The Irish Troubles, 1912–1922*. London: Hamish Hamilton, 1975.

O'Toole, Bridget. "J. G. Farrell." In *Contemporary Novelists*. Edited by James Vinson. London: St. James, 1976.

Page, Bruce, David Leitch, and Phillip Knightley. *The Philby Conspiracy*. New York: Signet-NAL, 1968. Published in England as *Philby: The Spy Who Betrayed a Generation*. London: Sphere, 1967.

Pascal, Roy. "Tense and Novel." *Modern Language Review* 57 (1962): 1–11.

Payne, Robert. *The Life and Death of Trotsky*. New York: McGraw-Hill, 1977.

Philby, Eleanor. *Kim Philby: The Spy I Loved*. London: Hamish Hamilton, 1968.

Philby, Kim. *My Silent War*. London: McGibbon and Kee, 1968.

Poole, Michael. "The Demography of Violence." In *Northern Ireland: The Background to the Conflict*. Edited by John Darby. Syracuse: Syracuse University Press, 1983.

Poster, Mark. *Foucault, Marxism, and History: Mode of Production versus Mode of Information*. Cambridge: Polity Press, 1984.

Pritchett, V. S. "The Human Factor in Greene." *New York Times Magazine* 26 February 1978, 33–36, 38, 40–42, 44, 46.

Queneau, Raymond. *We Always Treat Women Too Well*. Translated by Barbara Wright. New York: New Directions, 1981.

Rao, K. Bhaskara. *Paul Scott*. Boston: Twayne, 1980.

The Report of the American Committee for Relief in Ireland. New York: n.p., n.d.

Ridley, Hugh. *Images of Imperial Rule*. New York: St. Martin's, 1983.

Rubin, David. *After the Raj: British Novels of India since 1947*. Hanover, N.H.: University Press of New England, 1986.

Scholes, Robert and A. Walton Litz, eds. *Dubliners: Text, Criticism, and Notes*. Harmondsworth: Penguin, 1969.

Scott, Paul. *The Day of the Scorpion*. Vol. 2 of *The Raj Quartet*. 4 vols. 1968. New York: Avon, 1979.

———. *A Division of the Spoils*. Vol. 4 of *The Raj Quartet*. 4 vols. 1975. New York: Avon, 1979.

Scott, Paul. "India: A Post-Forsterian View." In *Essays by Divers Hands* n.s. 36 (1970): 113–32.

―――. *The Jewel in the Crown.* Vol. 1 of *The Raj Quartet.* 4 vols. 1966. New York: Avon, 1979.

―――. *The Towers of Silence.* Vol. 3 of *The Raj Quartet.* 4 vols. New York: Avon, 1979.

Seale, Patrick, and Maureen McConville. *Philby: The Long Road to Moscow.* London: Hamish Hamilton, 1973.

See, Katherine O'Sullivan. *First World Nationalisms: Class and Ethnic Politics in Northern Ireland and Quebec.* Chicago: University of Chicago Press, 1986.

Steele, Murray. *"Children of Violence* and Rhodesia: A Study of Doris Lessing as Historical Observer." Local Series Pamphlet No. 29. Salisbury: Central Africa Historical Association, 1974.

Steiner, George. "God's Spies." *New Yorker* no. 54, 8 May 1978, 149–54.

Stern, Frederic. "The Changing 'Voice' of Lessing's Characters: From Politics to Sci Fi." *World Literature Written in English* 21, no. 3 (1982): 456–67.

Stewart, A.T.Q. *The Narrow Ground: Aspects of Ulster, 1609–1969.* London: Faber, 1977.

Stimpson, Catharine R. "Doris Lessing and the Parables of Growth." In *The Voyage In.* Edited by Elizabeth Abel, Marianne Hirsch, and Elizabeth Langland. Hanover, N.H.: University Press of New England, 1983.

Swinden, Patrick. *The English Novel of History and Society, 1945–1980.* New York: St. Martin's, 1986.

―――. *Paul Scott: Images of India.* New York: St. Martin's, 1980.

Thomas, D. M. *The White Hotel.* New York: Pocket Books, 1982.

Thompson, William Irwin. *The Imagination of an Insurrection: Dublin, Easter 1916.* New York: Oxford University Press, 1967.

Trachtenberg, Alan. "The Journey Back: Myth and History in *Tender is the Night.*" In *Experience in the Novel.* Edited by Roy Harvey Pearce. New York: Columbia University Press, 1968.

Trevor-Roper, Hugh. *The Philby Affair.* London: William Kimber, 1968.

Wallbank, T. Walter. *A Short History of India and Pakistan.* 1951. New York: Mentor, 1958.

Weeks, Edward. Review of *The Red and the Green,* by Iris Murdoch. *Atlantic Monthly* December 1965, 138.

White, Hayden. "Fictions of Factual Representation." In *The Liter-*

ature of Fact. Edited by Angus Fletcher. New York: Columbia University Press, 1976.

———. "The Historical Text as Literary Artifact." In *The Writing of History.* Edited by Robert H. Canary and Henry Kozicki. Madison: University of Wisconsin Press, 1978.

———. *Metahistory.* Baltimore: Johns Hopkins University Press, 1973.

Wiesel, Elie. Interview on "Nightline." ABC television, 20 November 1983.

Williams, Alan. *Gentleman Traitor.* New York: Harcourt Brace, 1975.

Wright, Peter. *Spycatcher: The Candid Autobiography of a Senior Intelligence Officer.* New York: Dell, 1987.

Yeats, William Butler. *The Collected Poems of William Butler Yeats.* 2d ed. New York: Macmillan, 1951.

Index